The First

500
Chinese Character Practice Drills

Book 13

500 Chinese Hanzi Characters
for
Developing Writing Skills

毛猴子
Dà Máo Hóuzi
Big Hairy Monkey
www.SpeakandWriteChinese.com

[Type text]

All rights reserved. No part of this publication may be reproduced, photocopied, stored in a retrieval system, and transmitted in any form or by any means, electronic, mechanical, recording or otherwise, without the prior written permission of the author and publisher. But really, I am pretty flexible on this. My goal is to provide information to learn the written Chinese language so if you need copies for educational purposes or you are really cheap you can e-mail me for consent.

Library and Archives Canada Cataloguing in Publication

Dà, Máo Hóuzi, 1969-

Title: The First 500 Chinese Character Practice Drills:
Subtitle: 500 Chinese Hanzi Characters for Developing Writing Skills;
Book 13. / Dà Máo Hóuzi.

ISBN 978-1-926564-17-3

    1. Chinese Language--Writing--Problems, Exercises, etc. 2. Chinese Characters. 3. Chinese Language--Textbooks for Second Language Learners--English Speakers. I. Title. II. Title: First Five Hundred Chinese Character Practice Drills. III. Series: Comprehensive Approach to Learning Chinese Language; Book 13

PL1171.D37 2010   495.1'11   C2010-900438-8

Author: Dà Máo Hóuzi
Editor-in-Chief: Dà Máo Hóuzi
Authentic Chinese Editor: Lu XueFeng
Copy Editor: Dà Máo Hóuzi
Graphics / Tables / Covers: Dà Máo Hóuzi

This is Book 13 in the Series;

A Comprehensive Approach to Learning Chinese Language

Monkey Monk Publications
Stoney Creek, Ontario, Canada

Copyright © 2008 Dà Máo Hóuzi

[Type text]

Published by Monkey Monk Publications

1) Hanzi and the Kangxi Radicals

1a) The Rules of Chinese Characters and Mandarin

2) 425 Easy Chinese Characters

2a) 101 Easy Chinese Characters

2b) 300 Easy Chinese Characters

3) 425 Intermediate Chinese Characters

4) 425 Advanced Chinese Characters

5) 425 Chinese Characters Using 1 to 5 Strokes

6) The First 251 Most Common Chinese Characters

7) The Second 251 Most Common Chinese Characters

8) The Third 251 Most Common Chinese Characters

9) The Fourth 251 Most Common Chinese Characters

10) The First 1000 Most Common Chinese Characters

11) The Second 1000 Most Common Chinese Characters

12) The Third 1000 Most Common Chinese Characters

13) A Merciful Introduction to Chinese Grammar

14) Chinese Grammar for the Keener

15) Generally Clever Things to Say in Standard Mandarin Chinese

[Type text]

Preface to the General Introduction

Standard Mandarin is an official language of the United Nations. More people speak Mandarin than any other language. If you are a native English speaker you will need to turn on a part of your brain that is relatively dormant. This is the only language that exists that is not driven by a sound based signal system. A Chinese character is a logogram, a symbol. There are no consistent or reliable signals for meaning or sound in a character. After you learn a character you may be able to pick clues out of a small number of characters. If you never speak a word of Mandarin or travel to China you can still make a change in your brain that will open a whole new way to memorize.

The Chinese have always intrigued me. I was first exposed to them in university. I marvelled at how they could ace physics, math, chemistry, engineering and computer science yet barely speak English. It was not until I looked at their language that I began to understand. Their language is based on a system of a visual image representing meaning. Although each character has defined meanings, compiled together they may have totally different meanings. It would be nice if two characters beside each other as A and B equalled AB but in many situations it is more complex. A + B = AB exists but so does A + B = C. If you learn 200 characters in a paragraph and write all their meanings in an English sentence format, the product may be incomprehensible.

Initially you will struggle with learning complex characters. But like all skills you will improve. Many people lament the difficulty to me but my response is always, *2 billion people cannot be wrong*.

[Type text]

Table of Contents

#	Chapter	Page
1.	Title Page	1
2.	Published by Monkey Monk Publications	3
3.	Prelude to the General Introduction	4
4.	Table of Contents	5
5.	Introduction	6
6.	Using the Work Book	7
7.	500 Character Practice Drills	8
8.	Kangxi Radicals	515
9.	List of the 214 Kangxi Radicals	523
10.	Written Variants	537
11.	Stroke Order	540
12.	Basic and Compound Strokes	541
13.	Development of Stroke Order Rules	552
14.	The Six Single Strokes	556
15.	Stroke Variations and Additives	557
16.	Compound Strokes	559
17.	Exercise for Individual Strokes	565
18.	Eight Principles of Yong	620
19.	Guide to Pronunciation	623
20.	Initials	637
21.	Finals	631
22.	Tones	644
23.	Tonal Shift Patterns, or Tone Sandhi	645
24.	Hanyu Pinyin	650
25.	Rules of Pinyin	653
26.	Chinese Learning Websites	683
27.	How to Find the Ultimate Tools	684
28.	My Personal Favourites	686
29.	Using a Computer in China	691
31.	How to Spend Your Money	692

[Type text]

Introduction

The First 500 Chinese Character Practice Drills is a work book to practice writing the first 500 most common Chinese characters. These characters come from a list of the 3000 most common characters. This is list was compiled from a computer analysis of a recorded conversation database.

In writing this book series I first looked to see what was available in the local English bookstore's titles. I bought all the books I could find and was surprised at books that missed some of the most common characters and books that presented some very uncommon characters. I did not find one book that presented accepted common characters.

Perhaps my biggest pleasure was finding books that published 250 characters. 250 is somewhat of an insult in the Chinese language. The story is long and ancient and involves four men who stole 1000 monies and history records that the ruling judge called them each (二百五, **èr bǎi wǔ**, **250**). Get it? 1000 divided by 4 = 250. Four idiots. Then he ordered them executed.

Most (外国人, **wài guó rén**, **outside country person**) or *foreigners* make little effort to learn the written script of China. Given the very long learning curve to develop a functional writing skill, it is wise to first learn the most common characters. Knowing the 500 most common characters will give you a very good start to understanding the basics you will need to survive in China.

This book is written as a compliment to my first 16 books, detailed in the front inside cover. My first book ***Hanzi and the Kangxi Radicals*** is a 566 page 8 1/2 by 11 book that I feel is the most comprehensive book in English that details the essential components to writing Chinese characters. That is, the 50 plus named strokes, the 214 essential characters known as the Kangxi Radicals and guided practice drills. This book also includes all the rules of Pinyin and pronunciation.

Writing Chinese characters requires skills and a form of memory that is under-utilized in English speakers. Like all skills it develops with practice. You will not learn by looking at the drills. Like billions of Chinese over thousands of years, you must practice, practice, practice. 大毛猴子

[Type text]

Using the Work Book

What lies ahead are 500 tables. At the upper left of each table is a large Chinese character. This is of course the topic character for the work sheet.

Immediately below the topic character is a small box with the alphabetic sound that represents the usual sound of this character. The method of representing the sound of the character is called (拼音, **Pīnyīn**, **spell sound**). This use of the Roman alphabet was developed and embraced by China so that school children across China would have a standardized sound for each character.

China historically was unified by the written language. The spoken language had and has over 200 recognized very distinct variations. (拼音, **Pīnyīn**, **spell sound**) helped China develop a universal literacy of spoken language. At the back of this work book is a guide to pronunciation.

The third box, below the (拼音, **Pīnyīn**, **spell sound**) box, is the common or usual English translation. Like English, a Chinese character can have more than one meaning.

To the right of these first three boxes is an area to write your own notes and also a brief explanation of the meaning of the character along with the character and the (拼音, **Pīnyīn**, **spell sound**).

Below all of these, making the fourth row and crossing the page, is a long box in which the stroke order of the character is shown. As you move from left to right across the box, one extra stroke is added until finally the entire character is drawn.

Then come the practice boxes. Photocopy, overwrite or use a clear acetate with a wipe off marker and get to work using the correct stroke and stroke order. Chant the (拼音, **Pīnyīn**, **spell sound**) and the meaning. You will find it more useful if you pick about 10 lesson tables and do one character on each of all ten lessons and repeat this cycle.

There is no easy way to do this. Practice, repetition, frustration are all part of learning any language.

[Type text]

的 de particle	Notes: Grammatical Particle (的, **de**, **possessive particle**) (的, **de**, **grammatical particle**), has numerous uses in Hanyu. It can be used to make a personal pronoun into the possessive form. The form is (personal pronoun) + 的 = possessive pronoun. Example 我的, wǒ de, me + possessive particle = my / mine.

′　亻　竹　白　白　白′　的　的

的　的　的　的　的　的　的

一 yī one	Notes: Quantitative Adjective (一, **yī**, **one**, **a little**) is the number one. It can also be used to indicate a small amount. (一, **yī**, **diminutive verb prefix**) 一 can act to diminish verb intensity. The grammatical form is *verb 一 verb*. A typical example is (看一看, **kàn yī kàn**, **look little / quick look**).

一

一 一 一 一 一 一 一 一 一

一	一	一	一	一	一	一	一	一	一
yī	yī	yī	yī	yī	yī	yī	yī	yī	yī
one	one	one	one	one	one	one	one	one	one
一	一	一	一	一	一	一	一	一	一
yī	yī	yī	yī	yī	yī	yī	yī	yī	yī
one	one	one	one	one	one	one	one	one	one
一	一	一							
一	一	一							
一	一	一							
一	一	一							
一	一	一							
一	一	一							

[Type text]

是	Notes: Verb
shì is	(是, **shì**, **is**, **to be**) (是, **shì**, **is**) is the equivalent of the English verb ***to be***. Its use is near the same except that it is not used when the Topic - Subject is equated with an adjective and no target Object-Noun.

丨 冂 冃 日 旦 早 早 昰 是

是 是 是 是 是 是 是 是 是

是	是	是	是	是	是	是	是	是	是
shì	shì	shì	shì	shì	shì	shì	shì	shì	shì
is	is	is	is	is	is	is	is	is	is
是	是	是	是	是	是	是	是	是	是
shì	shì	shì	shì	shì	shì	shì	shì	shì	shì
is	is	is	is	is	is	is	is	is	is

不 bù not	Notes: Adverb (不, **bù**, **not**) (不, **bù**, **not**) is most commonly used to negate a verb. All Hanzi / Hanyu verbs except (有, **yǒu**, **have**) are negated in the form of (不, **bù**, **not**) preceding the verb.

一 丅 不 不

不 不 不 不 不 不 不 不

不	不	不	不	不	不	不	不	不	不
bù	bù	bù	bù	bù	bù	bù	bù	bù	bù
not	not	not	not	not	not	not	not	not	not
不	不	不	不	不	不	不	不	不	不
bù	bù	bù	bù	bù	bù	bù	bù	bù	bù
not	not	not	not	not	not	not	not	not	not

有	Notes: Verb
yǒu have	(有, **yǒu**, **have**) is the common Hanzi / Hanyu possessive verb. It can be used to form a question in the verb negation format by stating thus, (有没有, **yǒu méi yǒu**, **have not have**). (有, **yǒu**, **have**) is the only Hanzi / Hanyu verb not negated with the adverb (不, **bù**, **not**) but is negated with (没, **méi**, **not**).

一 ナ 广 冇 有 有

有 有 有 有 有 有 有 有 有

有	有	有	有	有	有	有	有	有	有
yǒu have	yǒu have	yǒu have	yǒu have	yǒu have	yǒu have	yǒu have	yǒu have	yǒu have	yǒu have
有	有	有	有	有	有	有	有	有	有
yǒu have	yǒu have	yǒu have	yǒu have	yǒu have	yǒu have	yǒu have	yǒu have	yǒu have	yǒu have

Notes: Noun

(人, **rén**, **person**)

(人, **rén**, **person**) is the character for person, people, man.

我	Notes: Singular First Person Pronoun
wǒ	(我, **wǒ**, **me**)
me	(我, **wǒ**, **me / I**) is the character for the Singular Personal Pronoun *me / I*.

丿 一 千 手 我 我 我

我 我 我 我 我 我 我 我 我

我	我	我	我	我	我	我	我	我	我
wǒ	wǒ	wǒ	wǒ	wǒ	wǒ	wǒ	wǒ	wǒ	wǒ
me	me	me	me	me	me	me	me	me	me
我	我	我	我	我	我	我	我	我	我
wǒ	wǒ	wǒ	wǒ	wǒ	wǒ	wǒ	wǒ	wǒ	wǒ
me	me	me	me	me	me	me	me	me	me

我	我	我	我	我		我	我	我	
我	我	我	我	我		我	我	我	
我	我	我	我	我		我	我	我	
我	我	我	我	我		我	我	我	
我	我	我	我	我		我	我	我	
我	我	我	我	我		我	我	我	
我	我	我	我	我		我	我	我	

[Type text]

在	Notes: Verb
zài at	(在, **zài, at, be at, be in, be on**) is a character that is used to precede a noun phrase that gives a location in a sentence. (在, **zài, to exist, to live, to live at, exist at**) (在, **zài, to depend on, rest with**)

一 ナ 广 圥 在 在

在 在 在 在 在 在 在 在 在

在	在	在	在	在	在	在	在	在
zài	zài	zài	zài	zài	zài	zài	zài	zài
at	at	at	at	at	at	at	at	at
在	在	在	在	在	在	在	在	在
zài	zài	zài	zài	zài	zài	zài	zài	zài
at	at	at	at	at	at	at	at	at

[Type text]

他	Notes: Singular Third Person Pronoun
tā he	(他, **tā**, **he**) (他, **tā**, **he**) is functionally the masculine Third Person Singular Pronoun. Although it is pronounced the same as (她, **tā**, **she**, **her**) the gender is preserved in the written character with the left sided gender specific Radical (亻, **rén**, **male**).

丿 亻 亻 仲 他

他 他 他 他 他 他 他 他 他

这 zhè this	Notes: Demonstrative Pronoun (这, **zhè**, **this**) (这, **zhè**, **this**) is a Demonstrative Pronoun that is used in the same way that the English ***this*** is used. The pronunciation is changed when it is used before a classifier. (这个, **zhèige**, **this one**).

丶 亠 ナ 文 文 议 这

这 这 这 这 这 这 这 这 这

这	这	这	这	这	这	这	这	这	这
zhè this	zhè this	zhè this	zhè this	zhè this	zhè this	zhè this	zhè this	zhè this	zhè this
这	这	这	这	这	这	这	这	这	这
zhè this	zhè this	zhè this	zhè this	zhè this	zhè this	zhè this	zhè this	zhè this	zhè this

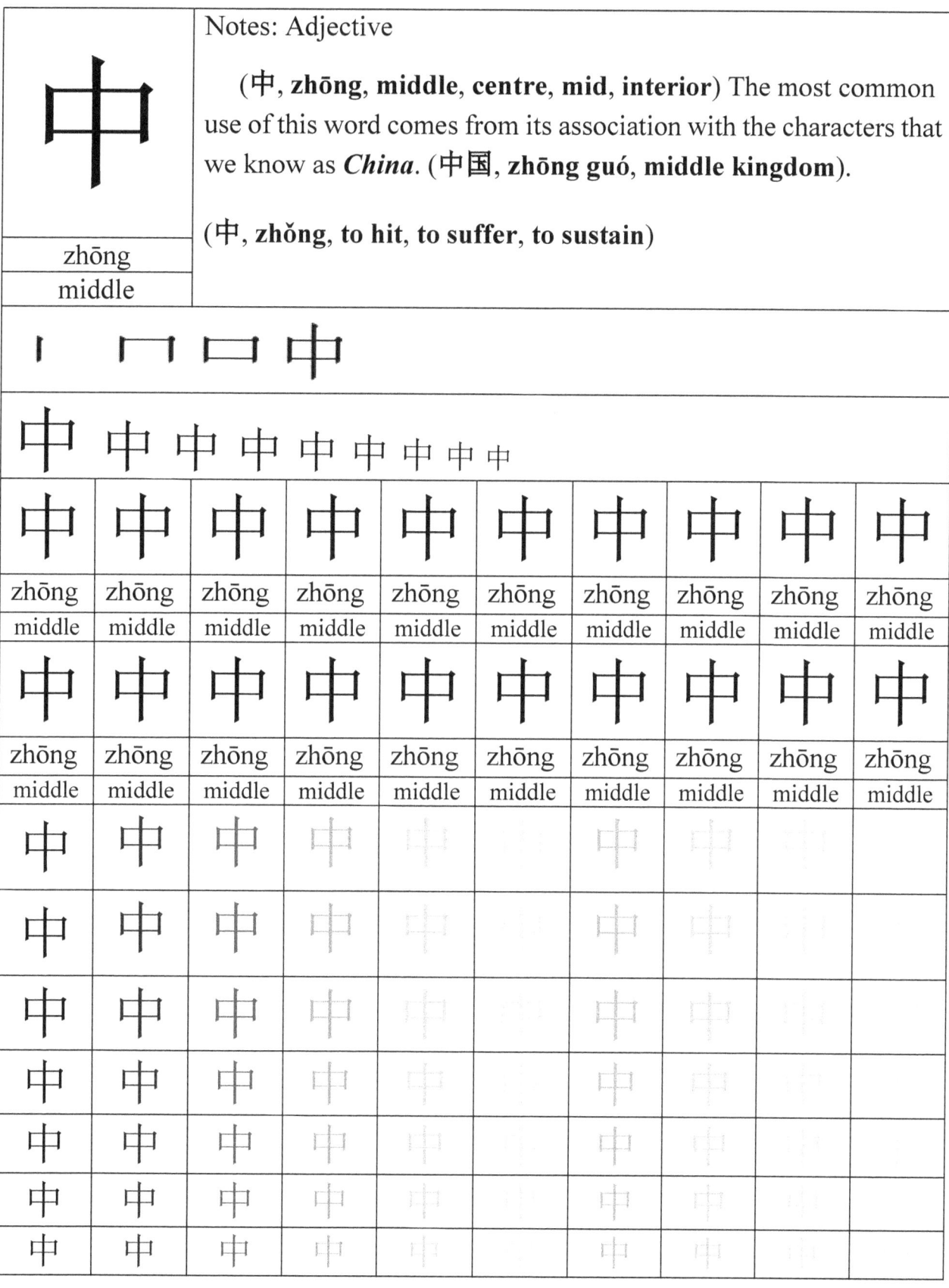

大	Notes: Quantitative Adjective (大, dà, big, huge, large, major, great, wide, deep) (大, dà, oldest, eldest, elder)
dà big	

一 ナ 大

大 大 大 大 大 大 大 大 大

大	大	大	大	大	大	大	大	大	大
dà	dà	dà	dà	dà	dà	dà	dà	dà	dà
big	big	big	big	big	big	big	big	big	big
大	大	大	大	大	大	大	大	大	大
dà	dà	dà	dà	dà	dà	dà	dà	dà	dà
big	big	big	big	big	big	big	big	big	big

[Type text]

来	Notes: Verb (来, **lái**, **come**) is the verb *to come*.
lái	
come	

一 丆 㓅 𠃓 平 来 来

来 来 来 来 来 来 来 来 来

来	来	来	来	来	来	来	来	来	来
lái	lái	lái	lái	lái	lái	lái	lái	lái	lái
come	come	come	come	come	come	come	come	come	come
来	来	来	来	来	来	来	来	来	来
lái	lái	lái	lái	lái	lái	lái	lái	lái	lái
come	come	come	come	come	come	come	come	come	come

来	来	来	来	来		来	来	来	
来	来	来	来	来		来	来	来	
来	来	来	来	来		来	来	来	
来	来	来	来	来		来	来	来	
来	来	来	来	来		来	来	来	
来	来	来	来	来		来	来	来	
来	来	来	来	来		来	来	来	

上 shàng on	Notes: Preposition (上, shàng, on, up, on top, upon, upper, higher, over, to climb up, to go into, above, to go up, upward, mount, to board) (上, shàng, first of two parts, primary, before, previous, last) (上, shàng, higher, superior, better) (上, shàng, go to, leave for, to)

丨 卜 上

上 上 上 上 上 上 上 上

上	上	上	上	上	上	上	上	上	上
shàng	shàng	shàng	shàng	shàng	shàng	shàng	shàng	shàng	shàng
on	on	on	on	on	on	on	on	on	on
上	上	上	上	上	上	上	上	上	上
shàng	shàng	shàng	shàng	shàng	shàng	shàng	shàng	shàng	shàng
on	on	on	on	on	on	on	on	on	on

国	Notes: Common Noun (国, **guó**, **kingdom**) (国, **guó**, **country, state, nation**)
guó	
kingdom	

丨 冂 冂 冃 冃 国 国 国

国 国 国 国 国 国 国 国 国

国	国	国	国	国	国	国	国	国	国
guó	guó	guó	guó	guó	guó	guó	guó	guó	guó
kingdom	kingdom	kingdom	kingdom	kingdom	kingdom	kingdom	kingdom	kingdom	kingdom
国	国	国	国	国	国	国	国	国	国
guó	guó	guó	guó	guó	guó	guó	guó	guó	guó
kingdom	kingdom	kingdom	kingdom	kingdom	kingdom	kingdom	kingdom	kingdom	kingdom

到	Notes: Verb (到, dào, to) (到, dào, to, to go to, towards, until, arrive, arrive at, reach)
dào to	

一 工 云 云 至 至 到 到

到 到 到 到 到 到 到 到 到

到	到	到	到	到	到	到	到	到	到
dào	dào	dào	dào	dào	dào	dào	dào	dào	dào
to	to	to	to	to	to	to	to	to	to
到	到	到	到	到	到	到	到	到	到
dào	dào	dào	dào	dào	dào	dào	dào	dào	dào
to	to	to	to	to	to	to	to	to	to

说	Notes: Verb
	(说, **shuō**, **to speak, to talk, to explain, to scold, to say, to state**)
	(说, **shuō**, **act as a matchmaker**)
	(说, **shuō**, **refer to, to indicate**)
shuō / speak	(说, **shuì**, **to persuade, to win over, to convince**)

丶 讠 讠 讠 讠 讲 讲 说 说

说 说 说 说 说 说 说 说 说

说	说	说	说	说	说	说	说	说	说
shuō	shuō	shuō	shuō	shuō	shuō	shuō	shuō	shuō	shuō
speak	speak	speak	speak	speak	speak	speak	speak	speak	speak
说	说	说	说	说	说	说	说	说	说
shuō	shuō	shuō	shuō	shuō	shuō	shuō	shuō	shuō	shuō
speak	speak	speak	speak	speak	speak	speak	speak	speak	speak

们 men particle	Notes: Grammatical Particle (们, **men**, **grammatical particle**) (们, **men**, **pluralizing suffix**) for Personal Pronouns and Person Nouns.

丿 亻 仁 仃 们

们 们 们 们 们 们 们 们 们

们	们	们	们	们	们	们	们	们	们
men particle	men particle	men particle	men particle	men particle	men particle	men particle	men particle	men particle	men particle
们	们	们	们	们	们	们	们	们	们
men particle	men particle	men particle	men particle	men particle	men particle	men particle	men particle	men particle	men particle

[Type text]

为	Notes: Preposition (为, wèi, stand for, support, for, on account of, on behalf of) (为, wèi, for, for the sake of, in order to) (为, wéi, do, act, act as, be, become)
wèi for	

丶 ヲ 为 为

为 为 为 为 为 为 为 为 为

和	Notes: Conjunction (和, **hé**, **and**) (和, **hé**, **together**, **with**, **union**, **harmony**) (和, **hé**, **gentle**, **mild**, **kind**, **peace**)
hé and	

丿 二 千 千 禾 和 和 和

和 和 和 和 和 和 和 和

和	和	和	和	和	和	和	和	和	和
hé and	hé and	hé and	hé and	hé and	hé and	hé and	hé and	hé and	hé and
和	和	和	和	和	和	和	和	和	和
hé and	hé and	hé and	hé and	hé and	hé and	hé and	hé and	hé and	hé and
和	和	和	和	和		和	和	和	
和	和	和	和	和		和	和		
和	和	和	和	和		和	和		
和	和	和	和	和		和	和		
和	和	和	和	和		和	和		
和	和	和	和	和		和	和	和	
和	和	和	和	和		和	和	和	

[Type text]

你

nǐ
you

Notes: Singular Second Person Pronoun

(你, **nǐ**, **you**)

(你, **nǐ**, **you**) is the Singular Second Personal Pronoun *you* and is used as the English *you*.

丿 亻 亻 伫 仔 你 你

地	Notes: Common Noun
	(地, de, **manner adverb forming particle, acts as -ly**) A common grammatical construction is to add 地 to an adjective to form a manner adverb.
dì	(地, dì, **earth, ground, dirt, soil, fields**)
earth	(地, dì, **place, position, distance**)

一 十 土 圠 圳 地

地 地 地 地 地 地 地 地 地

地	地	地	地	地	地	地	地	地	地
dì	dì	dì	dì	dì	dì	dì	dì	dì	dì
earth	earth	earth	earth	earth	earth	earth	earth	earth	earth
地	地	地	地	地	地	地	地	地	地
dì	dì	dì	dì	dì	dì	dì	dì	dì	dì
earth	earth	earth	earth	earth	earth	earth	earth	earth	earth

[Type text]

道	Notes: Common Noun
	(道, dào, a way, a method, a doctrine)
	(道, dào, a way, a path, a channel, a road, streak of light)
	(道, dào, classifier for rivers, topics)
dào	(道, dǎo, to lead)
way	

丶 丷 䒑 䒑 产 芦 䒑 首 首 首 道 道

道 道 道 道 道 道 道 道 道

道	道	道	道	道	道	道	道	道	道
dào	dào	dào	dào	dào	dào	dào	dào	dào	dào
way	way	way	way	way	way	way	way	way	way
道	道	道	道	道	道	道	道	道	道
dào	dào	dào	dào	dào	dào	dào	dào	dào	dào
way	way	way	way	way	way	way	way	way	way

道	道	道	道	道		道	道		
道	道	道	道	道		道	道		
道	道	道	道	道		道	道		
道	道	道	道	道		道	道		
道	道	道	道	道		道	道		
道	道	道	道	道		道	道		
道	道	道	道	道		道	道		

[Type text]

也	Notes: Adverb (也, yě, also, too, as well) (也, yě, either, even, more or less, by and large)
yě also	

㇆ ㇂ 也

也 也 也 也 也 也 也 也

也	也	也	也	也	也	也	也	也	也
yě also	yě also	yě also	yě also	yě also	yě also	yě also	yě also	yě also	yě also
也	也	也	也	也	也	也	也	也	也
yě also	yě also	yě also	yě also	yě also	yě also	yě also	yě also	yě also	yě also

[Type text]

时	Notes: Common Noun (时, shí, period, season, o'clock, time, when, hour) (时, Shí, surname Shí)
shí period	

丨 冂 冃 日 旷 时 时

时 时 时 时 时 时 时 时 时

时	时	时	时	时	时	时	时	时	时
shí	shí	shí	shí	shí	shí	shí	shí	shí	shí
period	period	period	period	period	period	period	period	period	period
时	时	时	时	时	时	时	时	时	时
shí	shí	shí	shí	shí	shí	shí	shí	shí	shí
period	period	period	period	period	period	period	period	period	period

时	时	时	时	时		时	时	时
时	时	时	时	时		时	时	时
时	时	时	时	时		时	时	时
时	时	时	时	时		时	时	时
时	时	时	时	时		时	时	时
时	时	时	时	时		时	时	时
时	时	时	时	时		时	时	时

[Type text]

年	Notes: Common Noun
	(年, **nián**, **year**)
nián	(年, **Nián**, **surname Nián**)
year	

丿 　 午 　 年 　 年 　 年 　 年

年 年 年 年 年 年 年 年 年

年	年	年	年	年	年	年	年	年	年
nián	nián	nián	nián	nián	nián	nián	nián	nián	nián
year	year	year	year	year	year	year	year	year	year
年	年	年	年	年	年	年	年	年	年
nián	nián	nián	nián	nián	nián	nián	nián	nián	nián
year	year	year	year	year	year	year	year	year	year

| 得 | Notes: Grammatical Particle

(得, **de**, **adverbial particle**) The form of use is verb + 得 + adjective, (**走得快**, **zǒude kuài**, **walk quickly**)

(得, **dé**, **get**, **reach**, **achieve**)

(得, **děi**, **should**) |
|---|---|
| de particle | |

丿 彳 彳 彳 彴 彴 彴 得 得 得

得 得 得 得 得 得 得 得 得

得	得	得	得	得	得	得	得	得	得
de	de	de	de	de	de	de	de	de	de
particle	particle	particle	particle	particle	particle	particle	particle	particle	particle
得	得	得	得	得	得	得	得	得	得
de	de	de	de	de	de	de	de	de	de
particle	particle	particle	particle	particle	particle	particle	particle	particle	particle

就	Notes: Adverb
jiù	(就, jiù, just, simply, right away, at once, then, only)
just	(就, jiù, to approach, to move towards, to undertake)

丶 亠 艹 亣 古 亨 亨 京 京 訃 就 就

就 就 就 就 就 就 就 就 就

就	就	就	就	就	就	就	就	就	就
jiù	jiù	jiù	jiù	jiù	jiù	jiù	jiù	jiù	jiù
just	just	just	just	just	just	just	just	just	just
就	就	就	就	就	就	就	就	就	就
jiù	jiù	jiù	jiù	jiù	jiù	jiù	jiù	jiù	jiù
just	just	just	just	just	just	just	just	just	just

那	Notes: Demonstrative Pronoun (那, **nà**, **that**) (那, **nà**, **that**) is a Demonstrative Pronoun that is used similar to the English equivalent.
nà that	

フ ヲ ヨ 月 那 那

那 那 那 那 那 那 那 那 那

那	那	那	那	那	那	那	那	那	那
nà	nà	nà	nà	nà	nà	nà	nà	nà	nà
that	that	that	that	that	that	that	that	that	that
那	那	那	那	那	那	那	那	那	那
nà	nà	nà	nà	nà	nà	nà	nà	nà	nà
that	that	that	that	that	that	that	that	that	that

那	那	那	那	那		那	那	那	
那	那	那	那	那		那	那	那	
那	那	那	那	那		那	那	那	
那	那	那	那	那		那	那	那	
那	那	那	那	那	那	那	那	那	
那	那	那	那	那	那	那	那	那	
那	那	那	那	那	那	那	那	那	

[Type text]

要	Notes: Verb
	(要, yào, want)
	(要, yào, to want, vital, will, shall, need, to be going to, important, essential, must)
yào	
want	(要, yāo, demand, ask, request, coerce)

一 丆 丆 襾 襾 要 要 要

要 要 要 要 要 要 要 要 要

要	要	要	要	要	要	要	要	要	要
yào	yào	yào	yào	yào	yào	yào	yào	yào	yào
want	want	want	want	want	want	want	want	want	want
要	要	要	要	要	要	要	要	要	要
yào	yào	yào	yào	yào	yào	yào	yào	yào	yào
want	want	want	want	want	want	want	want	want	want
要	要	要	要	要	要	要	要	要	
要	要	要	要	要	要	要	要	要	
要	要	要	要	要	要	要	要	要	
要	要	要	要	要	要	要	要	要	
要	要	要	要	要	要	要	要	要	
要	要	要	要	要	要	要	要	要	
要	要	要	要	要	要	要	要	要	

下	Notes: Adverb
	(下, **xià, below, under, go down, underneath**)
	(下, **xià, to decline, to go down**)
xià	(下, **xià, second of two parts, next, latter**)
below	

一 丁 下

下 下 下 下 下 下 下 下 下

下	下	下	下	下	下	下	下	下	下
xià	xià	xià	xià	xià	xià	xià	xià	xià	xià
below	below	below	below	below	below	below	below	below	below
下	下	下	下	下	下	下	下	下	下
xià	xià	xià	xià	xià	xià	xià	xià	xià	xià
below	below	below	below	below	below	below	below	below	below

yǐ
take

Notes: Verb

(以, **yǐ**, **take**, **use**)

(以, **yǐ**, **according to**, **because of**, **in order to**, **so as to**)

(以, **yǐ**, **empty verb suffix**) is added after some verbs to create a two character verb to give it spoken balance.

生

shēng
to bear

Notes: Verb

(生, **shēng, to bear**)

(生, **shēng, give birth, to be born, life, to grow, to bear, to produce**)

丿 𠂉 𠂇 牛 生

生 生 生 生 生 生 生 生 生

生	生	生	生	生	生	生	生	生	生
shēng	shēng	shēng	shēng	shēng	shēng	shēng	shēng	shēng	shēng
to bear	to bear	to bear	to bear	to bear	to bear	to bear	to bear	to bear	to bear
生	生	生	生	生	生	生	生	生	生
shēng	shēng	shēng	shēng	shēng	shēng	shēng	shēng	shēng	shēng
to bear	to bear	to bear	to bear	to bear	to bear	to bear	to bear	to bear	to bear

会

huì / able

Notes: Verb

(会, **huì, know how to, can, able**)

(会, **huì, meet, meeting, society, union, party**)

(会, **kuài, accounting**)

(会, **huǐ, moment**)

Stroke order: 丿 人 亼 亽 会 会

会	会	会	会	会	会	会	会	会	会
huì	huì	huì	huì	huì	huì	huì	huì	huì	huì
able	able	able	able	able	able	able	able	able	able
会	会	会	会	会	会	会	会	会	会
huì	huì	huì	huì	huì	huì	huì	huì	huì	huì
able	able	able	able	able	able	able	able	able	able

着	Notes: Grammatical Particle
zhe particle	(着, **zhe, verb particle marking a continuing progress state**)
	(着, **zháo, touch**)
	(着, **zhuó, wear clothes, dress**)
	(着, **zhāo, put in, add**)

丶 丷 䒑 䒑 羊 羊 差 着 着 着

着 着 着 着 着 着 着 着

着	着	着	着	着	着	着	着	着	着
zhe	zhe	zhe	zhe	zhe	zhe	zhe	zhe	zhe	zhe
particle	particle	particle	particle	particle	particle	particle	particle	particle	particle
着	着	着	着	着	着	着	着	着	着
zhe	zhe	zhe	zhe	zhe	zhe	zhe	zhe	zhe	zhe
particle	particle	particle	particle	particle	particle	particle	particle	particle	particle

去	Notes: Verb
	(去, qù, go, to go, to leave, to depart)
	(去, qù, get rid of, remove, cast out)
	(去, qù, be apart)
qù	
go	

一 十 土 去 去

去 去 去 去 去 去 去 去 去

去	去	去	去	去	去	去	去	去	去
qù	qù	qù	qù	qù	qù	qù	qù	qù	qù
go	go	go	go	go	go	go	go	go	go
去	去	去	去	去	去	去	去	去	去
qù	qù	qù	qù	qù	qù	qù	qù	qù	qù
go	go	go	go	go	go	go	go	go	go

	Notes: Personal Pronoun (之, **zhī**, **it**) in classical writing. (之, **zhī**, **subordinator similar to** 的 **de**)
zhī	
it	

丶 ㇋ 之

之 之 之 之 之 之 之 之 之

之	之	之	之	之	之	之	之	之	之
zhī	zhī	zhī	zhī	zhī	zhī	zhī	zhī	zhī	zhī
it	it	it	it	it	it	it	it	it	it
之	之	之	之	之	之	之	之	之	之
zhī	zhī	zhī	zhī	zhī	zhī	zhī	zhī	zhī	zhī
it	it	it	it	it	it	it	it	it	it

[Type text]

过	Notes: Grammatical Particle
guò particle	(过, **guò**, **particle**)
	(过, **guò**, **pass**, **cross**, **go by**, **exceed**)
	(过, **guò**, **experiential verb particle**) marking that someone has had the experience of doing something, that it has happened at least once in the past.

一 寸 寸 寸 讨 过

过 过 过 过 过 过 过 过 过

家 jiā home	Notes: Common Noun (家, jiā, home, household, family) (家, Jiā, surname Jiā) (家, jiā, school of thought) (家, jiā, as a suffix to form Reflexive Personal Pronouns)

丶 丷 宀 宁 宀 宁 穷 家 家 家

家 家 家 家 家 家 家 家 家

家	家	家	家	家	家	家	家	家	家
jiā	jiā	jiā	jiā	jiā	jiā	jiā	jiā	jiā	jiā
home	home	home	home	home	home	home	home	home	home
家	家	家	家	家	家	家	家	家	家
jiā	jiā	jiā	jiā	jiā	jiā	jiā	jiā	jiā	jiā
home	home	home	home	home	home	home	home	home	home

学	Notes: Verb
	(学, xué, study, learn, knowledge)
	(学, xué, to imitate, to mimic)
	(学, xué, branch of study as –ology, subject of study)
xué learn	(学, xué, school, college, university)

丶 ⸍ ⸌ ⹁⹁ ⺌ 兴 学 学 学

学 学 学 学 学 学 学 学 学

学	学	学	学	学	学	学	学	学	学
xué	xué	xué	xué	xué	xué	xué	xué	xué	xué
learn	learn	learn	learn	learn	learn	learn	learn	learn	learn
学	学	学	学	学	学	学	学	学	学
xué	xué	xué	xué	xué	xué	xué	xué	xué	xué
learn	learn	learn	learn	learn	learn	learn	learn	learn	learn
学	学	学	学	学		学	学		
学	学	学	学	学		学	学		
学	学	学	学	学		学	学		
学	学	学	学	学		学	学		
学	学	学	学	学		学	学		

[Type text]

对	Notes: Verb
	(对, **duì**, **answer**, **reply**)
	(对, **duì**, **correct**, **agree**, **right**)
dui	(对, **duì**, **mutual**, **pair**)
correct	

フ ヌ ヌ˙ 对 对

对 对 对 对 对 对 对 对 对

对	对	对	对	对	对	对	对	对	对
duì	duì	duì	duì	duì	duì	duì	duì	duì	duì
correct	correct	correct	correct	correct	correct	correct	correct	correct	correct
对	对	对	对	对	对	对	对	对	对
duì	duì	duì	duì	duì	duì	duì	duì	duì	duì
correct	correct	correct	correct	correct	correct	correct	correct	correct	correct

对	对	对	对	对		对	对	对	
对	对	对	对	对		对	对	对	
对	对	对	对	对		对	对	对	
对	对	对	对	对		对	对	对	
对	对	对	对	对		对	对	对	
对	对	对	对	对		对	对	对	
对	对	对	对	对		对	对	对	

[Type text]

可	Notes: Co-Verb (可, **kě**, **able**) (可, **kě**, **+able**, **may**, **can**) can be used to create the possibility of the action of a verb.
kě able	

她	Notes: Singular Third Person Pronoun
tā	(她, **tā**, **she**, **her**) is functionally the feminine Third Person Singular Pronoun.
she	

く 纟 女 幻 妣 她

她 她 她 她 她 她 她 她

后	Notes: Preposition (后, hòu, after, behind) (后, hòu, queen)
hòu	
behind	

一 厂 厂 斤 后 后

后 后 后 后 后 后 后 后 后

后	后	后	后	后	后	后	后	后	后
hòu	hòu	hòu	hòu	hòu	hòu	hòu	hòu	hòu	hòu
behind	behind	behind	behind	behind	behind	behind	behind	behind	behind
后	后	后	后	后	后	后	后	后	后
hòu	hòu	hòu	hòu	hòu	hòu	hòu	hòu	hòu	hòu
behind	behind	behind	behind	behind	behind	behind	behind	behind	behind

[Type text]

小	Notes: Quantitative Adjective (小, **xiǎo**, **small**, **tiny**, **few**, **young**)
xiǎo small	

亅 丿 小

小 小 小 小 小 小 小 小 小

小	小	小	小	小	小	小	小	小	小
xiǎo	xiǎo	xiǎo	xiǎo	xiǎo	xiǎo	xiǎo	xiǎo	xiǎo	xiǎo
small	small	small	small	small	small	small	small	small	small
小	小	小	小	小	小	小	小	小	小
xiǎo	xiǎo	xiǎo	xiǎo	xiǎo	xiǎo	xiǎo	xiǎo	xiǎo	xiǎo
small	small	small	small	small	small	small	small	small	small

Notes: Interrogative Grammatical Particle

(么, **me**, **grammatical particle**)

(么, **me**, **interrogative suffix**)

me / particle

心	Notes: Common Noun (心, xīn, heart)
xīn	
heart	

丿 心 心 心

心 心 心 心 心 心 心 心 心

心	心	心	心	心	心	心	心	心	心
xīn	xīn	xīn	xīn	xīn	xīn	xīn	xīn	xīn	xīn
heart	heart	heart	heart	heart	heart	heart	heart	heart	heart
心	心	心	心	心	心	心	心	心	心
xīn	xīn	xīn	xīn	xīn	xīn	xīn	xīn	xīn	xīn
heart	heart	heart	heart	heart	heart	heart	heart	heart	heart

心	心	心	心	心		心	心		
心	心	心	心	心		心	心		
心	心	心	心	心		心	心		
心	心	心	心	心		心	心		
心	心	心	心	心		心	心		
心	心	心	心	心		心	心		
心	心	心	心	心		心	心		

[Type text]

多

duō — many

Notes: Quantitative Adjective

(多, duō, many, much, more)

Stroke order: 丿 ク 夕 夕 多 多

天	Notes: Common Noun
tiān	(天, tiān, day, sky)
day	(天, tiān, heaven, god)

一 二 テ 天

天 天 天 天 天 天 天 天 天

天	天	天	天	天	天	天	天	天	天
tiān	tiān	tiān	tiān	tiān	tiān	tiān	tiān	tiān	tiān
day	day	day	day	day	day	day	day	day	day
天	天	天	天	天	天	天	天	天	天
tiān	tiān	tiān	tiān	tiān	tiān	tiān	tiān	tiān	tiān
day	day	day	day	day	day	day	day	day	day

天	天	天	天	天		天	天	天	
天	天	天	天	天		天	天	天	
天	天	天	天	天		天	天	天	
天	天	天	天	天		天	天	天	
天	天	天	天	天		天	天	天	
天	天	天	天	天		天	天	天	
天	天	天	天	天		天	天	天	

而	Notes: Conjunction
ér / and	(而, ér, and, and yet) (而, ér, furthermore, as well as, but not, yet not) (而, ér, shows causal relation, shows change of state, shows contrast)

一 丆 丆 丙 而 而

能	Notes: Co-Verb
néng	(能, **néng**, **can**)
can	(能, **néng**, **can, be able**)

⼂ ⼛ 乍 奆 奆 斻 能 能 能

能 能 能 能 能 能 能 能

能	能	能	能	能	能	能	能	能	能
néng	néng	néng	néng	néng	néng	néng	néng	néng	néng
can	can	can	can	can	can	can	can	can	can
能	能	能	能	能	能	能	能	能	能
néng	néng	néng	néng	néng	néng	néng	néng	néng	néng
can	can	can	can	can	can	can	can	can	can

能	能	能	能	能		能	能	能
能	能	能	能	能		能	能	能
能	能	能	能	能		能	能	能
能	能	能	能	能		能	能	能
能	能	能	能	能		能	能	能
能	能	能	能	能		能	能	能
能	能	能	能	能		能	能	能

[Type text]

好	Notes: Qualitative Adjective
hǎo / good	(好, **hǎo**, **good**)
	(好, **hǎo**, **good, good to..., easy to…**)
	(好, **hào**, **to like**)
	(好, **hāo**, **in good condition**)

く 女 女 奵 奵 好

好 好 好 好 好 好 好 好 好

好	好	好	好	好	好	好	好	好	好
hǎo	hǎo	hǎo	hǎo	hǎo	hǎo	hǎo	hǎo	hǎo	hǎo
good	good	good	good	good	good	good	good	good	good
好	好	好	好	好	好	好	好	好	好
hǎo	hǎo	hǎo	hǎo	hǎo	hǎo	hǎo	hǎo	hǎo	hǎo
good	good	good	good	good	good	good	good	good	good

都 dōu all	Notes: Adverb of Degree (都, dōu, all, always) (都, dōu, even, already) (都, dū, capital city)

一 十 土 耂 耂 者 者 者 都 都

都 都 都 都 都 都 都 都

都	都	都	都	都	都	都	都	都	都
dōu	dōu	dōu	dōu	dōu	dōu	dōu	dōu	dōu	dōu
all	all	all	all	all	all	all	all	all	all
都	都	都	都	都	都	都	都	都	都
dōu	dōu	dōu	dōu	dōu	dōu	dōu	dōu	dōu	dōu
all	all	all	all	all	all	all	all	all	all

然	Notes: Adverb (然, rán, right) (然, rán, so, like that)
rán	
right	

丿 ク 夕 夕 夕 ー 夕十 夕大 夕大 夕大 然 然 然

然 然 然 然 然 然 然 然 然

然	然	然	然	然	然	然	然	然	然
rán right	rán right	rán right	rán right	rán right	rán right	rán right	rán right	rán right	rán right
然	然	然	然	然	然	然	然	然	然
rán right	rán right	rán right	rán right	rán right	rán right	rán right	rán right	rán right	rán right
然	然	然	然	然		然	然		
然	然	然	然	然		然	然		
然	然	然	然	然		然	然		
然	然	然	然	然		然	然		
然	然	然	然	然		然	然		
然	然	然	然	然		然	然		
然	然	然	然	然		然	然		

没	Notes: Adverb
méi / not	(没, **méi**, **not**) is used to negate the verb (有, **yǒu**, **have**).
	(没, **mò**, **drown, sink, submerge, overflow**)
	(没, **mò**, **conceal, vanish, confiscate**)
	(没, **mò**, **die**)

丶 丶 氵 氵 沪 汐 没

没 没 没 没 没 没 没 没 没

Notes: Common Noun

(日, **rì**, **sun**, **day**)

rì
sun

起	Notes: Verb
	(起, qǐ, to arise, get up, start)
	(起, qǐ, to unload, to remove)
	(起, qǐ, to raise, to build)
qǐ	(起, qi, when used as a verb complement)
rise	

一 十 土 キ キ 丰 走 起 起 起

还	Notes: Adverb
	(还, hái, still, yet, even, still more, also, too, as well as)
hái	(还, hái, passably, fairly)
still	(还, huán, return, give back)

一 丆 不 不 不 还 还

发	Notes: Verb
	(发, fā, send out, deliver, distribute)
	(发, fā, to utter, express, shoot, emit, develop, expand)
	(发, fà, hair)
fā deliver	(发, fà, to make a fortune (slang))

一 ナ 岁 发 发

发 发 发 发 发 发 发 发 发

发	发	发	发	发	发	发	发	发	发
fā	fā	fā	fā	fā	fā	fā	fā	fā	fā
deliver	deliver	deliver	deliver	deliver	deliver	deliver	deliver	deliver	deliver
发	发	发	发	发	发	发	发	发	发
fā	fā	fā	fā	fā	fā	fā	fā	fā	fā
deliver	deliver	deliver	deliver	deliver	deliver	deliver	deliver	deliver	deliver

| 成 chéng become | Notes: Verb (成, **chéng**, **become, finish, complete, succeed, accomplish**) (成, **chéng**, **win**) (成, **Chéng**, **surname Chéng**) (成, **chéng**, one tenth) |

一 厂 厂 成 成 成

成 成 成 成 成 成 成 成 成

成	成	成	成	成	成	成	成	成	成
chéng	chéng	chéng	chéng	chéng	chéng	chéng	chéng	chéng	chéng
become	become	become	become	become	become	become	become	become	become
成	成	成	成	成	成	成	成	成	成
chéng	chéng	chéng	chéng	chéng	chéng	chéng	chéng	chéng	chéng
become	become	become	become	become	become	become	become	become	become

[Type text]

事	Notes: Common Noun
	(事, shì, matter)
	(事, shì, matter, affair, thing, event, accident, job, responsibility)
shì	
matter	(事, shì, job)

一 亅 亅 口 寸 写 写 写 事

事 事 事 事 事 事 事 事 事

事	事	事	事	事	事	事	事	事	事
shì	shì	shì	shì	shì	shì	shì	shì	shì	shì
matter	matter	matter	matter	matter	matter	matter	matter	matter	matter
事	事	事	事	事	事	事	事	事	事
shì	shì	shì	shì	shì	shì	shì	shì	shì	shì
matter	matter	matter	matter	matter	matter	matter	matter	matter	matter

[practice grid]

[Type text]

只	Notes: Adverb
zhǐ	(只, **zhǐ, only, single, one, just, merely**)
only	(只, **zhī, measure word for one of a pair**)
	(只, **zhī, measure word, for birds and some animals**)

丨 冂 口 叧 只

只 只 只 只 只 只 只 只 只

只	只	只	只	只	只	只	只	只	只
zhǐ	zhǐ	zhǐ	zhǐ	zhǐ	zhǐ	zhǐ	zhǐ	zhǐ	zhǐ
only	only	only	only	only	only	only	only	only	only
只	只	只	只	只	只	只	只	只	只
zhǐ	zhǐ	zhǐ	zhǐ	zhǐ	zhǐ	zhǐ	zhǐ	zhǐ	zhǐ
only	only	only	only	only	only	only	only	only	only

作 zuò do	Notes: Verb (作, **zuò**, **do**, **make**) (作, **zuó**, **spoil**, **waste**, **humiliate**, **insult**) (作, **zuó**, **humiliate**, **insult**)

丿 亻 伄 仁 仵 作 作

作 作 作 作 作 作 作 作 作

作	作	作	作	作	作	作	作	作	作
zuò do	zuò do	zuò do	zuò do	zuò do	zuò do	zuò do	zuò do	zuò do	zuò do
作	作	作	作	作	作	作	作	作	作
zuò do	zuò do	zuò do	zuò do	zuò do	zuò do	zuò do	zuò do	zuò do	zuò do

当	Notes: Verb
	(当, dāng, accept, serve as)
dāng	(当, dàng, proper, right, equal, at or in the very same..., to pawn, suitable, adequate, fitting, replace, represent)
accept	

丨 丶 ⺌ 半 当 当

当	当	当	当	当	当	当	当	当

当	当	当	当	当	当	当	当	当	当
dāng	dāng	dāng	dāng	dāng	dāng	dāng	dāng	dāng	dāng
accept	accept	accept	accept	accept	accept	accept	accept	accept	accept
当	当	当	当	当	当	当	当	当	当
dāng	dāng	dāng	dāng	dāng	dāng	dāng	dāng	dāng	dāng
accept	accept	accept	accept	accept	accept	accept	accept	accept	accept

[Type text]

想	Notes: Verb (想, **xiǎng**, **desire**) (想, **xiǎng**, **think, feel, consider, want, remember, desire**)
xiǎng	
desire	

一 十 才 木 利 机 桕 相 相 相 想 想 想

想 想 想 想 想 想 想 想 想

想	想	想	想	想	想	想	想	想	想
xiǎng	xiǎng	xiǎng	xiǎng	xiǎng	xiǎng	xiǎng	xiǎng	xiǎng	xiǎng
desire	desire	desire	desire	desire	desire	desire	desire	desire	desire
想	想	想	想	想	想	想	想	想	想
xiǎng	xiǎng	xiǎng	xiǎng	xiǎng	xiǎng	xiǎng	xiǎng	xiǎng	xiǎng
desire	desire	desire	desire	desire	desire	desire	desire	desire	desire

[Type text]

看	Notes: Verb
kàn	(看, kàn, look)
look	(看, kàn, see, look, look at, read, think, consider)
	(看, kān, look after, tend, take care of)

一 二 三 手 チ 丢 看 看 看

看 看 看 看 看 看 看 看 看

看	看	看	看	看	看	看	看	看	看
kàn	kàn	kàn	kàn	kàn	kàn	kàn	kàn	kàn	kàn
look	look	look	look	look	look	look	look	look	look
看	看	看	看	看	看	看	看	看	看
kàn	kàn	kàn	kàn	kàn	kàn	kàn	kàn	kàn	kàn
look	look	look	look	look	look	look	look	look	look

文	Notes: Common Noun (文, **wén**, **script**) (文, **wén**, **language**, **literature**)
wén script	

丶 亠 ナ 文

文 文 文 文 文 文 文 文 文

文	文	文	文	文	文	文	文	文	文
wén script	wén script	wén script	wén script	wén script	wén script	wén script	wén script	wén script	wén script
文	文	文	文	文	文	文	文	文	文
wén script	wén script	wén script	wén script	wén script	wén script	wén script	wén script	wén script	wén script
文	文	文	文	文	文	文	文	文	
文	文	文	文	文	文	文	文	文	
文	文	文	文	文	文	文	文	文	
文	文	文	文	文	文	文	文	文	
文	文	文	文	文	文	文	文	文	
文	文	文	文	文	文	文	文	文	
文	文	文	文	文	文	文	文	文	

无	Notes: Adverb
wú	(无, **wú**, **not**)
not	(无, **wú**, **without, nothingness, have not**)

一 二 チ 无

无 无 无 无 无 无 无 无 无

无	无	无	无	无	无	无	无	无	无
wú	wú	wú	wú	wú	wú	wú	wú	wú	wú
not	not	not	not	not	not	not	not	not	not
无	无	无	无	无	无	无	无	无	无
wú	wú	wú	wú	wú	wú	wú	wú	wú	wú
not	not	not	not	not	not	not	not	not	not

开	Notes: Verb (开, kāi, open, initiate, begin, start) (开, kāi, to operate a…, to start)
kāi open	

一 二 开 开

开 开 开 开 开 开 开 开 开

开	开	开	开	开	开	开	开	开	开
kāi	kāi	kāi	kāi	kāi	kāi	kāi	kāi	kāi	kāi
open	open	open	open	open	open	open	open	open	open
开	开	开	开	开	开	开	开	开	开
kāi	kāi	kāi	kāi	kāi	kāi	kāi	kāi	kāi	kāi
open	open	open	open	open	open	open	open	open	open

开	开	开	开	开	开	开	开	开	开
开	开	开	开	开	开	开	开	开	开
开	开	开	开	开	开	开	开	开	开
开	开	开	开	开	开	开	开	开	开
开	开	开	开	开	开	开	开	开	开
开	开	开	开	开	开	开	开	开	开
开	开	开	开	开	开	开	开	开	开

[Type text]

手 shǒu hand	Notes: Common Noun (手, shǒu, hand) (手, shǒu, a person skilled in something)

一 二 三 手

手 手 手 手 手 手 手 手 手

手	手	手	手	手	手	手	手	手	手
shǒu	shǒu	shǒu	shǒu	shǒu	shǒu	shǒu	shǒu	shǒu	shǒu
hand	hand	hand	hand	hand	hand	hand	hand	hand	hand
手	手	手	手	手	手	手	手	手	手
shǒu	shǒu	shǒu	shǒu	shǒu	shǒu	shǒu	shǒu	shǒu	shǒu
hand	hand	hand	hand	hand	hand	hand	hand	hand	hand

[Type text]

用	Notes: Verb (用, **yòng, to use**)
yòng use	

丿 冂 月 月 用

用 用 用 用 用 用 用

用	用	用	用	用	用	用	用	用	用
yòng	yòng	yòng	yòng	yòng	yòng	yòng	yòng	yòng	yòng
use	use	use	use	use	use	use	use	use	use
用	用	用	用	用	用	用	用	用	用
yòng	yòng	yòng	yòng	yòng	yòng	yòng	yòng	yòng	yòng
use	use	use	use	use	use	use	use	use	use
用	用	用	用	用		用	用	用	
用	用	用	用	用		用	用	用	
用	用	用	用	用		用	用	用	
用	用	用	用	用		用	用	用	
用	用	用	用	用		用	用	用	
用	用	用	用	用		用	用	用	
用	用	用	用	用		用	用	用	

所

Notes: Common Noun

(所, **suǒ**, **place**)

suǒ — place

丶 厂 斤 斤 斤 斤 斤 所

所 所 所 所 所 所 所 所 所

所	所	所	所	所	所	所	所	所	所
suǒ	suǒ	suǒ	suǒ	suǒ	suǒ	suǒ	suǒ	suǒ	suǒ
place	place	place	place	place	place	place	place	place	place
所	所	所	所	所	所	所	所	所	所
suǒ	suǒ	suǒ	suǒ	suǒ	suǒ	suǒ	suǒ	suǒ	suǒ
place	place	place	place	place	place	place	place	place	place

方	Notes: Common Noun
fāng / side	(方, **fāng**, **side, direction, place, region, position**)
	(方, **fāng**, **side, a carpenter's square**)
	(方, **fāng**, **prescription, recipe**)
	(方, **fāng**, **method, way**)

丶 亠 亏 方

方 方 方 方 方 方 方 方 方

方	方	方	方	方	方	方	方	方	方
fāng side	fāng side	fāng side	fāng side	fāng side	fāng side	fāng side	fāng side	fāng side	fāng side
方	方	方	方	方	方	方	方	方	方
fāng side	fāng side	fāng side	fāng side	fāng side	fāng side	fāng side	fāng side	fāng side	fāng side

又	Notes: Adverb
yòu	(又, **yòu**, **again**)
again	(又, **yòu**, **again**, **both... and...**)

丿 又

又

如	Notes: Verb
rú	(如, rú, like, similar, such as, as if, for example, measure up)
like	(如, rú, as, as if)
	(如, rú, be in accord with, according to, in accordance with)

く 夊 女 奴 如 如

如 如 如 如 如 如 如 如 如

前	Notes: Preposition (前, qián, front, in front of, previous, ago, before, former, first, preceding, formerly, ahead)
qián front	

丶 丷 䒑 产 产 肯 甘 前 前

前 前 前 前 前 前 前 前

前	前	前	前	前	前	前	前	前	前
qián	qián	qián	qián	qián	qián	qián	qián	qián	qián
front	front	front	front	front	front	front	front	front	front
前	前	前	前	前	前	前	前	前	前
qián	qián	qián	qián	qián	qián	qián	qián	qián	qián
front	front	front	front	front	front	front	front	front	front

本 běn basis	Notes: Common Noun (本, běn, basis) (本, běn, basis, origin, edition, foundation) (本, běn, classifier for books, periodicals, files)

一 十 才 木 本

本 本 本 本 本 本 本 本 本

本	本	本	本	本	本	本	本	本	本
běn	běn	běn	běn	běn	běn	běn	běn	běn	běn
basis	basis	basis	basis	basis	basis	basis	basis	basis	basis
本	本	本	本	本	本	本	本	本	本
běn	běn	běn	běn	běn	běn	běn	běn	běn	běn
basis	basis	basis	basis	basis	basis	basis	basis	basis	basis

[Type text]

三	Notes: Quantitative Adjective (三, sān, three, 3) (三, sān, more than two, several, many)
sān	
three	

一 二 三

三 三 三 三 三 三 三 三

三	三	三	三	三	三	三	三	三	三
sān	sān	sān	sān	sān	sān	sān	sān	sān	sān
three	three	three	three	three	three	three	three	three	three
三	三	三	三	三	三	三	三	三	三
sān	sān	sān	sān	sān	sān	sān	sān	sān	sān
three	three	three	three	three	three	three	three	three	three
三	三	三	三	三	三	三	三	三	三
三	三	三	三	三	三	三	三	三	三
三	三	三	三	三	三	三	三	三	三
三	三	三	三	三	三	三	三	三	三
三	三	三	三	三	三	三	三	三	三
三	三	三	三	三	三	三	三	三	三
三	三	三	三	三	三	三	三	三	三

[Type text]

见	Notes: Verb
jiàn meet	(见, **jiàn**, **meet**) (见, **jiàn**, appear to be, meet with, call on) (见, **jiàn**, to show, appear, become visible)

丨 冂 刂 见

见 见 见 见 见 见 见 见 见

见	见	见	见	见	见	见	见	见	见
jiàn	jiàn	jiàn	jiàn	jiàn	jiàn	jiàn	jiàn	jiàn	jiàn
meet	meet	meet	meet	meet	meet	meet	meet	meet	meet
见	见	见	见	见	见	见	见	见	见
jiàn	jiàn	jiàn	jiàn	jiàn	jiàn	jiàn	jiàn	jiàn	jiàn
meet	meet	meet	meet	meet	meet	meet	meet	meet	meet

经

jīng — classics

Notes: Verb

(经, jīng, pass through, to undergo, to endure)

(经, jīng, classics, sacred book, scripture, canon)

(经, Jīng, surname Jīng)

头	Notes: Common Noun
	(头, tóu, head, a head of)
	(头, tóu, top, first)
tóu	(头, tóu, classifier for livestock, garlic)
head	

丶 丷 丷 头 头

头 头 头 头 头 头 头 头 头

头	头	头	头	头	头	头	头	头	头
tóu	tóu	tóu	tóu	tóu	tóu	tóu	tóu	tóu	tóu
head	head	head	head	head	head	head	head	head	head
头	头	头	头	头	头	头	头	头	头
tóu	tóu	tóu	tóu	tóu	tóu	tóu	tóu	tóu	tóu
head	head	head	head	head	head	head	head	head	head

[Type text]

公	Notes: Common Noun
gōng public	(公, **gōng**, **public affairs, official duties**)
	(公, **gōng**, **following a surname, a respectful form of address for an elderly or married man**)
	(公, **gōng**, **common, accepted**)

丿 八 公 公

公 公 公 公 公 公 公 公 公

公	公	公	公	公	公	公	公	公	公
gōng public	gōng public	gōng public	gōng public	gōng public	gōng public	gōng public	gōng public	gōng public	gōng public
公	公	公	公	公	公	公	公	公	公
gōng public	gōng public	gōng public	gōng public	gōng public	gōng public	gōng public	gōng public	gōng public	gōng public

[Type text]

已	Notes: Verb (已, yǐ, stop, cease, end, finish, complete) (已, yǐ, already, thereafter, afterward)
yǐ	
stop	

㇐ ㇒ 已

已 已 已 已 已 已 已 已 已 已

已	已	已	已	已	已	已	已	已	已
yǐ	yǐ	yǐ	yǐ	yǐ	yǐ	yǐ	yǐ	yǐ	yǐ
stop	stop	stop	stop	stop	stop	stop	stop	stop	stop
已	已	已	已	已	已	已	已	已	已
yǐ	yǐ	yǐ	yǐ	yǐ	yǐ	yǐ	yǐ	yǐ	yǐ
stop	stop	stop	stop	stop	stop	stop	stop	stop	stop
已	已	已	已						
已	已	已	已						
已	已	已	已						
已	已	已	已						
已	已	已	已						
已	已	已	已						
已	已	已	已						

[Type text]

行	Notes: Adjective
	(行, xíng, okay, capable, competent, acceptable, all right)
	(行, xíng, go, walk, travel, circulate, prevail)
	(行, xíng, overflow, rise beyond)
xíng okay	行, háng, héng, a line, a row)

丿 彳 彳 彳 彳 行

行 行 行 行 行 行 行 行 行

行	行	行	行	行	行	行	行	行	行
xíng	xíng	xíng	xíng	xíng	xíng	xíng	xíng	xíng	xíng
okay	okay	okay	okay	okay	okay	okay	okay	okay	okay
行	行	行	行	行	行	行	行	行	行
xíng	xíng	xíng	xíng	xíng	xíng	xíng	xíng	xíng	xíng
okay	okay	okay	okay	okay	okay	okay	okay	okay	okay

老	Notes: Adjective (老, lǎo, old, outdated) (老, lǎo, venerable) (老, lǎo, always)
lǎo old	

一 十 土 耂 耂 老

老 老 老 老 老 老 老 老 老

老	老	老	老	老	老	老	老	老	老
lǎo	lǎo	lǎo	lǎo	lǎo	lǎo	lǎo	lǎo	lǎo	lǎo
old	old	old	old	old	old	old	old	old	old
老	老	老	老	老	老	老	老	老	老
lǎo	lǎo	lǎo	lǎo	lǎo	lǎo	lǎo	lǎo	lǎo	lǎo
old	old	old	old	old	old	old	old	old	old

老	老	老	老	老		老	老	老
老	老	老	老	老		老	老	老
老	老	老	老	老		老	老	老
老	老	老	老	老		老	老	老
老	老	老	老	老	老	老	老	老
老	老	老	老	老	老	老	老	老
老	老	老	老	老	老	老	老	老

[Type text]

| 从 cóng from | Notes: Preposition
(从, **cóng**, **from**, **follow**)
(从, **cóng**, **from**, **through**, **join**)
(从, **cóng**, **follower**, **secondary**) |

丿 亻 从 从

老 老 老 老 老 老 老 老 老

从	从	从	从	从	从	从	从	从	从
cóng	cóng	cóng	cóng	cóng	cóng	cóng	cóng	cóng	cóng
from	from	from	from	from	from	from	from	from	from
从	从	从	从	从	从	从	从	从	从
cóng	cóng	cóng	cóng	cóng	cóng	cóng	cóng	cóng	cóng
from	from	from	from	from	from	from	from	from	from

动	Notes: Verb (动, **dòng**, **to use**) (动, **dòng**, to act, to move, to change)
dòng	
to use	

一 二 云 云 幻 动

动 动 动 动 动 动 动 动 动

动	动	动	动	动	动	动	动	动	动
dòng	dòng	dòng	dòng	dòng	dòng	dòng	dòng	dòng	dòng
to use	to use	to use	to use	to use	to use	to use	to use	to use	to use
动	动	动	动	动	动	动	动	动	动
dòng	dòng	dòng	dòng	dòng	dòng	dòng	dòng	dòng	dòng
to use	to use	to use	to use	to use	to use	to use	to use	to use	to use
动	动	动	动	动	动	动	动	动	动
动	动	动	动	动	动	动	动	动	动
动	动	动	动	动	动	动	动	动	动
动	动	动	动	动	动	动	动	动	动
动	动	动	动	动	动	动	动	动	动
动	动	动	动	动	动	动	动	动	动
动	动	动	动	动	动	动	动	动	动

[Type text]

两	Notes: Quantitative Adjective
liǎng two	(两, liǎng, two)
	(两, liǎng, both, some, a few)
	(两, liǎng, either side, both sides)
	(两, liǎng, measure word for tael weight)

一 厂 冂 冋 丙 两 两

两 两 两 两 两 两 两 两 两

两	两	两	两	两	两	两	两	两	两
liǎng	liǎng	liǎng	liǎng	liǎng	liǎng	liǎng	liǎng	liǎng	liǎng
two	two	two	two	two	two	two	two	two	two
两	两	两	两	两	两	两	两	两	两
liǎng	liǎng	liǎng	liǎng	liǎng	liǎng	liǎng	liǎng	liǎng	liǎng
two	two	two	two	two	two	two	two	two	two

	Notes: Adjective
cháng / long	(长, **cháng, long, lasting, length**)
	(长, **zhǎng, grow up, chief, head, older, elder**)
	(长, **cháng, steadily, regularly**)

ノ 一 长 长

知	Notes: Verb (知, **zhī**, **to know**) (知, **zhī**, **realize, sense, to be aware of**) (知, **zhī**, **to inform, to notify, to tell**)
zhī	
to know	

丿 ㄥ 乍 矢 矢 知 知 知

知 知 知 知 知 知 知 知

知	知	知	知	知	知	知	知	知	知
zhī	zhī	zhī	zhī	zhī	zhī	zhī	zhī	zhī	zhī
know	know	know	know	know	know	know	know	know	know
知	知	知	知	知	知	知	知	知	知
zhī	zhī	zhī	zhī	zhī	zhī	zhī	zhī	zhī	zhī
know	know	know	know	know	know	know	know	know	know

民	Notes: Common Noun (民, **mín**, **citizen**) (民, **mín**, **the people, nationality, citizen**)
mín citizen	

フ ⇁ ⼸ ⼸ 民

民 民 民 民 民 民 民 民 民

民	民	民	民	民	民	民	民	民	民
mín	mín	mín	mín	mín	mín	mín	mín	mín	mín
citizen	citizen	citizen	citizen	citizen	citizen	citizen	citizen	citizen	citizen
民	民	民	民	民	民	民	民	民	民
mín	mín	mín	mín	mín	mín	mín	mín	mín	mín
citizen	citizen	citizen	citizen	citizen	citizen	citizen	citizen	citizen	citizen

[Type text]

样

Notes: Common Noun

(样, **yàng**, **appearance**, **shape**, **form**, **manner**)

(样, **yàng**, **sample**, **model**, **pattern**)

(样, **yàng**, **kind**, **type**, **class**)

yàng — manner

一 十 才 木 木̍ 术̍ 栏 栏 栏 样

现

xiàn
current

Notes: Adverb

(现, **xiàn**, **current**, **present**)

(现, **xiàn**, **show**, **appear**)

一 丁 干 王 王 玎 玑 现 现

分	Notes: Verb
fēn divide	(分, fēn, to divide, separate, distribute, allot) (分, fēn, distinguish, differentiate, discriminate) (分, fēn, classifier for length, area, weight, money, time) (分, fēn, fraction, one-tenth, percent)

丿 八 分 分

分 分 分 分 分 分 分 分 分

分	分	分	分	分	分	分	分	分	分
fēn	fēn	fēn	fēn	fēn	fēn	fēn	fēn	fēn	fēn
divide	divide	divide	divide	divide	divide	divide	divide	divide	divide
分	分	分	分	分	分	分	分	分	分
fēn	fēn	fēn	fēn	fēn	fēn	fēn	fēn	fēn	fēn
divide	divide	divide	divide	divide	divide	divide	divide	divide	divide

将	Notes: Verb
jiāng shall	(将, jiāng, to take)
	(将, jiàng, just, a short time ago)
	(将, jiāng, about to)
	(将, jiāng, partly...partly...)

丶 丷 丬 丬 护 护 护 将 将

将 将 将 将 将 将 将 将 将

外

wài
outside

Notes: Preposition

(外, wài, outside)

(外, wài, outside, outer, other, foreign, beyond)

(外, wài, relative on one's mother's / sister's / wife's family)

丿 ク 夕 列 外

但	Notes: Conjunction
dàn	(但, dàn, but, yet, still, nevertheless, however)
but	(但, dàn, only, merely)

丿 亻 仍 仍 佀 但 但

但 但 但 但 但 但 但 但 但

身	Notes: Common Noun
	(身, shēn, life)
	(身, shēn, incarnation)
	(身, shēn, body)
shēn life	(身, shēn, classifier for suits of clothing)

丶 丨 勹 勹 身 身 身

身 身 身 身 身 身 身 身 身

身	身	身	身	身	身	身	身	身	身
shēn	shēn	shēn	shēn	shēn	shēn	shēn	shēn	shēn	shēn
life	life	life	life	life	life	life	life	life	life
身	身	身	身	身	身	身	身	身	身
shēn	shēn	shēn	shēn	shēn	shēn	shēn	shēn	shēn	shēn
life	life	life	life	life	life	life	life	life	life

些

xiē — few

Notes: Adjective

(些, xiē, few, some)

(些, xiē, classifier for plural or indefinite or small amount)

Stroke order: 丨 卜 𠄌 止 止' 此 此 些

与 yǔ give	Notes: Verb (与, yǔ, give) (与, yǔ, give, offer, help, support) (与, yǔ, interrogative exclamative particle)

一 与 与

与 与 与 与 与 与 与 与 与

与	与	与	与	与	与	与	与	与	与
yǔ give	yǔ give	yǔ give	yǔ give	yǔ give	yǔ give	yǔ give	yǔ give	yǔ give	yǔ give
与	与	与	与	与	与	与	与	与	与
yǔ give	yǔ give	yǔ give	yǔ give	yǔ give	yǔ give	yǔ give	yǔ give	yǔ give	yǔ give

高	Notes: Attributive Adjective
gāo	(高, **gāo**, **high**)
high	(高, **gāo**, **high**, **tall**, **loud**)

丶 亠 广 产 亩 声 亭 高 高 高

高 高 高 高 高 高 高 高 高

高	高	高	高	高	高	高	高	高	高
gāo	gāo	gāo	gāo	gāo	gāo	gāo	gāo	gāo	gāo
high	high	high	high	high	high	high	high	high	high
高	高	高	高	高	高	高	高	高	高
gāo	gāo	gāo	gāo	gāo	gāo	gāo	gāo	gāo	gāo
high	high	high	high	high	high	high	high	high	high

高	高	高	高	高		高	高		
高	高	高	高	高		高	高		
高	高	高	高	高		高	高		
高	高	高	高	高		高	高		
高	高	高	高	高		高	高		
高	高	高	高	高		高	高		
高	高	高	高	高		高	高		

意	Notes: Common Noun (意, yì, idea) (意, yì, idea, meaning, wish, desire)
yì	
idea	

丶 亠 亠 产 产 产 产 音 音 音 音 意 意 意

意 意 意 意 意 意 意 意 意

意	意	意	意	意	意	意	意	意	意
yì	yì	yì	yì	yì	yì	yì	yì	yì	yì
idea	idea	idea	idea	idea	idea	idea	idea	idea	idea
意	意	意	意	意	意	意	意	意	意
yì	yì	yì	yì	yì	yì	yì	yì	yì	yì
idea	idea	idea	idea	idea	idea	idea	idea	idea	idea

[Type text]

进	Notes: Verb
	(进, jìn, advance, go forward)
	(进, jìn, enter, come into, go into)
	((进, jìn, drink, eat, receive)
jìn	(进, jìn, submit)
enter	

一 二 二 井 井 讲 进

进 进 进 进 进 进 进 进 进

进	进	进	进	进	进	进	进	进	进
jìn	jìn	jìn	jìn	jìn	jìn	jìn	jìn	jìn	jìn
enter	enter	enter	enter	enter	enter	enter	enter	enter	enter
进	进	进	进	进	进	进	进	进	进
jìn	jìn	jìn	jìn	jìn	jìn	jìn	jìn	jìn	jìn
enter	enter	enter	enter	enter	enter	enter	enter	enter	enter

进	进	进	进	进	进	进	进	进
进	进	进	进	进	进	进	进	进
进	进	进	进	进	进	进	进	进
进	进	进	进	进	进	进	进	进
进	进	进	进	进	进	进	进	进
进	进	进	进	进	进	进	进	进
进	进	进	进	进	进	进	进	进

把 bǎ grasp	Notes: Verb (把, bǎ, grasp) (把, bǎ, grasp, hold, handle) (把, bǎ, classifier for things with handles, handfuls, chairs)

一 十 扌 扌㇆ 扌㇆ 扌巴 把

把 把 把 把 把 把 把 把 把

把	把	把	把	把	把	把	把	把	把
bǎ	bǎ	bǎ	bǎ	bǎ	bǎ	bǎ	bǎ	bǎ	bǎ
grasp	grasp	grasp	grasp	grasp	grasp	grasp	grasp	grasp	grasp
把	把	把	把	把	把	把	把	把	把
bǎ	bǎ	bǎ	bǎ	bǎ	bǎ	bǎ	bǎ	bǎ	bǎ
grasp	grasp	grasp	grasp	grasp	grasp	grasp	grasp	grasp	grasp

法	Notes: Common Noun (法, fǎ, method, law, way) (法, fǎ, Buddhist teaching)
fǎ method	

丶 丶 氵 氵 汁 汒 法 法

法 法 法 法 法 法 法 法 法

法	法	法	法	法	法	法	法	法	法
fǎ	fǎ	fǎ	fǎ	fǎ	fǎ	fǎ	fǎ	fǎ	fǎ
method	method	method	method	method	method	method	method	method	method
法	法	法	法	法	法	法	法	法	法
fǎ	fǎ	fǎ	fǎ	fǎ	fǎ	fǎ	fǎ	fǎ	fǎ
method	method	method	method	method	method	method	method	method	method

[Type text]

此

cǐ — this

Notes: Demonstrative Pronoun

(此, **cǐ**, **this**)

Stroke order: 丨 卜 卝 止 止̇ 此

实	Notes: Adjective (实, shí, real) (实, shí, solid, true, real)
shí real	

丶 丷 宀 宀 宀 宀 实 实

实 实 实 实 实 实 实 实 实

实	实	实	实	实	实	实	实	实	实
shí real	shí real	shí real	shí real	shí real	shí real	shí real	shí real	shí real	shí real
实	实	实	实	实	实	实	实	实	实
shí real	shí real	shí real	shí real	shí real	shí real	shí real	shí real	shí real	shí real
实	实	实	实	实	实	实	实	实	
实	实	实	实	实	实	实	实	实	
实	实	实	实	实	实	实	实	实	
实	实	实	实	实	实	实	实	实	
实	实	实	实	实	实	实	实	实	
实	实	实	实	实	实	实	实	实	
实	实	实	实	实	实	实	实	实	

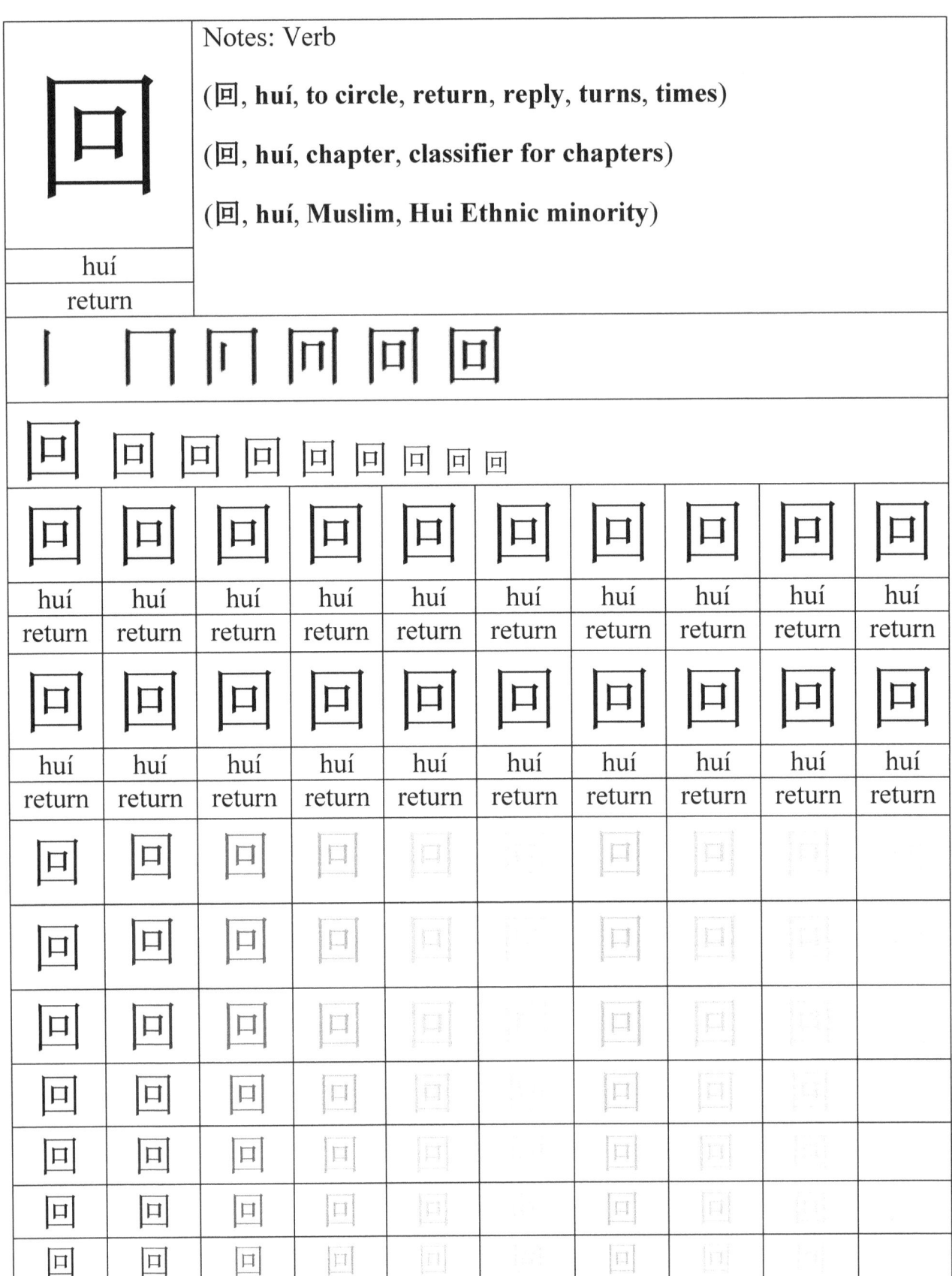

Notes: Quantitative Adjective

(二, èr, two, 2)

èr — two

理

lǐ

Notes: Common Noun

(理, lǐ, principle)

(理, lǐ, reason, logic, truth)

一 二 丅 王 邘 玑 玑 珇 珇 珋 理 理

理 理 理 理 理 理 理 理

理	理	理	理	理	理	理	理	理	理
lǐ	lǐ	lǐ	lǐ	lǐ	lǐ	lǐ	lǐ	lǐ	lǐ
reason	reason	reason	reason	reason	reason	reason	reason	reason	reason
理	理	理	理	理	理	理	理	理	理
lǐ	lǐ	lǐ	lǐ	lǐ	lǐ	lǐ	lǐ	lǐ	lǐ
reason	reason	reason	reason	reason	reason	reason	reason	reason	reason

[Type text]

美	Notes: Qualitative Adjective (美, **měi**, **beautiful**)
měi beautiful	

丶 丷 丷 䒑 㠯 羊 羊 美 美

美	美	美	美	美	美	美	美	美

美	美	美	美	美	美	美	美	美	美
měi	měi	měi	měi	měi	měi	měi	měi	měi	měi
beautiful	beautiful	beautiful	beautiful	beautiful	beautiful	beautiful	beautiful	beautiful	beautiful
美	美	美	美	美	美	美	美	美	美
měi	měi	měi	měi	měi	měi	měi	měi	měi	měi
beautiful	beautiful	beautiful	beautiful	beautiful	beautiful	beautiful	beautiful	beautiful	beautiful
美	美	美	美	美	美	美	美	美	
美	美	美	美	美	美	美	美	美	
美	美	美	美	美	美	美	美	美	
美	美	美	美	美	美	美	美	美	
美	美	美	美	美	美	美	美	美	
美	美	美	美	美	美	美	美	美	
美	美	美	美	美	美	美	美	美	
美	美	美	美	美	美	美	美	美	

[Type text]

点	Notes: Common Noun
	(点, diǎn, a tear drop shaped stroke)
	(点, diǎn, a drop of liquid, dot, decimal point, a little, a bit)
	(点, diǎn, appoint time, select, choose, order food / drink)
diǎn a drop	(点, diǎn, classifier for small amounts)

丨 丨- 广 占 占 卢 点 点 点

点 点 点 点 点 点 点 点 点

点	点	点	点	点	点	点	点	点	点
diǎn	diǎn	diǎn	diǎn	diǎn	diǎn	diǎn	diǎn	diǎn	diǎn
drop	drop	drop	drop	drop	drop	drop	drop	drop	drop
点	点	点	点	点	点	点	点	点	点
diǎn	diǎn	diǎn	diǎn	diǎn	diǎn	diǎn	diǎn	diǎn	diǎn
drop	drop	drop	drop	drop	drop	drop	drop	drop	drop

月	Notes: Common Noun (月, **yuè**, **month**, **moon**)
yuè	
month	

丿 几 月 月

月 月 月 月 月 月 月 月

月	月	月	月	月	月	月	月	月	月
yuè	yuè	yuè	yuè	yuè	yuè	yuè	yuè	yuè	yuè
month	month	month	month	month	month	month	month	month	month
月	月	月	月	月	月	月	月	月	月
yuè	yuè	yuè	yuè	yuè	yuè	yuè	yuè	yuè	yuè
month	month	month	month	month	month	month	month	month	month

[Type text]

明	Notes: Adjective
	(明, míng, bright, clear, distinct, open, obvious, overt)
	(明, míng, *next* as a prefix in compound Temporal Adverbs)
	(明, Míng, surname Míng)
míng bright	(明, míng, sense of vision, sight, sharp eyed, clear sighted)

丨 冂 冃 日 町 明 明 明

明 明 明 明 明 明 明 明

明	明	明	明	明	明	明	明	明	明
míng	míng	míng	míng	míng	míng	míng	míng	míng	míng
bright	bright	bright	bright	bright	bright	bright	bright	bright	bright
明	明	明	明	明	明	明	明	明	明
míng	míng	míng	míng	míng	míng	míng	míng	míng	míng
bright	bright	bright	bright	bright	bright	bright	bright	bright	bright

其	Notes: Personal Pronoun
qí	(其, qí, his, her, its, their, they, them, he, she, it)
such	(其, qí, such)
	(其, qí, that)

一 十 卄 廾 甘 甘 其 其

其 其 其 其 其 其 其 其 其

其	其	其	其	其	其	其	其	其	其
qí	qí	qí	qí	qí	qí	qí	qí	qí	qí
such	such	such	such	such	such	such	such	such	such
其	其	其	其	其	其	其	其	其	其
qí	qí	qí	qí	qí	qí	qí	qí	qí	qí
such	such	such	such	such	such	such	such	such	such

种	Notes: Common Noun (种, **zhǒng**, **species, breed, race, type, kind of, sort of**) (种, **zhòng**, **to plant, cultivate**)
zhǒng type of	

丿 二 千 千 禾 禾 和 和 种

种 种 种 种 种 种 种 种 种

种	种	种	种	种	种	种	种	种	种
zhǒng	zhǒng	zhǒng	zhǒng	zhǒng	zhǒng	zhǒng	zhǒng	zhǒng	zhǒng
type	type	type	type	type	type	type	type	type	type
种	种	种	种	种	种	种	种	种	种
zhǒng	zhǒng	zhǒng	zhǒng	zhǒng	zhǒng	zhǒng	zhǒng	zhǒng	zhǒng
type	type	type	type	type	type	type	type	type	type

声	Notes: Common Noun
shēng / voice	(声, **shēng**, **voice**) (声, **shēng**, **classifier for sounds**) (声, **shēng**, **voice, tone, noise, declaration**)

一 十 士 圥 声 声 声 声

全	Notes: Adjective (全, **quán**, **whole**, **entire**, **total**, **complete**) (全, **quán**, **surname Quan**)
quán entire	

丿 人 入 仝 仝 全

全 全 全 全 全 全 全 全 全

全	全	全	全	全	全	全	全	全	全
quán entire	quán entire	quán entire	quán entire	quán entire	quán entire	quán entire	quán entire	quán entire	quán entire
全	全	全	全	全	全	全	全	全	全
quán entire	quán entire	quán entire	quán entire	quán entire	quán entire	quán entire	quán entire	quán entire	quán entire

工	Notes: Common Noun (工, **gōng**, **work**, **job**)
quán work	

一 丁 工

工 工 工 工 工 工 工 工

工	工	工	工	工	工	工	工	工	工
gōng	gōng	gōng	gōng	gōng	gōng	gōng	gōng	gōng	gōng
work	work	work	work	work	work	work	work	work	work
工	工	工	工	工	工	工	工	工	工
gōng	gōng	gōng	gōng	gōng	gōng	gōng	gōng	gōng	gōng
work	work	work	work	work	work	work	work	work	work

[Type text]

己

jǐ
self

Notes: Reflexive Pronoun

(己, **jǐ**, **self**)

Stroke order: 𠃍 → コ → 己

话	Notes: Common Noun (话, **huà**, **speech**, **word**, **language**, **dialect**, **language**)
huà	
speech	

丶 讠 讠 讠 讠 讠 话 话

话 话 话 话 话 话 话 话 话

话 话 话 话 话 话 话 话 话

话	话	话	话	话	话	话	话	话	话
huà	huà	huà	huà	huà	huà	huà	huà	huà	huà
speech	speech	speech	speech	speech	speech	speech	speech	speech	speech
话	话	话	话	话	话	话	话	话	话
huà	huà	huà	huà	huà	huà	huà	huà	huà	huà
speech	speech	speech	speech	speech	speech	speech	speech	speech	speech

[Type text]

儿	Notes: Person Noun (儿, **ér**, **child**) (儿, **ér**) also acts as a noun suffix for interrogative and demonstrative pronouns to mean *place*.
ér	
child	

丿 儿

儿 儿 儿 儿 儿 儿 儿 儿 儿

儿	儿	儿	儿	儿	儿	儿	儿	儿	儿
ér	ér	ér	ér	ér	ér	ér	ér	ér	ér
child	child	child	child	child	child	child	child	child	child
儿	儿	儿	儿	儿	儿	儿	儿	儿	儿
ér	ér	ér	ér	ér	ér	ér	ér	ér	ér
child	child	child	child	child	child	child	child	child	child

zhě / -er	Notes: Grammatical Particle (者, **zhě**, **-er, one who**...) acts as a grammatical nominalizer, that is, it indicates one who does a certain task. (者, **zhě**, **used after a word, phrase, or clause to mark a pause**)

一 十 土 耂 耂 者 者 者

者 者 者 者 者 者 者 者

者	者	者	者	者	者	者	者	者	者
zhě	zhě	zhě	zhě	zhě	zhě	zhě	zhě	zhě	zhě
-er	-er	-er	-er	-er	-er	-er	-er	-er	-er
者	者	者	者	者	者	者	者	者	者
zhě	zhě	zhě	zhě	zhě	zhě	zhě	zhě	zhě	zhě
-er	-er	-er	-er	-er	-er	-er	-er	-er	-er

(practice grid)

[Type text]

向	Notes: Verb (向, **xiàng, to face, turn toward, to side with, be partial to, towards, to**) (向, **xiàng, to side with, be partial to, towards, to**)
xiàng to face	

丿 亻 冂 向 向 向

向 向 向 向 向 向 向 向

向	向	向	向	向	向	向	向	向	向
xiàng	xiàng	xiàng	xiàng	xiàng	xiàng	xiàng	xiàng	xiàng	xiàng
to face	to face	to face	to face	to face	to face	to face	to face	to face	to face
向	向	向	向	向	向	向	向	向	向
xiàng	xiàng	xiàng	xiàng	xiàng	xiàng	xiàng	xiàng	xiàng	xiàng
to face	to face	to face	to face	to face	to face	to face	to face	to face	to face

[Type text]

情

qíng — mood

Notes: Abstract Noun

(情, qíng, mood, feelings, emotions)

Stroke order: 丶 丷 忄 忄 忄 忄 忄 情 情 情

部

bù — section

Notes: Common Noun

(部, **bù**, **part, section, unit**)

(部, **bù**, **classifier for film, large books, machines**)

Stroke order: 丶 亠 䒑 立 产 产 咅 音 咅阝 部

正	Notes: Adverb (正, zhèng, right, straight, upright, correct)
zhèng	
right	

一 丁 下 正 正

正 正 正 正 正 正 正 正 正

正	正	正	正	正	正	正	正	正	正
zhèng	zhèng	zhèng	zhèng	zhèng	zhèng	zhèng	zhèng	zhèng	zhèng
right	right	right	right	right	right	right	right	right	right
正	正	正	正	正	正	正	正	正	正
zhèng	zhèng	zhèng	zhèng	zhèng	zhèng	zhèng	zhèng	zhèng	zhèng
right	right	right	right	right	right	right	right	right	right

[Type text]

名	Notes: Common Noun (名, **míng**, **name, personal name, reputation, famous**) (名, **míng**, **classifier for persons with professional or prominent social identities**)
míng name	

丿 ク 夕 夕 名 名

名 名 名 名 名 名 名 名 名

名	名	名	名	名	名	名	名	名	名
míng	míng	míng	míng	míng	míng	míng	míng	míng	míng
name	name	name	name	name	name	name	name	name	name
名	名	名	名	名	名	名	名	名	名
míng	míng	míng	míng	míng	míng	míng	míng	míng	míng
name	name	name	name	name	name	name	name	name	name

定

dìng
settle

Notes: Verb

(定, **dìng**, **fix, settle, calm, stable**)

(定, **dìng**, **to subscribe**)

丶 丷 宀 宀 宁 宇 㝎 定

女	Notes: Common Noun
nǚ female	(女, nǚ, female)

く 夊 女

女 女 女 女 女 女 女 女 女

女	女	女	女	女	女	女	女	女	女
nǚ	nǚ	nǚ	nǚ	nǚ	nǚ	nǚ	nǚ	nǚ	nǚ
female	female	female	female	female	female	female	female	female	female
女	女	女	女	女	女	女	女	女	女
nǚ	nǚ	nǚ	nǚ	nǚ	nǚ	nǚ	nǚ	nǚ	nǚ
female	female	female	female	female	female	female	female	female	female

力	Notes: Common Noun (力, lì, **energy, vitality**) (力, Lì, **surname Lì**)
lì energy	

フ 力

力 力 力 力 力 力 力 力

力	力	力	力	力	力	力	力	力	力
lì	lì	lì	lì	lì	lì	lì	lì	lì	lì
energy	energy	energy	energy	energy	energy	energy	energy	energy	energy
力	力	力	力	力	力	力	力	力	力
lì	lì	lì	lì	lì	lì	lì	lì	lì	lì
energy	energy	energy	energy	energy	energy	energy	energy	energy	energy

机	Notes: Common Noun (机, **jī**, **machine**)
jī machine	

一 十 才 木 机 机

机 机 机 机 机 机 机 机 机

机	机	机	机	机	机	机	机	机	机
jī	jī	jī	jī	jī	jī	jī	jī	jī	jī
machine	machine	machine	machine	machine	machine	machine	machine	machine	machine
机	机	机	机	机	机	机	机	机	机
jī	jī	jī	jī	jī	jī	jī	jī	jī	jī
machine	machine	machine	machine	machine	machine	machine	machine	machine	machine
机	机	机	机	机		机	机	机	
机	机	机	机	机		机	机	机	
机	机	机	机	机		机	机	机	
机	机	机	机	机		机	机	机	
机	机	机	机	机		机	机	机	
机	机	机	机	机		机	机	机	
机	机	机	机	机		机	机	机	
机	机	机	机	机		机	机	机	

[Type text]

给

gěi
give

Notes: Verb

(给, gěi, give, give to, for, for the benefit of)

(给, jǐ, supply, provide)

Stroke order: 乚 纟 纟 纟 纟 纟 纟 给 给

等

děng — wait

Notes: Verb

(等, děng, wait, class, equal, and so on, etc.)

Stroke order: 丿 ⺁ ⺮ ⺮ ⺮ ⺮ 竺 竺 竺 竺 等 等

几

jī — table

Notes: Common Noun

(几, **jī**, **small table**)

(几, **jī**, **nearly**)

(几, **jǐ**, **how many**)

(几, **jǐ**, **few, several, some**)

Strokes: 丿 几

很

hěn — very

Notes: Quantitative Adjective

(很, **hěn**, **very**, **quite**)

Stroke order: 丿 彳 彳 彳 彳 彳 很 很 很

业	Notes: Common Noun (业, yè, line of business, trade, occupation, profession, course of study, engage in) (业, Yè, surname Yè)
yè	
trade	

丨 丨丨 业 业 业

业 业 业 业 业 业 业 业 业

业	业	业	业	业	业	业	业	业	业
yè	yè	yè	yè	yè	yè	yè	yè	yè	yè
trade	trade	trade	trade	trade	trade	trade	trade	trade	trade
业	业	业	业	业	业	业	业	业	业
yè	yè	yè	yè	yè	yè	yè	yè	yè	yè
trade	trade	trade	trade	trade	trade	trade	trade	trade	trade
业	业	业	业	业		业	业		
业	业	业	业	业		业	业		
业	业	业	业	业		业	业		
业	业	业	业	业		业	业		
业	业	业	业	业		业	业		
业	业	业	业	业		业	业		
业	业	业	业	业		业	业		
业	业	业	业	业		业	业		

[Type text]

最

zuì
most

Notes: Superlative Adjective

(最, zuì, most)

最	最	最	最	最	最	最	最	最	最
zuì	zuì	zuì	zuì	zuì	zuì	zuì	zuì	zuì	zuì
most	most	most	most	most	most	most	most	most	most
最	最	最	最	最	最	最	最	最	最
zuì	zuì	zuì	zuì	zuì	zuì	zuì	zuì	zuì	zuì
most	most	most	most	most	most	most	most	most	most

	Notes: Common Noun
间 jiàn room	(间, **jiān**, **room**) (间, **jiān**, **classifier for rooms**) (间, **jiàn**, **gap, interval, between, time duration, among, within a given time or space**)

丶 亻 门 门 问 间 间

间 间 间 间 间 间 间 间

间	间	间	间	间	间	间	间	间	间
jiàn	jiàn	jiàn	jiàn	jiàn	jiàn	jiàn	jiàn	jiàn	jiàn
room	room	room	room	room	room	room	room	room	room
间	间	间	间	间	间	间	间	间	间
jiàn	jiàn	jiàn	jiàn	jiàn	jiàn	jiàn	jiàn	jiàn	jiàn
room	room	room	room	room	room	room	room	room	room
间	间	间	间	间		间	间	间	
间	间	间	间	间		间	间	间	
间	间	间	间	间		间	间	间	
间	间	间	间	间		间	间	间	
间	间	间	间	间		间	间	间	
间	间	间	间	间		间	间	间	
间	间	间	间	间		间	间	间	
间	间	间	间	间		间	间	间	

新

Notes: Qualitative Adjective

(新, xīn, new, renew)

xīn
new

丶 亠 产 立 立 辛 辛 亲 亲 新 新 新

什	Notes: Interrogative Pronoun (什, **shén**, **what**) (什, **shí**, **ten**, **10**)
shén / what	

丿 亻 仁 什

什 什 什 什 什 什 什 什 什

什	什	什	什	什	什	什	什	什	什
shén	shén	shén	shén	shén	shén	shén	shén	shén	shén
what	what	what	what	what	what	what	what	what	what
什	什	什	什	什	什	什	什	什	什
shén	shén	shén	shén	shén	shén	shén	shén	shén	shén
what	what	what	what	what	what	what	what	what	what

[Type text]

打	Notes: Verb (打, dǎ, strike, hit, get, play)
dǎ strike	

一 十 扌 扩 打

打 打 打 打 打 打 打 打 打

打	打	打	打	打	打	打	打	打	打
dǎ	dǎ	dǎ	dǎ	dǎ	dǎ	dǎ	dǎ	dǎ	dǎ
strike	strike	strike	strike	strike	strike	strike	strike	strike	strike
打	打	打	打	打	打	打	打	打	打
dǎ	dǎ	dǎ	dǎ	dǎ	dǎ	dǎ	dǎ	dǎ	dǎ
strike	strike	strike	strike	strike	strike	strike	strike	strike	strike

打	打	打	打	打		打	打	打	
打	打	打	打	打		打	打	打	
打	打	打	打	打		打	打	打	
打	打	打	打	打		打	打	打	
打	打	打	打	打		打	打	打	
打	打	打	打	打		打	打	打	
打	打	打	打	打		打	打	打	
打	打	打	打	打		打	打	打	

便

biàn — then

Notes: Adverb

(便, **biàn**, then, in that case)

(便, **biàn**, as early as, as little as)

Stroke order: ノ 亻 丆 仃 仃 仴 伊 便

位

wèi — place

Notes: Common Noun

(位, **wèi**, **place, location, position**)

(位, **wèi**, **polite classifier for people**)

Stroke order: 丿 亻 亻 仁 位 位 位

因	Notes: Verb (因, **yīn**, **to cause**)
yīn	
cause	

丨 冂 冂 因 因 因

因 因 因 因 因 因 因 因 因

因	因	因	因	因	因	因	因	因	因
yīn	yīn	yīn	yīn	yīn	yīn	yīn	yīn	yīn	yīn
cause	cause	cause	cause	cause	cause	cause	cause	cause	cause
因	因	因	因	因	因	因	因	因	因
yīn	yīn	yīn	yīn	yīn	yīn	yīn	yīn	yīn	yīn
cause	cause	cause	cause	cause	cause	cause	cause	cause	cause

[Type text]

重	Notes: Adjective
	(重, zhòng, weight, heavy)
	(重, zhòng, important, considerable in amount or value)
	(重, chóng, again, once more, repeat, duplicate)
zhòng	
weight	(重, chóng, layers)

一 亠 广 六 亐 盲 育 重 重

重 重 重 重 重 重 重 重 重

被 bèi cover

Notes: Common Noun

(被, **bèi**, **cover, quilt**)

(被, **bèi**, **by**)

丶 冫 礻 礻 衤 衤 衤 衤 衤 被 被

走	Notes: Verb
	(走, zǒu, walk, go, leave)
	(走, zǒu, visit, call on)
	(走, zǒu, leak, go through, pass through)
zǒu	
walk	

一 十 土 キ キ 走 走

走 走 走 走 走 走 走 走 走

走	走	走	走	走	走	走	走	走	走
zǒu	zǒu	zǒu	zǒu	zǒu	zǒu	zǒu	zǒu	zǒu	zǒu
walk	walk	walk	walk	walk	walk	walk	walk	walk	walk
走	走	走	走	走	走	走	走	走	走
zǒu	zǒu	zǒu	zǒu	zǒu	zǒu	zǒu	zǒu	zǒu	zǒu
walk	walk	walk	walk	walk	walk	walk	walk	walk	walk

Notes: Quantitative Adjective

(四, sì, four, 4)

第	Notes: Grammatical Particle
dì -th/#	(第, **dì**, **-th / #**) this character is used to indicate ordinal numbers. Grammatically, it precedes the number. Example: 第 + (一, **yī**, **one**, 1) = (第一) = 1st 　　　　第 + (三, **sān**, **three**, 3) = (第三) = 3rd (第, **dì**, sequence, order)

丿 ⺈ 竹 笅 笃 笃 笃 笃 第 第

第 第 第 第 第 第 第 第 第

cì
times

Notes: Grammatical Particle

(次, **cì**, **times, occurence, second, inferior, number of times**)

Grammatically (次, **cì**, **number of times**) is placed after a number to indicate the number of times of repetition. Example:

(两, **liǎng, two**) + (次, **cì, number of times**) = (两次, **liǎng, cì, twice**)

东 dōng east	Notes: Common Noun (东, **dōng**, **east**) (东, **dōng**, **master, owner**) (东, **dōng**, **host**) (东, **Dōng**, **surname Dōng**)

一 左 庄 东 东

东 东 东 东 东 东 东 东 东

东	东	东	东	东	东	东	东	东	东
dōng	dōng	dōng	dōng	dōng	dōng	dōng	dōng	dōng	dōng
east	east	east	east	east	east	east	east	east	east
东	东	东	东	东	东	东	东	东	东
dōng	dōng	dōng	dōng	dōng	dōng	dōng	dōng	dōng	dōng
east	east	east	east	east	east	east	east	east	east

政

zhèng — government

Notes: Common Noun

(政, zhèng, government)

Stroke order: 一 丁 下 正 正 政 政 政 政

海	Notes: Common Noun (海, **hǎi**, **sea**) (海, **Hǎi**, **surname Hǎi**)
hǎi	
sea	

丶 丶 氵 氵 氵 汇 海 海 海 海

海 海 海 海 海 海 海 海 海

海	海	海	海	海	海	海	海	海	海
hǎi	hǎi	hǎi	hǎi	hǎi	hǎi	hǎi	hǎi	hǎi	hǎi
sea	sea	sea	sea	sea	sea	sea	sea	sea	sea
海	海	海	海	海	海	海	海	海	海
hǎi	hǎi	hǎi	hǎi	hǎi	hǎi	hǎi	hǎi	hǎi	hǎi
sea	sea	sea	sea	sea	sea	sea	sea	sea	sea

口	Notes: Common Noun
kǒu	(口, kǒu, mouth, opening, entrance, hole, cut)
mouth	(口, kǒu, classifier for mouthfuls, people, wells, openings)
	(口, kǒu, measure word for people in a family)

丨 冂 口

口 口 口 口 口 口 口 口

口	口	口	口	口	口	口	口	口	口
kǒu	kǒu	kǒu	kǒu	kǒu	kǒu	kǒu	kǒu	kǒu	kǒu
mouth	mouth	mouth	mouth	mouth	mouth	mouth	mouth	mouth	mouth
口	口	口	口	口	口	口	口	口	口
kǒu	kǒu	kǒu	kǒu	kǒu	kǒu	kǒu	kǒu	kǒu	kǒu
mouth	mouth	mouth	mouth	mouth	mouth	mouth	mouth	mouth	mouth

使	Notes: Verb
shǐ / make	(使, shǐ, make, cause to do)
	(使, shǐ, have somebody do something)
	(使, shǐ, employ, apply)
	(使, shǐ, to send as an envoy)

丿 亻 仁 仨 仁 仨 伊 使

使 使 使 使 使 使 使 使 使

使	使	使	使	使	使	使	使	使	使
shǐ	shǐ	shǐ	shǐ	shǐ	shǐ	shǐ	shǐ	shǐ	shǐ
make	make	make	make	make	make	make	make	make	make
使	使	使	使	使	使	使	使	使	使
shǐ	shǐ	shǐ	shǐ	shǐ	shǐ	shǐ	shǐ	shǐ	shǐ
make	make	make	make	make	make	make	make	make	make

教	Notes: Verb (教, **jiāo**, **teach**) (教, **jiào**, **to cause to, ask to**)
jiāo teach	

一 十 土 耂 耂 考 孝 孝 孝 教 教

教 教 教 教 教 教 教 教 教

教	教	教	教	教	教	教	教	教	教
jiāo	jiāo	jiāo	jiāo	jiāo	jiāo	jiāo	jiāo	jiāo	jiāo
teach	teach	teach	teach	teach	teach	teach	teach	teach	teach
教	教	教	教	教	教	教	教	教	教
jiāo	jiāo	jiāo	jiāo	jiāo	jiāo	jiāo	jiāo	jiāo	jiāo
teach	teach	teach	teach	teach	teach	teach	teach	teach	teach

西	Notes: Common Noun (西, xī, west, western)
xī	
west	

一 丆 冂 丙 西 西

西 西 西 西 西 西 西 西 西

平	Notes: Adjective
	(平, **píng**, **flat, level, even**)
	(平, **píng**, **ordinary, common, uniform**)
	(平, **píng**, **safe and sound, peaceful, calm**)
píng flat	(平, **píng**, **fair, just, objective**)

一 丆 万 平 平

平 平 平 平 平 平 平 平 平

平	平	平	平	平	平	平	平	平	平
píng flat	píng flat	píng flat	píng flat	píng flat	píng flat	píng flat	píng flat	píng flat	píng flat
平	平	平	平	平	平	平	平	平	平
píng flat	píng flat	píng flat	píng flat	píng flat	píng flat	píng flat	píng flat	píng flat	píng flat

真	Notes: Adverb
	(真, zhēn, really, truly, indeed)
	(真, zhēn, true, genuine, real)
	(真, zhēn, original character of human beings)
zhēn really	(真, zhēn, newcomer among the immortals)

一 十 亠 亣 古 肯 盲 直 真 真

真 真 真 真 真 真 真 真 真

真	真	真	真	真	真	真	真	真	真
zhēn	zhēn	zhēn	zhēn	zhēn	zhēn	zhēn	zhēn	zhēn	zhēn
really	really	really	really	really	really	really	really	really	really
真	真	真	真	真	真	真	真	真	真
zhēn	zhēn	zhēn	zhēn	zhēn	zhēn	zhēn	zhēn	zhēn	zhēn
really	really	really	really	really	really	really	really	really	really

真	真	真	真	真		真	真		
真	真	真	真	真		真	真		
真	真	真	真	真		真	真		
真	真	真	真	真		真	真		
真	真	真	真	真		真	真		
真	真	真	真	真		真	真		
真	真	真	真	真		真	真		
真	真	真	真	真		真	真		

[Type text]

听

tīng
listen

Notes: Verb

(听, **tīng, listen, hear, heed, obey**)

(听, **tīng, to administer, allow, let**)

(听, **tīng, measure word for tin can or pop can**)

丨 冂 口 口⺁ 吖 听 听

听 听 听 听 听 听 听 听 听

听	听	听	听	听	听	听	听	听	听
tīng	tīng	tīng	tīng	tīng	tīng	tīng	tīng	tīng	tīng
listen	listen	listen	listen	listen	listen	listen	listen	listen	listen
听	听	听	听	听	听	听	听	听	听
tīng	tīng	tīng	tīng	tīng	tīng	tīng	tīng	tīng	tīng
listen	listen	listen	listen	listen	listen	listen	listen	listen	listen

气	Notes: Common Noun (气, qì, air, gas, vapour, spirit) (气, qì, vital energy)
qì	
air	

丿 ⺁ ⺭ 气

气 气 气 气 气 气 气 气 气

气	气	气	气	气	气	气	气	气	气
qì	qì	qì	qì	qì	qì	qì	qì	qì	qì
air	air	air	air	air	air	air	air	air	air
气	气	气	气	气	气	气	气	气	气
qì	qì	qì	qì	qì	qì	qì	qì	qì	qì
air	air	air	air	air	air	air	air	air	air

气	气	气	气	气		气	气		
气	气	气	气	气		气	气		
气	气	气	气	气		气	气		
气	气	气	气	气		气	气		
气	气	气	气	气		气	气		
气	气	气	气	气		气	气		
气	气	气	气	气		气	气		
气	气	气	气	气		气	气		

[Type text]

信

xìn — letter

Notes: Common Noun

(信, xìn, letter, message, information)

(信, xìn, believe, credibility, give credence to)

Stroke order: 丿 亻 亻 仁 仁 仨 信 信 信

北	Notes: Common Noun (北, **běi**, **north**)
běi	
north	

丨 亅 扌 北 北

北 北 北 北 北 北 北 北 北

北	北	北	北	北	北	北	北	北	北
běi	běi	běi	běi	běi	běi	běi	běi	běi	běi
north	north	north	north	north	north	north	north	north	north
北	北	北	北	北	北	北	北	北	北
běi	běi	běi	běi	běi	běi	běi	běi	běi	běi
north	north	north	north	north	north	north	north	north	north

Notes: Quantitative Adjective

(少, shǎo, few, little, less, lack)

(少, shào, young)

shǎo
few

丨 丿 小 少

少 少 少 少 少 少 少 少 少

关	Notes: Verb (关, guān, shut, close, turn off, close down) (关, guān, concern, key part)
guān shut	

丶 丷 䒑 兰 关 关

关 关 关 关 关 关 关 关 关

关	关	关	关	关	关	关	关	关	关
guān shut	guān shut	guān shut	guān shut	guān shut	guān shut	guān shut	guān shut	guān shut	guān shut
关	关	关	关	关	关	关	关	关	关
guān shut	guān shut	guān shut	guān shut	guān shut	guān shut	guān shut	guān shut	guān shut	guān shut

并	Notes: Verb
bìng shut	(并, bìng, combine, merge) (并, bìng, equally, simultaneously) (并, bìng, actually, truly (as a pre-negation intensifier))

丶 丷 兰 兰 䒑 并

内	Notes: Preposition (内, **nèi**, inside)
nèi	
inside	

丨 冂 内 内

内 内 内 内 内 内 内 内 内

内	内	内	内	内	内	内	内	内	内
nèi	nèi	nèi	nèi	nèi	nèi	nèi	nèi	nèi	nèi
inside	inside	inside	inside	inside	inside	inside	inside	inside	inside
内	内	内	内	内	内	内	内	内	内
nèi	nèi	nèi	nèi	nèi	nèi	nèi	nèi	nèi	nèi
inside	inside	inside	inside	inside	inside	inside	inside	inside	inside

加	Notes: Verb
jiā	(加, **jiā**, **add**, **plus**, **append**)
add	

フ 力 加 加 加

加 加 加 加 加 加 加 加 加

加	加	加	加	加	加	加	加	加	加
jiā	jiā	jiā	jiā	jiā	jiā	jiā	jiā	jiā	jiā
add	add	add	add	add	add	add	add	add	add
加	加	加	加	加	加	加	加	加	加
jiā	jiā	jiā	jiā	jiā	jiā	jiā	jiā	jiā	jiā
add	add	add	add	add	add	add	add	add	add

[Type text]

化	Notes: Verb
	(化, huà, change, transform, convert)
huà	(化, huà, melt, dissolve, thaw, digest, incinerate)
change	

丿 亻 亻 化

化 化 化 化 化 化 化 化 化

化	化	化	化	化	化	化	化	化	化
huà	huà	huà	huà	huà	huà	huà	huà	huà	huà
change	change	change	change	change	change	change	change	change	change
化	化	化	化	化	化	化	化	化	化
huà	huà	huà	huà	huà	huà	huà	huà	huà	huà
change	change	change	change	change	change	change	change	change	change

[Type text]

却

què — however

Notes: Adverb

(却, què, however, yet, but)

Stroke order: 一 十 土 去 去 却 却

代

Notes: Verb

(代, dài, act as, take the place of)

dài — act as

丿 亻 仁 代 代

代 代 代 代 代 代 代 代 代

代	代	代	代	代	代	代	代	代	代
dài	dài	dài	dài	dài	dài	dài	dài	dài	dài
act as	act as	act as	act as	act as	act as	act as	act as	act as	act as
代	代	代	代	代	代	代	代	代	代
dài	dài	dài	dài	dài	dài	dài	dài	dài	dài
act as	act as	act as	act as	act as	act as	act as	act as	act as	act as

军	Notes: Common Noun (军, **jūn**, **army**, **military**, **troops**)
jūn	
army	

丶 宀 冖 冝 军 军

军 军 军 军 军 军 军 军 军

军	军	军	军	军	军	军	军	军	军
jūn	jūn	jūn	jūn	jūn	jūn	jūn	jūn	jūn	jūn
army	army	army	army	army	army	army	army	army	army
军	军	军	军	军	军	军	军	军	军
jūn	jūn	jūn	jūn	jūn	jūn	jūn	jūn	jūn	jūn
army	army	army	army	army	army	army	army	army	army

军	军	军	军	军		军	军		
军	军	军	军	军		军	军		
军	军	军	军	军		军	军		
军	军	军	军	军		军	军		
军	军	军	军	军		军	军		
军	军	军	军	军		军	军		
军	军	军	军	军		军	军		
军	军	军	军	军		军	军		

产	Notes: Verb (产, **chǎn**, **give birth**, **produce**, **to produce**, **product**)
chǎn produce	

丶 亠 产 立 产 产

产 产 产 产 产 产 产 产 产

产	产	产	产	产	产	产	产	产	产
chǎn	chǎn	chǎn	chǎn	chǎn	chǎn	chǎn	chǎn	chǎn	chǎn
produce	produce	produce	produce	produce	produce	produce	produce	produce	produce
产	产	产	产	产	产	产	产	产	产
chǎn	chǎn	chǎn	chǎn	chǎn	chǎn	chǎn	chǎn	chǎn	chǎn
produce	produce	produce	produce	produce	produce	produce	produce	produce	produce

先

xiān — first

Notes: Temporal Adverb

(先, xiān, first, before, earlier)

Stroke order: 丿 ⺊ 斗 生 ⺌ 先

五

Notes: Quantitative Adjective

(五, **wǔ**, **five**, 5)

wǔ
five

一 丁 开 五

五 五 五 五 五 五 五 五 五

五	五	五	五	五	五	五	五	五	五
wǔ	wǔ	wǔ	wǔ	wǔ	wǔ	wǔ	wǔ	wǔ	wǔ
five	five	five	five	five	five	five	five	five	five
五	五	五	五	五	五	五	五	五	五
wǔ	wǔ	wǔ	wǔ	wǔ	wǔ	wǔ	wǔ	wǔ	wǔ
five	five	five	five	five	five	five	five	five	five

Notes: Adjective

(太, **tài**, **too**, **great**, **very**)

tài
too

一 ナ 大 太

水	Notes: Common Noun
shuǐ	(水, shuǐ, water, liquid)
water	(水, Shuǐ, surname Shuǐ)

丨 刁 氺 水

水 水 水 水 水 水 水 水 水

水	水	水	水	水	水	水	水	水	水
shuǐ	shuǐ	shuǐ	shuǐ	shuǐ	shuǐ	shuǐ	shuǐ	shuǐ	shuǐ
water	water	water	water	water	water	water	water	water	water
水	水	水	水	水	水	水	水	水	水
shuǐ	shuǐ	shuǐ	shuǐ	shuǐ	shuǐ	shuǐ	shuǐ	shuǐ	shuǐ
water	water	water	water	water	water	water	water	water	water

万	Notes: Quantitative Adjective (万, **wàn**, **10,000, ten thousand, myriad**) (万, **Wàn, surname Wàn**)
wàn 10,000	

一 丁 万

万 万 万 万 万 万 万 万

万	万	万	万	万	万	万	万	万	万
wàn	wàn	wàn	wàn	wàn	wàn	wàn	wàn	wàn	wàn
10,000	10,000	10,000	10,000	10,000	10,000	10,000	10,000	10,000	10,000
万	万	万	万	万	万	万	万	万	万
wàn	wàn	wàn	wàn	wàn	wàn	wàn	wàn	wàn	wàn
10,000	10,000	10,000	10,000	10,000	10,000	10,000	10,000	10,000	10,000
万	万	万	万	万	万	万	万	万	
万	万	万	万	万	万	万	万	万	
万	万	万	万	万	万	万	万	万	
万	万	万	万	万	万	万	万	万	
万	万	万	万	万	万	万	万	万	
万	万	万	万	万	万	万	万	万	
万	万	万	万	万	万	万	万	万	
万	万	万	万	万	万	万	万	万	

市	Notes: Common Noun (市, shì, market, city, town)
shì market	

丶 亠 广 亣 市

市 市 市 市 市 市 市 市 市

市	市	市	市	市	市	市	市	市	市
shì	shì	shì	shì	shì	shì	shì	shì	shì	shì
market	market	market	market	market	market	market	market	market	market
市	市	市	市	市	市	市	市	市	市
shì	shì	shì	shì	shì	shì	shì	shì	shì	shì
market	market	market	market	market	market	market	market	market	market

眼

yǎn
eye

Notes: Common Noun

(眼, **yǎn**, **eye, small hole, aperture**)

(眼, **yǎn**, **salient point, weighted point**)

(眼, **yǎn**, **trap**)

(眼, **yǎn**, **measure word for wells and caves**)

体

tǐ
body

Notes: Common Noun

(体, **tǐ**, body)

丿 亻 仁 什 休 休 体

体 体 体 体 体 体 体 体 体

体	体	体	体	体	体	体	体	体	体
tǐ	tǐ	tǐ	tǐ	tǐ	tǐ	tǐ	tǐ	tǐ	tǐ
body	body	body	body	body	body	body	body	body	body
体	体	体	体	体	体	体	体	体	体
tǐ	tǐ	tǐ	tǐ	tǐ	tǐ	tǐ	tǐ	tǐ	tǐ
body	body	body	body	body	body	body	body	body	body

别 bié leave	Notes: Verb (别, bié, to leave) (别, bié, to differentiate) (别, bié, other, another) (别, Bié, surname Bié)

丨 冂 口 㕣 另 别 别

别 别 别 别 别 别 别 别 别

别	别	别	别	别	别	别	别	别	别
bié	bié	bié	bié	bié	bié	bié	bié	bié	bié
leave	leave	leave	leave	leave	leave	leave	leave	leave	leave
别	别	别	别	别	别	别	别	别	别
bié	bié	bié	bié	bié	bié	bié	bié	bié	bié
leave	leave	leave	leave	leave	leave	leave	leave	leave	leave

处

chù
place

Notes: Common Noun

(处, chù, place, part, point, department, office)

(处, chǔ, deal with, get along with somebody, interact)

丿 ク 夂 处 处

总	Notes: Adverb (总, **zǒng, general, overall, total, comprehensive, always**)
zǒng	
general	

丶 丷 丷 丷 丷 丷 总 总 总

总 总 总 总 总 总 总 总 总

总	总	总	总	总	总	总	总	总	总
zǒng	zǒng	zǒng	zǒng	zǒng	zǒng	zǒng	zǒng	zǒng	zǒng
general	general	general	general	general	general	general	general	general	general
总	总	总	总	总	总	总	总	总	总
zǒng	zǒng	zǒng	zǒng	zǒng	zǒng	zǒng	zǒng	zǒng	zǒng
general	general	general	general	general	general	general	general	general	general

才	Notes: Common Noun
	(才, cái, talent, ability, skill)
	(才, cái, then and only then, just now)
cái	(才, cái, only (before a number to limit the number))
talent	

一 十 才

才 才 才 才 才 才 才 才

才	才	才	才	才	才	才	才	才	才
cái	cái	cái	cái	cái	cái	cái	cái	cái	cái
talent	talent	talent	talent	talent	talent	talent	talent	talent	talent
才	才	才	才	才	才	才	才	才	才
cái	cái	cái	cái	cái	cái	cái	cái	cái	cái
talent	talent	talent	talent	talent	talent	talent	talent	talent	talent

场 chǎng field	Notes: Common Noun (场, **chǎng**, **field, place where people gather, stage, level open ground, country fair**) (场, **chǎng**, **classifier for games**) (场, **cháng**, **classifier for events, performances, happenings**)

一 十 土 圢 场 场

场 场 场 场 场 场 场 场 场

场	场	场	场	场	场	场	场	场	场
chǎng	chǎng	chǎng	chǎng	chǎng	chǎng	chǎng	chǎng	chǎng	chǎng
field	field	field	field	field	field	field	field	field	field
场	场	场	场	场	场	场	场	场	场
chǎng	chǎng	chǎng	chǎng	chǎng	chǎng	chǎng	chǎng	chǎng	chǎng
field	field	field	field	field	field	field	field	field	field

师

Notes: Person Noun

(师, shī, teacher)

shī — teacher

丨 丿 广 𠂇 师 师

师 师 师 师 师 师 师 师 师

书	Notes: Common Noun (书, shū, book, style of calligraphy)
shū	
book	

㇀ 乛 书 书

书 书 书 书 书 书 书 书 书

书	书	书	书	书	书	书	书	书	书
shū	shū	shū	shū	shū	shū	shū	shū	shū	shū
book	book	book	book	book	book	book	book	book	book
书	书	书	书	书	书	书	书	书	书
shū	shū	shū	shū	shū	shū	shū	shū	shū	shū
book	book	book	book	book	book	book	book	book	book

比	Notes: Verb (比, bǐ, compare, contrast, as compared to, than)
bǐ	
compare	

一 ト ヒ 比

比 比 比 比 比 比 比 比 比

比	比	比	比	比	比	比	比	比	比
bǐ	bǐ	bǐ	bǐ	bǐ	bǐ	bǐ	bǐ	bǐ	bǐ
than	than	than	than	than	than	than	than	than	than
比	比	比	比	比	比	比	比	比	比
bǐ	bǐ	bǐ	bǐ	bǐ	bǐ	bǐ	bǐ	bǐ	bǐ
than	than	than	than	than	than	than	than	than	than

住	Notes: Verb (住, zhù, live in, live in a place, live at a place, reside at, stay at)
zhù live in	

丿 亻 亻 仁 仁 住 住

住 住 住 住 住 住 住 住 住

住	住	住	住	住	住	住	住	住	住
zhù	zhù	zhù	zhù	zhù	zhù	zhù	zhù	zhù	zhù
live	live	live	live	live	live	live	live	live	live
住	住	住	住	住	住	住	住	住	住
zhù	zhù	zhù	zhù	zhù	zhù	zhù	zhù	zhù	zhù
live	live	live	live	live	live	live	live	live	live

[Type text]

员	Notes: Common Noun
	(员, **yuán**, **member of**, **member**)
yuán	(员, **yuán**, **-ist**, **-er**)
member	

丨　冂　口　尸　吊　吊　员

员 员 员 员 员 员 员 员 员

员	员	员	员	员	员	员	员	员	员
yuán	yuán	yuán	yuán	yuán	yuán	yuán	yuán	yuán	yuán
member	member	member	member	member	member	member	member	member	member
员	员	员	员	员	员	员	员	员	员
yuán	yuán	yuán	yuán	yuán	yuán	yuán	yuán	yuán	yuán
member	member	member	member	member	member	member	member	member	member

九

jiǔ
nine

Notes: Quantitative Adjective

(九, **jiǔ**, **nine**)

笑

xiào
laugh

Notes: Verb

(笑, xiào, laugh)

丿 亠 𠂉 𠂉 𥫗 竹 竹 竹 笑 笑

性	Notes: Common Noun (性, xìng, sex, gender) (性, xìng, having the character of, nature, disposition, ~ness)
xìng	
gender	

丶 丶 忄 忄 忄 忏 性 性

性 性 性 性 性 性 性 性 性

性	性	性	性	性	性	性	性	性	性
xìng	xìng	xìng	xìng	xìng	xìng	xìng	xìng	xìng	xìng
gender	gender	gender	gender	gender	gender	gender	gender	gender	gender
性	性	性	性	性	性	性	性	性	性
xìng	xìng	xìng	xìng	xìng	xìng	xìng	xìng	xìng	xìng
gender	gender	gender	gender	gender	gender	gender	gender	gender	gender

[Type text]

通	Notes: Verb
	(通, tōng, to communicate, notify, connect, join)
	(通, tōng, know very well, authority on, expert)
	(通, tōng, classifier for telegrams)
tōng expert	(通, Tōng, surname Tōng)

フ マ マ 甬 甬 甬 甬 甬 诵 通

通 通 通 通 通 通 通 通

通	通	通	通	通	通	通	通	通	通
tōng	tōng	tōng	tōng	tōng	tōng	tōng	tōng	tōng	tōng
expert	expert	expert	expert	expert	expert	expert	expert	expert	expert
通	通	通	通	通	通	通	通	通	通
tōng	tōng	tōng	tōng	tōng	tōng	tōng	tōng	tōng	tōng
expert	expert	expert	expert	expert	expert	expert	expert	expert	expert

目	Notes: Common Noun (目, **mù**, **eye**)
mù	
eye	

| 丨 | 冂 | 冃 | 目 | 目 |

| 目 | 目 | 目 | 目 | 目 | 目 | 目 | 目 |

目	目	目	目	目	目	目	目	目	目
mù	mù	mù	mù	mù	mù	mù	mù	mù	mù
eye	eye	eye	eye	eye	eye	eye	eye	eye	eye
目	目	目	目	目	目	目	目	目	目
mù	mù	mù	mù	mù	mù	mù	mù	mù	mù
eye	eye	eye	eye	eye	eye	eye	eye	eye	eye

[Type text]

华	Notes: Common Noun (华, huá, glory, splendour, magnificent) (华, Huá, surname Huá)
huá glory	

丿 亻 仁 化 化 华

华 华 华 华 华 华 华 华 华

华	华	华	华	华	华	华	华	华	华
huá	huá	huá	huá	huá	huá	huá	huá	huá	huá
glory	glory	glory	glory	glory	glory	glory	glory	glory	glory
华	华	华	华	华	华	华	华	华	华
huá	huá	huá	huá	huá	huá	huá	huá	huá	huá
glory	glory	glory	glory	glory	glory	glory	glory	glory	glory

报

bào — report

Notes: Verb

(报, bào, report, reply)

Stroke order: 一 十 扌 护 护 报 报

立	Notes: Verb (立, lì, to stand, erect)
lì stand	

丶 亠 立 立 立

立 立 立 立 立 立 立 立 立

立	立	立	立	立	立	立	立	立	立
lì	lì	lì	lì	lì	lì	lì	lì	lì	lì
stand	stand	stand	stand	stand	stand	stand	stand	stand	stand
立	立	立	立	立	立	立	立	立	立
lì	lì	lì	lì	lì	lì	lì	lì	lì	lì
stand	stand	stand	stand	stand	stand	stand	stand	stand	stand

[Type text]

马	Notes: Common Noun (马, **mǎ**, **horse**)
mǎ	
horse	

フ 马 马

马 马 马 马 马 马 马 马 马

马	马	马	马	马	马	马	马	马	马
mǎ	mǎ	mǎ	mǎ	mǎ	mǎ	mǎ	mǎ	mǎ	mǎ
horse	horse	horse	horse	horse	horse	horse	horse	horse	horse
马	马	马	马	马	马	马	马	马	马
mǎ	mǎ	mǎ	mǎ	mǎ	mǎ	mǎ	mǎ	mǎ	mǎ
horse	horse	horse	horse	horse	horse	horse	horse	horse	horse

命	Notes: Common Noun (命, **mìng**, **life**, **fate**, **destiny**)
mìng	
life	

丿 ㇏ 亽 亽 合 合 合 命

命 命 命 命 命 命 命 命 命

命	命	命	命	命	命	命	命	命	命
mìng	mìng	mìng	mìng	mìng	mìng	mìng	mìng	mìng	mìng
life	life	life	life	life	life	life	life	life	life
命	命	命	命	命	命	命	命	命	命
mìng	mìng	mìng	mìng	mìng	mìng	mìng	mìng	mìng	mìng
life	life	life	life	life	life	life	life	life	life

[Type text]

张	Notes: Common Noun
zhāng	(张, zhāng, sheet, sheet of paper)
sheet	(张, zhāng, stretch, spread, expand)
	(张, zhāng, classifier for flat surfaces, tables, postcards)

フ ㄱ 弓 弓' 弓' 张 张

活	Notes: Verb (活, **huó**, **live, alive, living, vivid, save someone's life**) (活, **huó**, **stretch, spread, expand**)
huó live	

丶 冫 氵 汀 汙 汗 浐 活 活

活 活 活 活 活 活 活 活 活

活	活	活	活	活	活	活	活	活	活
huó	huó	huó	huó	huó	huó	huó	huó	huó	huó
live	live	live	live	live	live	live	live	live	live
活	活	活	活	活	活	活	活	活	活
huó	huó	huó	huó	huó	huó	huó	huó	huó	huó
live	live	live	live	live	live	live	live	live	live

[Type text]

难

nán — difficult

Notes: Adjective

(难, **nán**, **difficult**)

(难, **nàn**, **disaster**)

Stroke order: 乛 又 groupsize 刈 对 attended 𠁣 𠁣 难 难

神	Notes: Common Noun (神, **shén**, spirit, god)
shén spirit	

丶 ｚ 礻 礻 礻 初 礻 礻 神

神 神 神 神 神 神 神 神 神

（character practice grid with 神, shén, spirit repeated）

数 shù number	Notes: Common Noun
	(数, shù, number, figure)
	(数, shù, fate, plan, destiny)
	(数, shǔ, count, enumerate, list)
	(数, shuò, frequently, repeatedly)

丶 丷 丼 半 米 米 米 娄 娄 娄 娄 数 数

数 数 数 数 数 数 数 数 数

数	数	数	数	数	数	数	数	数	数
shù	shù	shù	shù	shù	shù	shù	shù	shù	shù
number	number	number	number	number	number	number	number	number	number
数	数	数	数	数	数	数	数	数	数
shù	shù	shù	shù	shù	shù	shù	shù	shù	shù
number	number	number	number	number	number	number	number	number	number

件	Notes: Common Noun
jiàn item	(件, **jiàn, item, correspondence, document**) (件, **jiàn, classifier for articles and items**)

丿 亻 亻 仁 伫 件

件 件 件 件 件 件 件 件 件

件	件	件	件	件	件	件	件	件
jiàn	jiàn	jiàn	jiàn	jiàn	jiàn	jiàn	jiàn	jiàn
item	item	item	item	item	item	item	item	item
件	件	件	件	件	件	件	件	件
jiàn	jiàn	jiàn	jiàn	jiàn	jiàn	jiàn	jiàn	jiàn
item	item	item	item	item	item	item	item	item

安 ān peace

Notes: Abstract Noun

(安, ān, peace, still, quiet)

丶 丷 宀 宀 安 安

安 安 安 安 安 安 安 安 安

安	安	安	安	安	安	安	安	安	安
ān	ān	ān	ān	ān	ān	ān	ān	ān	ān
peace	peace	peace	peace	peace	peace	peace	peace	peace	peace
安	安	安	安	安	安	安	安	安	安
ān	ān	ān	ān	ān	ān	ān	ān	ān	ān
peace	peace	peace	peace	peace	peace	peace	peace	peace	peace

表	Notes: Verb
biǎo show	(表, biǎo, to show, to list) (表, biǎo, table, form) (表, biǎo, a meter)

一 二 キ 主 声 声 表 表

表 表 表 表 表 表 表 表 表

原

yuán — simple

(原, **yuán, simple, originally**)

(原, **Yuán, surname Yuán**)

Notes: Adjective

Stroke order: 一 厂 厂 厂 厉 厉 盾 原 原 原

车 chē vehicle

Notes: Common Noun

(车, chē, vehicle, car, chariot, vehicle with wheels)

(车, Chē, surname Chē)

一 ナ 넋 车

白 bái white	Notes: Adjective (白, **bái**, **white, clear, pure**) (白, **bái**, **plain, obvious**) (白, **bái**, **free of charge**) (白, **Bái**, **surname Bái**)

丿 亻 𣅜 白 白

应	Notes: Verb (应, yīng, promise to do something, answer, respond) (应, Yīng, surname Yīng)
yīng promise	

丶 亠 广 广 应 应 应

应 应 应 应 应 应 应 应 应

应	应	应	应	应	应	应	应	应	应
yīng	yīng	yīng	yīng	yīng	yīng	yīng	yīng	yīng	yīng
promise	promise	promise	promise	promise	promise	promise	promise	promise	promise
应	应	应	应	应	应	应	应	应	应
yīng	yīng	yīng	yīng	yīng	yīng	yīng	yīng	yīng	yīng
promise	promise	promise	promise	promise	promise	promise	promise	promise	promise

路	Notes: Common Noun (路, lù, road, path, way, journey, distance, means) (路, lù, sequence, logic, sort, grade, class)
lù	
road	

丨 冂 口 呂 呂 昂 足 足 跂 跂 跤 路 路

路 路 路 路 路 路 路 路

路	路	路	路	路	路	路	路	路	路
lù	lù	lù	lù	lù	lù	lù	lù	lù	lù
road	road	road	road	road	road	road	road	road	road
路	路	路	路	路	路	路	路	路	路
lù	lù	lù	lù	lù	lù	lù	lù	lù	lù
road	road	road	road	road	road	road	road	road	road
路	路	路	路	路	路	路	路	路	
路	路	路	路	路	路	路	路	路	
路	路	路	路	路	路	路	路	路	
路	路	路	路	路	路	路	路	路	
路	路	路	路	路	路	路	路	路	
路	路	路	路	路	路	路	路	路	
路	路	路	路	路	路	路	路	路	

[Type text]

期

qī — time

Notes: Common Noun

(期, **qī**, **time, period of time, time interval, phase, stage**)

(期, **qī**, **classifier for issues of periodicals**)

(期, **jī**, **anniversary**)

Stroke order: 一 十 卄 甘 甘 甚 其 其 其 期 期 期

叫	Notes: Verb (叫, **jiào**, **called**, **cry out**, **call**, **shout out**, **greet**)
jiào called	

| 丨 | 冂 | 口 | 叫 | 叫 |

| 叫 | 叫 | 叫 | 叫 | 叫 | 叫 | 叫 | 叫 | 叫 |

叫	叫	叫	叫	叫	叫	叫	叫	叫	叫
jiào	jiào	jiào	jiào	jiào	jiào	jiào	jiào	jiào	jiào
called	called	called	called	called	called	called	called	called	called
叫	叫	叫	叫	叫	叫	叫	叫	叫	叫
jiào	jiào	jiào	jiào	jiào	jiào	jiào	jiào	jiào	jiào
called	called	called	called	called	called	called	called	called	called

[Type text]

死	Notes: Verb (死, sǐ, die, death)
sǐ die	

一 厂 歹 歹 歹 死

死 死 死 死 死 死 死 死 死

死 (sǐ / die) × 10

死 (sǐ / die) × 10

常

cháng — often

Notes: Adverb

(常, cháng, often, constant, ordinary)

Stroke order: 丨 丷 ⺌ ⺌ 屮 屮 ⺻ 崊 ⺼ 常 常

提

tí — lift

Notes: Verb

(提, **tí**, **lift, raise, pick up, carry**)

(提, **dī**, **ward off, defend against**)

Stroke order: 一 十 扌 扌' 扩 扩 扩 担 担 捍 提 提

提 提 提 提 提 提 提 提 提

提	提	提	提	提	提	提	提	提	提
tí	tí	tí	tí	tí	tí	tí	tí	tí	tí
lift	lift	lift	lift	lift	lift	lift	lift	lift	lift
提	提	提	提	提	提	提	提	提	提
tí	tí	tí	tí	tí	tí	tí	tí	tí	tí
lift	lift	lift	lift	lift	lift	lift	lift	lift	lift

感

gǎn — emotion

Notes: Abstract Noun

(感, gǎn, emotion, feeling)

一 厂 厂 厂 厉 后 咸 咸 咸 咸 感 感 感

金

jīn
gold

Notes: Common Noun

(金, jīn, gold, metal)

丿 人 𠆢 亼 仐 㑒 金 金

金 金 金 金 金 金 金 金 金

金	金	金	金	金	金	金	金	金	金
jīn	jīn	jīn	jīn	jīn	jīn	jīn	jīn	jīn	jīn
gold	gold	gold	gold	gold	gold	gold	gold	gold	gold
金	金	金	金	金	金	金	金	金	金
jīn	jīn	jīn	jīn	jīn	jīn	jīn	jīn	jīn	jīn
gold	gold	gold	gold	gold	gold	gold	gold	gold	gold

何	Notes: Responsive Interrogative Pronoun (何, hé, what?, where?, why?, how?) (何, Hé, surname Hé)
hé what?	

丿 亻 亻 伃 伃 何 何

何 何 何 何 何 何 何 何 何

何	何	何	何	何	何	何	何	何	何
hé	hé	hé	hé	hé	hé	hé	hé	hé	hé
what?	what?	what?	what?	what?	what?	what?	what?	what?	what?
何	何	何	何	何	何	何	何	何	何
hé	hé	hé	hé	hé	hé	hé	hé	hé	hé
what?	what?	what?	what?	what?	what?	what?	what?	what?	what?

更

gèng / still

Notes: Verb

(更, **gēng**, **change**, **replace**, **transform**)

(更, **gèng**, **more**, **still**, **even more**, **further**, **furthermore**)

(更, **gēng**, **night watch**)

一 丆 丆 亓 亘 百 更 更

反	Notes: Verb
fǎn return	(反, **fǎn, turn over, return, revolt, counter, rebel**)

一 厂 厅 反

Notes: Verb

(合, hé, close, shut)

(合, hé, accord with, conform to, be equal to, together, jointly)

(合, hé, classifier for rounds)

(合, gě, unit of dry measure for grain, equal to one deciliter)

放

fàng — put

Notes: Verb

(放, fàng, to put, to place, release, set free, give out)

(放, fàng, expand, blossom, bloom)

Stroke order: 丶 亠 方 方 방 放 放

做	Notes: Verb (做, **zuò**, **to do, do, act, make, produce**) (做, **zuò**, **write, compose**)
zuò	
to do	

丿 亻 仁 什 什 估 估 估 估 做 做

做 做 做 做 做 做 做 做 做

做	做	做	做	做	做	做	做	做	做
zuò	zuò	zuò	zuò	zuò	zuò	zuò	zuò	zuò	zuò
to do	to do	to do	to do	to do	to do	to do	to do	to do	to do
做	做	做	做	做	做	做	做	做	做
zuò	zuò	zuò	zuò	zuò	zuò	zuò	zuò	zuò	zuò
to do	to do	to do	to do	to do	to do	to do	to do	to do	to do

254

系	Notes: Verb (系, xì, relate to, to bear on) (系, jì, tie, fasten, do up, button up) (系, xì, system, series)
xì	
relate	

一 ⺄ 幺 幺 乎 系 系

系 系 系 系 系 系 系 系 系

系	系	系	系	系	系	系	系	系	系
xì	xì	xì	xì	xì	xì	xì	xì	xì	xì
relate	relate	relate	relate	relate	relate	relate	relate	relate	relate
系	系	系	系	系	系	系	系	系	系
xì	xì	xì	xì	xì	xì	xì	xì	xì	xì
relate	relate	relate	relate	relate	relate	relate	relate	relate	relate

计	Notes: Verb (计, jì, count, calculate, plot, plan) (计, Jì, surname Jì)
jì	
count	

丶 讠 计 计

计 计 计 计 计 计 计 计 计

计	计	计	计	计	计	计	计	计	计
jì	jì	jì	jì	jì	jì	jì	jì	jì	jì
count	count	count	count	count	count	count	count	count	count
计	计	计	计	计	计	计	计	计	计
jì	jì	jì	jì	jì	jì	jì	jì	jì	jì
count	count	count	count	count	count	count	count	count	count

或

huò — perhaps

Notes: Adverb

(或, **huò, perhaps, maybe, probably**)

Stroke order: 一 丆 口 口 口 戓 或 或

利

lì — profit

Notes: Common Noun

(利, **lì, profit, interest, benefit**)

(利, **Lì, surname Lì**)

一 二 千 禾 禾 利 利

受

shòu — receive

Notes: Verb

(受, shòu, receive, accept)

(受, shòu, endure, suffer, be subjected to)

光	Notes: Common Noun
	(光, guāng, light, ray, brightness)
	(光, guāng, honour, glory, lustre)
	(光, guāng, smooth, glossy)
guāng light	(光, guāng, to be bare, naked)

丨 丷 ⺌ 业 乎 光

光 光 光 光 光 光 光 光 光

光	光	光	光	光	光	光	光	光	光
guāng light	guāng light	guāng light	guāng light	guāng light	guāng light	guāng light	guāng light	guāng light	guāng light
光	光	光	光	光	光	光	光	光	光
guāng light	guāng light	guāng light	guāng light	guāng light	guāng light	guāng light	guāng light	guāng light	guāng light

[Type text]

王 wáng king	Notes: Common Noun (王, **wáng, king, sovereign, prince**) (王, **Wáng, surname Wáng**) (王, **wàng, to rule**) (王, **wáng, grand, great, honourable**)

一 二 干 王

王 王 王 王 王 王 王 王 王

王	王	王	王	王	王	王	王	王	王
wáng king	wáng king	wáng king	wáng king	wáng king	wáng king	wáng king	wáng king	wáng king	wáng king
王	王	王	王	王	王	王	王	王	王
wáng king	wáng king	wáng king	wáng king	wáng king	wáng king	wáng king	wáng king	wáng king	wáng king

[Type text]

果	Notes: Common Noun (果, **guǒ**, **fruit**) (果, **guǒ**, **surely**, **truly**, **as expected**)
guǒ	
fruit	

丨 冂 冃 日 旦 早 果 果

果 果 果 果 果 果 果 果 果

果	果	果	果	果	果	果	果	果	果
guǒ	guǒ	guǒ	guǒ	guǒ	guǒ	guǒ	guǒ	guǒ	guǒ
fruit	fruit	fruit	fruit	fruit	fruit	fruit	fruit	fruit	fruit
果	果	果	果	果	果	果	果	果	果
guǒ	guǒ	guǒ	guǒ	guǒ	guǒ	guǒ	guǒ	guǒ	guǒ
fruit	fruit	fruit	fruit	fruit	fruit	fruit	fruit	fruit	fruit

亲	Notes: Verb (亲, **qīn**, **kiss**) (亲, **qīn**, *close relative*)
qīn kiss	

丶 亠 产 立 䒑 辛 亲 亲

亲 亲 亲 亲 亲 亲 亲 亲 亲

亲	亲	亲	亲	亲	亲	亲	亲	亲	亲
qīn	qīn	qīn	qīn	qīn	qīn	qīn	qīn	qīn	qīn
kiss	kiss	kiss	kiss	kiss	kiss	kiss	kiss	kiss	kiss
亲	亲	亲	亲	亲	亲	亲	亲	亲	亲
qīn	qīn	qīn	qīn	qīn	qīn	qīn	qīn	qīn	qīn
kiss	kiss	kiss	kiss	kiss	kiss	kiss	kiss	kiss	kiss

界	Notes: Common Noun (界, jiè, boundary, limit)
jiè limit	

丨 冂 日 冃 田 甼 毘 界 界

及	Notes: Verb (及, jí, reach, come up to) (及, jí, and, in, on, to)
jí reach	

丿 乃 及

及 及 及 及 及 及 及 及 及

及	及	及	及	及	及	及	及	及	及
jí	jí	jí	jí	jí	jí	jí	jí	jí	jí
reach	reach	reach	reach	reach	reach	reach	reach	reach	reach
及	及	及	及	及	及	及	及	及	及
jí	jí	jí	jí	jí	jí	jí	jí	jí	jí
reach	reach	reach	reach	reach	reach	reach	reach	reach	reach

及	及	及	及	及		及	及	及	
及	及	及	及	及		及	及	及	
及	及	及	及	及		及	及	及	
及	及	及	及	及		及	及	及	
及	及	及	及	及		及	及	及	
及	及	及	及	及		及	及	及	
及	及	及	及	及		及	及	及	
及	及	及	及	及		及	及		

[Type text]

今	Notes: Temporal Adverb (今, **jīn**, **now**, **current**, **presently**)
jīn	
current	

丿 人 𠆢 今

今 今 今 今 今 今 今 今 今

今	今	今	今	今	今	今	今	今	今
jīn	jīn	jīn	jīn	jīn	jīn	jīn	jīn	jīn	jīn
current	current	current	current	current	current	current	current	current	current
今	今	今	今	今	今	今	今	今	今
jīn	jīn	jīn	jīn	jīn	jīn	jīn	jīn	jīn	jīn
current	current	current	current	current	current	current	current	current	current
今	今	今	今	今		今	今		
今	今	今	今	今		今	今		
今	今	今	今	今		今	今		
今	今	今	今	今		今	今		
今	今	今	今	今		今	今		
今	今	今	今	今		今	今		
今	今	今	今	今		今	今		
今	今	今	今	今		今	今		

[Type text]

京

Notes: Proper Noun

(京, jīng, capital city)

jīng / capital

丶 亠 广 亣 古 宁 京 京

务	Notes: Common Noun (务, wù, event, affair, business)
wù	
affair	

丿 夂 夂 冬 务

务 务 务 务 务 务 务 务 务

务	务	务	务	务	务	务	务	务	务
wù	wù	wù	wù	wù	wù	wù	wù	wù	wù
affair	affair	affair	affair	affair	affair	affair	affair	affair	affair
务	务	务	务	务	务	务	务	务	务
wù	wù	wù	wù	wù	wù	wù	wù	wù	wù
affair	affair	affair	affair	affair	affair	affair	affair	affair	affair
务	务	务	务	务		务	务	务	
务	务	务	务	务		务	务	务	
务	务	务	务	务		务	务	务	
务	务	务	务	务		务	务	务	
务	务	务	务	务		务	务	务	
务	务	务	务	务		务	务	务	
务	务	务	务	务		务	务	务	
务	务	务	务	务		务	务	务	

[Type text]

制	Notes: Verb (制, zhì, restrict, control) (制, zhì, work out, formulate, stipulate)
zhì control	

丿 丄 匕 乍 낰 制 制

制 制 制 制 制 制 制 制

制	制	制	制	制	制	制	制	制	制
zhì	zhì	zhì	zhì	zhì	zhì	zhì	zhì	zhì	zhì
control	control	control	control	control	control	control	control	control	control
制	制	制	制	制	制	制	制	制	制
zhì	zhì	zhì	zhì	zhì	zhì	zhì	zhì	zhì	zhì
control	control	control	control	control	control	control	control	control	control

[Type text]

| 解 jiě explain | Notes: Verb

(解, jiě, explain)

(解, jiě, separate, untie, undo, take off, dissolve)

(解, jiě, mathematic solution)

(解, Xiè, surname Xiè) |

丿 ⺈ ⺈ 𠂊 角 角 角 角 解 解 解 解 解

解 解 解 解 解 解 解 解 解

解	解	解	解	解	解	解	解	解	解
jiě	jiě	jiě	jiě	jiě	jiě	jiě	jiě	jiě	jiě
explain	explain	explain	explain	explain	explain	explain	explain	explain	explain
解	解	解	解	解	解	解	解	解	解
jiě	jiě	jiě	jiě	jiě	jiě	jiě	jiě	jiě	jiě
explain	explain	explain	explain	explain	explain	explain	explain	explain	explain

各

gè — each

Notes: Adverb

(各, **gè**, **each**, **every**)

(各, **gè**, **different**, **separately**)

丿 ク 夂 各 各 各

各 各 各 各 各 各 各 各 各

任	Notes: Verb
rèn allow	(任, rèn, appoint, serve a position, official post)
	(任, rèn, classifier for terms of office)
	(任, rèn, allow, trust)
	(任, Rèn, surname Rèn)

ノ 亻 亻 仁 仟 任

任 任 任 任 任 任 任 任 任

任	任	任	任	任	任	任	任	任	任
rèn allow	rèn allow	rèn allow	rèn allow	rèn allow	rèn allow	rèn allow	rèn allow	rèn allow	rèn allow
任	任	任	任	任	任	任	任	任	任
rèn allow	rèn allow	rèn allow	rèn allow	rèn allow	rèn allow	rèn allow	rèn allow	rèn allow	rèn allow

至

zhì — arrive

Notes: Verb

(至, **zhì, arrive, reach**)

(至, **zhì, to, until, till**)

(至, **zhì, extremely, most**)

Stroke order: 一 丆 厼 至 至 至

至 至 至 至 至 至 至 至 至

至	至	至	至	至	至	至	至	至	至
zhì	zhì	zhì	zhì	zhì	zhì	zhì	zhì	zhì	zhì
arrive	arrive	arrive	arrive	arrive	arrive	arrive	arrive	arrive	arrive
至	至	至	至	至	至	至	至	至	至
zhì	zhì	zhì	zhì	zhì	zhì	zhì	zhì	zhì	zhì
arrive	arrive	arrive	arrive	arrive	arrive	arrive	arrive	arrive	arrive

清	Notes: Adjective
	(清, qīng, clear, pure, fresh, cool)
	(清, qīng, clear up, settle, clean up, purge)
	(清, qīng, count)
qīng / clear	(清, qīng, lonely, poor)

丶 丶 氵 氵 氵 浐 浐 浐 清 清 清

物	Notes: Common Noun (物, wù, thing, matter)
wù thing	

丿 丨 亻 牛 牜 牞 物 物

物 物 物 物 物 物 物 物 物

物	物	物	物	物	物	物	物	物	物
wù thing	wù thing	wù thing	wù thing	wù thing	wù thing	wù thing	wù thing	wù thing	wù thing
物	物	物	物	物	物	物	物	物	物
wù thing	wù thing	wù thing	wù thing	wù thing	wù thing	wù thing	wù thing	wù thing	wù thing
物	物	物	物	物		物	物	物	
物	物	物	物	物		物	物	物	
物	物	物	物	物		物	物	物	
物	物	物	物	物		物	物	物	
物	物	物	物	物		物	物	物	
物	物	物	物	物		物	物	物	
物	物	物	物	物		物	物	物	
物	物	物	物	物		物	物	物	

[Type text]

台	Notes: Common Noun
	(台, **tái**, **platform, stage, terrace, stand, support, station**)
tái	(台, **tái**, **classifier for performances, engines, electronic devises**)
stage	(台, **Tái**, **surname Tái**)

厶 厶 仒 台 台

台 台 台 台 台 台 台 台 台

(practice grid of 台 / tái / stage repeated)

象 xiàng image	Notes: Common Noun (象, xiàng, appearance, shape, image, likeness) (象, xiàng, be like, resemble, similar too) (象, xiàng, look as if, seem)

⁄ 厶 scriptsize 产 台 台

象 象 象 象 象 象 象 象 象

象	象	象	象	象	象	象	象	象	象
xiàng image	xiàng image	xiàng image	xiàng image	xiàng image	xiàng image	xiàng image	xiàng image	xiàng image	xiàng image
象	象	象	象	象	象	象	象	象	象
xiàng image	xiàng image	xiàng image	xiàng image	xiàng image	xiàng image	xiàng image	xiàng image	xiàng image	xiàng image

记

Notes: Verb

(记, jì, remember, recall)

jì
recall

丶 讠 讠̄ 讠̄ 记

记 记 记 记 记 记 记 记 记

记	记	记	记	记	记	记	记	记	记
jì	jì	jì	jì	jì	jì	jì	jì	jì	jì
recall	recall	recall	recall	recall	recall	recall	recall	recall	recall
记	记	记	记	记	记	记	记	记	记
jì	jì	jì	jì	jì	jì	jì	jì	jì	jì
recall	recall	recall	recall	recall	recall	recall	recall	recall	recall

边

biān — side

Notes: Common Noun

(边, **biān**, side, on the side of something, margin, limit)

(边, **Biān**, surname Biān)

Stroke order: 乛 力 ⺌力 边 边

共	Notes: Verb
gòng / share	(共, gòng, share, commonly possess) (共, gòng, common, general)

一 十 廾 共 共 共

共 共 共 共 共 共 共 共 共

共	共	共	共	共	共	共	共	共	共
gòng share	gòng share	gòng share	gòng share	gòng share	gòng share	gòng share	gòng share	gòng share	gòng share
共	共	共	共	共	共	共	共	共	共
gòng share	gòng share	gòng share	gòng share	gòng share	gòng share	gòng share	gòng share	gòng share	gòng share

风 fēng share	Notes: Common Noun (风, **fēng**, **wind**) (风, **fēng**, **common practice, custom, general mood, style**)

丿 几 风 风

风 风 风 风 风 风 风 风 风

风	风	风	风	风	风	风	风	风	风
fēng	fēng	fēng	fēng	fēng	fēng	fēng	fēng	fēng	fēng
share	share	share	share	share	share	share	share	share	share
风	风	风	风	风	风	风	风	风	风
fēng	fēng	fēng	fēng	fēng	fēng	fēng	fēng	fēng	fēng
share	share	share	share	share	share	share	share	share	share
风	风	风	风	风	风	风	风	风	风
风	风	风	风	风	风	风	风	风	风
风	风	风	风	风	风	风	风	风	风
风	风	风	风	风	风	风	风	风	风
风	风	风	风	风	风	风	风	风	风
风	风	风	风	风	风	风	风	风	风
风	风	风	风	风	风	风	风	风	风
风	风	风	风	风	风	风	风	风	风

[Type text]

战

zhàn — war

Notes: Common Noun

(战, **zhàn**, **war**, **warfare**, **battle**)

Stroke order: 丨 卜 ⺊ 占 占 占 战 战 战

战 战 战 战 战 战 战 战 战

战	战	战	战	战	战	战	战	战	战
zhàn	zhàn	zhàn	zhàn	zhàn	zhàn	zhàn	zhàn	zhàn	zhàn
war	war	war	war	war	war	war	war	war	war
战	战	战	战	战	战	战	战	战	战
zhàn	zhàn	zhàn	zhàn	zhàn	zhàn	zhàn	zhàn	zhàn	zhàn
war	war	war	war	war	war	war	war	war	war

干	Notes: Common Noun
	(干, **gān**, **stem**)
	(干, **gān**, **to dry**)
	(干, **gān**, **dry**)
	(干, **gān**, **in vain**)
gān	(干, **gān**, **only, simply**)
dry	

一 二 干

干 干 干 干 干 干 干 干 干

干	干	干	干	干	干	干	干	干	干
gān	gān	gān	gān	gān	gān	gān	gān	gān	gān
dry	dry	dry	dry	dry	dry	dry	dry	dry	dry
干	干	干	干	干	干	干	干	干	干
gān	gān	gān	gān	gān	gān	gān	gān	gān	gān
dry	dry	dry	dry	dry	dry	dry	dry	dry	dry

接	Notes: Verb
jiē join	(接, jiē, connect, join, put together, come in contact) (接, jiē, catch, take hold of) (接, jiē, receive, meet, welcome)

一 扌 扌 扩 扩 扩 护 护 挼 接 接

接 接 接 接 接 接 接 接 接

它	Notes: Personal Pronoun
tā	(它, tā, it, its')
it	

丶 丶 宀 宁 它

它 它 它 它 它 它 它 它 它

许 xǔ allow	Notes: Verb (许, xǔ, allow, permit, promise) (许, xǔ, be betrothed to) (许, Xǔ, surname Xǔ) (许, xǔ, maybe, perhaps, somewhat)

丶 讠 讠 讠 许 许

特	Notes: Adjective
	(特, tè, special, particular, exceptional)
tè	(特, tè, especially)
special	

丿 丨 牜 牛 牜 牜 牜 牪 特 特

特 特 特 特 特 特 特 特 特

觉

Notes: Verb

(觉, jiào, sleep)

(觉, jué, perceive, think of)

jiào — sleep

丶 丶 丷 ⺍ ⺍ 兴 兴 觉 觉

觉 觉 觉 觉 觉 觉 觉 觉 觉

觉	觉	觉	觉	觉	觉	觉	觉	觉	觉
jiào	jiào	jiào	jiào	jiào	jiào	jiào	jiào	jiào	jiào
sleep	sleep	sleep	sleep	sleep	sleep	sleep	sleep	sleep	sleep
觉	觉	觉	觉	觉	觉	觉	觉	觉	觉
jiào	jiào	jiào	jiào	jiào	jiào	jiào	jiào	jiào	jiào
sleep	sleep	sleep	sleep	sleep	sleep	sleep	sleep	sleep	sleep
觉	觉	觉	觉	觉		觉	觉	觉	
觉	觉	觉	觉	觉		觉	觉		
觉	觉	觉	觉	觉		觉	觉		
觉	觉	觉	觉	觉		觉	觉		
觉	觉	觉	觉	觉		觉	觉		
觉	觉	觉	觉	觉		觉	觉		
觉	觉	觉	觉	觉		觉	觉		
觉	觉	觉	觉	觉		觉	觉		

[Type text]

望	Notes: Verb (望, **wàng**, **look**) (望, **wàng**, **full moon**)
wàng	
look	

望 (stroke order practice)

直

Notes: Adjective

(直, zhí, straight, directly)

zhí — straight

一 十 𠂇 𠂋 古 古 盲 直

Stroke practice: 直 直 直 直 直 直 直 直 直

直	直	直	直	直	直	直	直	直	直
zhí	zhí	zhí	zhí	zhí	zhí	zhí	zhí	zhí	zhí
straight	straight	straight	straight	straight	straight	straight	straight	straight	straight
直	直	直	直	直	直	直	直	直	直
zhí	zhí	zhí	zhí	zhí	zhí	zhí	zhí	zhí	zhí
straight	straight	straight	straight	straight	straight	straight	straight	straight	straight

服	Notes: Verb (服, **fú**, serve) (服, **fú**, dose)
fú	
serve	

丿 几 月 月 朋 朋 服 服

服 服 服 服 服 服 服 服 服

毛

máo — hair

Notes: Common Noun

(毛, **máo**, **hair**)

Stroke order: 一 二 三 毛

林

lín — forest

Notes: Common Noun

(林, **lín**, **forest**)

(林, **Lín**, **surname Lín**)

Stroke order: 一 十 才 木 木 村 村 林

题

tí
problem

Notes: Common Noun

(题, **tí**, **topic**, **problem**)

(题, **tí**, inscribe)

建

jiàn — make

Notes: Verb

(建, jiàn, make, construct, establish)

Stroke order: 乛 ⺕ ⺕ ⺕ 킈 聿 建 建

建 建 建 建 建 建 建 建 建

建	建	建	建	建	建	建	建	建	建
jiàn	jiàn	jiàn	jiàn	jiàn	jiàn	jiàn	jiàn	jiàn	jiàn
make	make	make	make	make	make	make	make	make	make
建	建	建	建	建	建	建	建	建	建
jiàn	jiàn	jiàn	jiàn	jiàn	jiàn	jiàn	jiàn	jiàn	jiàn
make	make	make	make	make	make	make	make	make	make

南

nán — south

(南, **nán**, **south**)

Stroke order: 一 十 ナ 门 冇 冇 肖 南 南

度	Notes: Common Noun
	(度, dù, degrees, kWh, angle, temperature)
dù	(度, dù, classifier for units of measurement, occasions, times)
degrees	

丶 亠 广 广 庐 庐 庐 庐 度 度

度 度 度 度 度 度 度 度 度

统

Notes: Verb

(统, tǒng, order, unite)

tǒng
order

色	Notes: Adjective (色, **sè**, **colour**) (色, **shǎi**, **colour**)
sè	
colour	

丿 ⺈ 刀 匂 匂 色

色 色 色 色 色 色 色 色 色

色	色	色	色	色	色	色	色	色	色
sè	sè	sè	sè	sè	sè	sè	sè	sè	sè
colour	colour	colour	colour	colour	colour	colour	colour	colour	colour
色	色	色	色	色	色	色	色	色	色
sè	sè	sè	sè	sè	sè	sè	sè	sè	sè
colour	colour	colour	colour	colour	colour	colour	colour	colour	colour
色	色	色	色	色		色	色	色	
色	色	色	色	色		色	色	色	
色	色	色	色	色		色	色	色	
色	色	色	色	色		色	色	色	
色	色	色	色	色		色	色	色	
色	色	色	色	色		色	色	色	
色	色	色	色	色		色	色	色	
色	色	色	色	色		色	色	色	

[Type text]

字	Notes: Common Noun
zì	(字, zì, written Chinese character, Hanzi)
Hanzi	

丶 丷 宀 宀 宁 字

字 字 字 字 字 字 字 字 字

字	字	字	字	字	字	字	字	字	字
zì	zì	zì	zì	zì	zì	zì	zì	zì	zì
Hanzi	Hanzi	Hanzi	Hanzi	Hanzi	Hanzi	Hanzi	Hanzi	Hanzi	Hanzi
字	字	字	字	字	字	字	字	字	字
zì	zì	zì	zì	zì	zì	zì	zì	zì	zì
Hanzi	Hanzi	Hanzi	Hanzi	Hanzi	Hanzi	Hanzi	Hanzi	Hanzi	Hanzi
字	字	字	字	字		字	字		
字	字	字	字	字		字	字		
字	字	字	字	字		字	字		
字	字	字	字	字		字	字		
字	字	字	字	字		字	字		
字	字	字	字	字		字	字		
字	字	字	字	字		字	字		
字	字	字	字	字		字	字		

[Type text]

请	Notes: Verb (请, **qǐng**, **request**, **invite**) (请, **qǐng**, **please**)
qǐng	
please	

丶 丨 讠 讠̄ 讠⁺ 讠⁼ 请 请 请

请 请 请 请 请 请 请 请 请

请	请	请	请	请	请	请	请	请	请
qǐng	qǐng	qǐng	qǐng	qǐng	qǐng	qǐng	qǐng	qǐng	qǐng
please	please	please	please	please	please	please	please	please	please
请	请	请	请	请	请	请	请	请	请
qǐng	qǐng	qǐng	qǐng	qǐng	qǐng	qǐng	qǐng	qǐng	qǐng
please	please	please	please	please	please	please	please	please	please

请	请	请	请	请		请	请		
请	请	请	请	请		请			
请	请	请	请	请		请	请		
请	请	请	请	请		请	请		
请	请	请	请	请		请	请		
请	请	请	请	请		请			
请	请	请	请	请		请	请		

[Type text]

交

Notes: Verb

(**交**, **jiāo**, **join**)

jiāo
join

丶 一 亠 六 亣 交

交 交 交 交 交 交 交 交 交

爱	Notes: Verb (爱, ài, love)
ài	
love	

一 ⼂ ⼀ ⼃ ⼍ ⺈ ⺌ ⺍ 爫 爱

爱 爱 爱 爱 爱 爱 爱 爱 爱

爱	爱	爱	爱	爱	爱	爱	爱	爱	爱
ài	ài	ài	ài	ài	ài	ài	ài	ài	ài
love	love	love	love	love	love	love	love	love	love
爱	爱	爱	爱	爱	爱	爱	爱	爱	爱
ài	ài	ài	ài	ài	ài	ài	ài	ài	ài
love	love	love	love	love	love	love	love	love	love

让

Notes: Verb

(让, ràng, let, allow)

ràng — allow

`丶 讠 让 让 让`

认	Notes: Verb
rèn	(认, rèn, recognize, know)
know	(认, rèn, enter into a certain relationship with)
	(认, rèn, accept as unavoidable)

丶 讠 认 认

算

suàn / plan

Notes: Verb

(算, **suàn**, **calculate, compute, figure**)

(算, **suàn**, **include, plan, think, suppose, consider**)

Stroke order: 丿 ⺮ ⺮ ⺮ ⺮ ⺮ 竹 竹 笁 筲 筲 筲 算 算

论

lùn — theory

Notes: Common Noun

(论, lùn, theory)

(论, lùn, discuss, talk about, discourse)

(论, lùn, decide on, determine)

丶 亠 讠 论 论 论

百

Notes: Quantitative Adjective

(百, **bǎi**, **hundred**, **100**)

bǎi
100

一 丆 丆 丆 百 百

百 百 百 百 百 百 百 百

百	百	百	百	百	百	百	百	百	百
bǎi	bǎi	bǎi	bǎi	bǎi	bǎi	bǎi	bǎi	bǎi	bǎi
100	100	100	100	100	100	100	100	100	100
百	百	百	百	百	百	百	百	百	百
bǎi	bǎi	bǎi	bǎi	bǎi	bǎi	bǎi	bǎi	bǎi	bǎi
100	100	100	100	100	100	100	100	100	100

吃	Notes: Verb (吃, **chī**, eat) (吃, **qī, the sound of giggling**)
chī	
eat	

丨 冂 口 口' 吃' 吃

吃 吃 吃 吃 吃 吃 吃 吃 吃

吃	吃	吃	吃	吃	吃	吃	吃	吃	吃
chī	chī	chī	chī	chī	chī	chī	chī	chī	chī
eat	eat	eat	eat	eat	eat	eat	eat	eat	eat
吃	吃	吃	吃	吃	吃	吃	吃	吃	吃
chī	chī	chī	chī	chī	chī	chī	chī	chī	chī
eat	eat	eat	eat	eat	eat	eat	eat	eat	eat

义	Notes: Common Noun (义, yì, **justice**, **righteousness**)
yì justice	

丶 丷 义

义 义 义 义 义 义 义 义 义

义	义	义	义	义	义	义	义	义	义
yì	yì	yì	yì	yì	yì	yì	yì	yì	yì
justice	justice	justice	justice	justice	justice	justice	justice	justice	justice
义	义	义	义	义	义	义	义	义	义
yì	yì	yì	yì	yì	yì	yì	yì	yì	yì
justice	justice	justice	justice	justice	justice	justice	justice	justice	justice

科	Notes: Common Noun
kē	(科, kē, department, branch of study, taxonomic family)
justice	(科, kē, rules, laws)
	(科, kē, levy taxes, levy fines)

丶 二 千 千 禾 禾 科 科 科

怎

Notes: Interrogative Pronoun

(怎, zěn, how)

zěn / how

元	Notes: Adjective
yuán first	(元, **yuán, first, primary**) (元, **yuán, Chinese monetary unit**) (元, **Yuán, Yuan dynasty**) (元, **Yuán, surname Yuán**)

一 二 テ 元

元 元 元 元 元 元 元 元 元

元	元	元	元	元	元	元	元	元	元
yuán first	yuán first	yuán first	yuán first	yuán first	yuán first	yuán first	yuán first	yuán first	yuán first
元	元	元	元	元	元	元	元	元	元
yuán first	yuán first	yuán first	yuán first	yuán first	yuán first	yuán first	yuán first	yuán first	yuán first

[Type text]

社

shè — club

Notes: Common Noun

(社, shè, club, organized body, agency, society)

Stroke order: 丶 亠 亣 礻 礻 礻 社 社

Notes: Common Noun

((术, shù, skill)

shù
skill

一 十 才 木 术

结

jié — knit

Notes: Verb

(结, **jié**, **tie, knit, knot, weave**)

(结, **jiē**, **bear fruit**)

(结, **jiē**, **congeal, form, forge, cement**)

(结, **jiē**, **join together**)

Stroke order: 乚 乡 纟 纟 纟 纣 纣 结 结

功	Notes: Common Noun (功, gōng, achievement, skill) (功, gōng, meritorious service, exploit) (功, gōng, achievement, result, effect)
gōng skill	

一 丁 工 功 功

功 功 功 功 功 功 功 功 功

功	功	功	功	功	功	功	功	功	功
gōng skill	gōng skill	gōng skill	gōng skill	gōng skill	gōng skill	gōng skill	gōng skill	gōng skill	gōng skill
功	功	功	功	功	功	功	功	功	功
gōng skill	gōng skill	gōng skill	gōng skill	gōng skill	gōng skill	gōng skill	gōng skill	gōng skill	gōng skill

指	Notes: Common Noun (指, zhǐ, point)
zhǐ	
point	

一 十 扌 扩 护 指 指 指 指

指 指 指 指 指 指 指 指 指

指	指	指	指	指	指	指	指	指	指
zhǐ	zhǐ	zhǐ	zhǐ	zhǐ	zhǐ	zhǐ	zhǐ	zhǐ	zhǐ
point	point	point	point	point	point	point	point	point	point
指	指	指	指	指	指	指	指	指	指
zhǐ	zhǐ	zhǐ	zhǐ	zhǐ	zhǐ	zhǐ	zhǐ	zhǐ	zhǐ
point	point	point	point	point	point	point	point	point	point

思

sī — think

Notes: Verb

(思, sī, think, consider, deliberate)

Stroke order: 丨 冂 日 田 田 思 思 思 思

流	Notes: Verb (流, liú, to flow, stream)
liú flow	

丶 丶 氵 氵 广 疒 产 浐 浐 流

流 流 流 流 流 流 流 流 流

流	流	流	流	流	流	流	流	流	流
liú	liú	liú	liú	liú	liú	liú	liú	liú	liú
flow	flow	flow	flow	flow	flow	flow	flow	flow	flow
流	流	流	流	流	流	流	流	流	流
liú	liú	liú	liú	liú	liú	liú	liú	liú	liú
flow	flow	flow	flow	flow	flow	flow	flow	flow	flow

流	流	流	流	流		流	流		
流	流	流	流	流		流	流		
流	流	流	流	流		流	流		
流	流	流	流	流		流	流		
流	流	流	流	流		流	流		
流	流	流	流	流		流	流		
流	流	流	流	流		流	流		
流	流	流	流	流		流	流		

[Type text]

每	Notes: Adjective (每, měi, every, each)
měi	
every	

丿 ㇇ 仁 每 每 每 每

每 每 每 每 每 每 每 每 每

每	每	每	每	每	每	每	每	每	每
měi	měi	měi	měi	měi	měi	měi	měi	měi	měi
every	every	every	every	every	every	every	every	every	every
每	每	每	每	每	每	每	每	每	每
měi	měi	měi	měi	měi	měi	měi	měi	měi	měi
every	every	every	every	every	every	every	every	every	every

[Type text]

青	Notes: Adjective (青, qīng, nature's colours of blue, green, black)
qīng blue	

一 二 十 丰 丰 青 青 青

青 青 青 青 青 青 青 青 青

青	青	青	青	青	青	青	青	青	青
qīng blue	qīng blue	qīng blue	qīng blue	qīng blue	qīng blue	qīng blue	qīng blue	qīng blue	qīng blue
青	青	青	青	青	青	青	青	青	青
qīng blue	qīng blue	qīng blue	qīng blue	qīng blue	qīng blue	qīng blue	qīng blue	qīng blue	qīng blue

管

Notes: Common Noun

(管, **guǎn**, **tube**, **pipe**)

guǎn
pipe

夫	Notes: Common Noun
fū	(夫, fū, man)
man	(夫, fú, formal classifier for this / that person)

一 二 廾 夫

夫 夫 夫 夫 夫 夫 夫 夫 夫

夫	夫	夫	夫	夫	夫	夫	夫	夫	夫
fū	fū	fū	fū	fū	fū	fū	fū	fū	fū
man	man	man	man	man	man	man	man	man	man
夫	夫	夫	夫	夫	夫	夫	夫	夫	夫
fū	fū	fū	fū	fū	fū	fū	fū	fū	fū
man	man	man	man	man	man	man	man	man	man

连	Notes: Verb
	(连, lián, connect, join, link, connect including)
	(连, lián, company)
	(连, Lián, surname Lián)
lián	
connect	

一 二 左 车 车 诈 连

连 连 连 连 连 连 连 连 连

连	连	连	连	连	连	连	连	连	连
lián	lián	lián	lián	lián	lián	lián	lián	lián	lián
connect	connect	connect	connect	connect	connect	connect	connect	connect	connect
连	连	连	连	连	连	连	连	连	连
lián	lián	lián	lián	lián	lián	lián	lián	lián	lián
connect	connect	connect	connect	connect	connect	connect	connect	connect	connect

远

Notes: Adjective

(远, **yuǎn**, **far**)

yuǎn
far

一 二 テ 元 沅 沅 远

远 远 远 远 远 远 远 远 远

资

Notes: Common Noun

(资, zī, money)

zī
money

丶 冫 氵 沪 汸 次 咨 咨 资 资

资	资	资	资	资	资	资	资	资	资
zī	zī	zī	zī	zī	zī	zī	zī	zī	zī
money	money	money	money	money	money	money	money	money	money
资	资	资	资	资	资	资	资	资	资
zī	zī	zī	zī	zī	zī	zī	zī	zī	zī
money	money	money	money	money	money	money	money	money	money
资	资	资	资	资		资	资		
资	资	资	资	资		资	资		
资	资	资	资	资		资	资		
资	资	资	资	资		资	资		
资	资	资	资	资		资	资		
资	资	资	资	资		资	资		
资	资	资	资	资		资	资		
资	资	资	资	资		资	资		

队

Notes: Common Noun

(队, **duì**, team)

duì — team

跟

gēn — follow

Notes: Verb

(跟, **gēn**, heel, follow)

(跟, **gēn**, with, and)

Stroke order: 丨 冂 口 ㅁ 尸 尸 足 足 趴 跟 跟 跟

带	Notes: Verb (带, dài, carry, bring, take) (带, dài, belt, zone)
dài	
take	

一 十 卄 卅 丗 芇 芇 带 带

带 带 带 带 带 带 带 带 带

带	带	带	带	带	带	带	带	带	带
dài	dài	dài	dài	dài	dài	dài	dài	dài	dài
take	take	take	take	take	take	take	take	take	take
带	带	带	带	带	带	带	带	带	带
dài	dài	dài	dài	dài	dài	dài	dài	dài	dài
take	take	take	take	take	take	take	take	take	take

[Type text]

花	Notes: Common Noun (花, **huā**, **flower**) (花, **huā**, **spend**)
huā	
flower	

一 十 艹 艹 艾 花 花

花 花 花 花 花 花 花 花 花

花	花	花	花	花	花	花	花	花	花
huā	huā	huā	huā	huā	huā	huā	huā	huā	huā
flower	flower	flower	flower	flower	flower	flower	flower	flower	flower
花	花	花	花	花	花	花	花	花	花
huā	huā	huā	huā	huā	huā	huā	huā	huā	huā
flower	flower	flower	flower	flower	flower	flower	flower	flower	flower

[Type text]

快

kuài — fast

Notes: Adjective

(快, **kuài**, **fast**, **sharp**)

一 十 卄 艹 艹 艿 花

快 快 快 快 快 快 快 快 快

条	Notes: Common Noun (条, tiáo, twig, strip, item) (条, tiáo, classifier for dogs, snakes, dragons)
tiáo	
twig	

丿 ク 夂 冬 冬 条 条

条 条 条 条 条 条 条 条 条

条	条	条	条	条	条	条	条	条	条
tiáo	tiáo	tiáo	tiáo	tiáo	tiáo	tiáo	tiáo	tiáo	tiáo
twig	twig	twig	twig	twig	twig	twig	twig	twig	twig
条	条	条	条	条	条	条	条	条	条
tiáo	tiáo	tiáo	tiáo	tiáo	tiáo	tiáo	tiáo	tiáo	tiáo
twig	twig	twig	twig	twig	twig	twig	twig	twig	twig

院

yuàn
twig

Notes: Common Noun

(院, **yuàn, courtyard, compound, court**)

阝 阝 阝 阝 阝 阝 阝 阝 院

| 变 biàn change | Notes: Verb
(变, biàn, change) |

丶 亠 十 六 亦 亦 变 变

变 变 变 变 变 变 变 变 变

变	变	变	变	变	变	变	变	变	变
biàn change	biàn change	biàn change	biàn change	biàn change	biàn change	biàn change	biàn change	biàn change	biàn change
变	变	变	变	变	变	变	变	变	变
biàn change	biàn change	biàn change	biàn change	biàn change	biàn change	biàn change	biàn change	biàn change	biàn change

联

lián — unite

Notes: Verb

(联, lián, unite, join)

Stroke order: 一 丆 丌 丌 月 耳 耳' 耳" 耳丷 耴 联 联

言

Notes: Common Noun

(言, **yán**, **words**)

yán — words

丶 一 亠 言 言 言 言

言 言 言 言 言 言 言 言 言

言	言	言	言	言	言	言	言	言	言
yán	yán	yán	yán	yán	yán	yán	yán	yán	yán
words	words	words	words	words	words	words	words	words	words
言	言	言	言	言	言	言	言	言	言
yán	yán	yán	yán	yán	yán	yán	yán	yán	yán
words	words	words	words	words	words	words	words	words	words

[Type text]

权	Notes: Common Noun
quán power	(权, **quán**, **power**) (权, **quán**, **right**)

一 十 才 木 权 权

权 权 权 权 权 权 权 权 权

权	权	权	权	权	权	权	权	权	权
quán	quán	quán	quán	quán	quán	quán	quán	quán	quán
power	power	power	power	power	power	power	power	power	power
权	权	权	权	权	权	权	权	权	权
quán	quán	quán	quán	quán	quán	quán	quán	quán	quán
power	power	power	power	power	power	power	power	power	power

往 wǎng toward

Notes: Preposition

(往, **wǎng**, **to**, **toward**)

丿 彳 彳 彳 广 彳 往 往

展	Notes: Verb
zhǎn expand	(展, zhǎn, expand, spread out) (展, zhǎn, family name)

㇐ ㇕ 尸 尸 屏 屏 屏 展 展 展

展 展 展 展 展 展 展 展 展

展	展	展	展	展	展	展	展	展	展
zhǎn	zhǎn	zhǎn	zhǎn	zhǎn	zhǎn	zhǎn	zhǎn	zhǎn	zhǎn
expand	expand	expand	expand	expand	expand	expand	expand	expand	expand
展	展	展	展	展	展	展	展	展	展
zhǎn	zhǎn	zhǎn	zhǎn	zhǎn	zhǎn	zhǎn	zhǎn	zhǎn	zhǎn
expand	expand	expand	expand	expand	expand	expand	expand	expand	expand

该	Notes: Adverb (该, gāi, should)
gāi should	

丶 亠 讠 讠ˊ 讠ˊ 讠亠 讠亥 该 该

该 (gāi, should) practice sheet

领

lǐng — lead

(领, **lǐng, to lead, collar**)

Notes: Verb

Stroke order: 丿 丶 ㇏ 今 令 令 㔾 领 领 领 领

传

chuán
pass

Notes: Verb

(传, **chuán**, **pass, pass on**)

(传, **zhuàn, Confucian classic**)

丿 亻 仁 仨 传 传

近

jìn — near

Notes: Verb

(近, jìn, preposition)

Stroke order: 一 厂 斤 斤 斤 近 近

留	Notes: Verb (留, liú, remain, stay)
liú	
stay	

留 (character stroke order practice grid)

红

hóng — red

Notes: Adjective

(红, **hóng**, red)

治	Notes: Verb
zhì	(治, zhì, govern)
govern	(治, zhì, cure)
	(治, zhì, punish)

丶 丶 冫 沪 沪 泸 治 治

决 jué decide

Notes: Verb

(决, jué, decide, resolve, make up one's mind, think)

丶 冫 冯 决 决 决

周

zhōu — circuit

Notes: Common Noun

(周, **zhōu**, **circuit, circumference, cycle, week**)

丿 冂 刀 円 用 周 周 周

保

(保, bǎo, protect)

Notes: Verb

bǎo — protect

丿 亻 亻 伊 伊 伊 保 保 保

达	Notes: Verb
dá	(达, dá, **reach, arrive**)
reach	(达, dā, referring to sounds of clocks or footsteps)
	(达, tà, walk casually to and fro)

一 ナ 大 犬 达 达

达 达 达 达 达 达 达 达 达

达	达	达	达	达	达	达	达	达	达
dá	dá	dá	dá	dá	dá	dá	dá	dá	dá
reach	reach	reach	reach	reach	reach	reach	reach	reach	reach
达	达	达	达	达	达	达	达	达	达
dá	dá	dá	dá	dá	dá	dá	dá	dá	dá
reach	reach	reach	reach	reach	reach	reach	reach	reach	reach

办	Notes: Verb
bàn / do	(办, **bàn**, **do**)

フ 力 办 办

办 办 办 办 办 办 办 办 办

办	办	办	办	办	办	办	办	办	办
bàn do	bàn do	bàn do	bàn do	bàn do	bàn do	bàn do	bàn do	bàn do	bàn do
办	办	办	办	办	办	办	办	办	办
bàn do	bàn do	bàn do	bàn do	bàn do	bàn do	bàn do	bàn do	bàn do	bàn do

运	Notes: Verb (运, **yùn**, **carry**, **transport**)
yùn	
carry	

一 二 テ 云 迓 沄 运

运 运 运 运 运 运 运 运 运

武

wǔ
army

Notes: Common Noun

(武, wǔ, military, army)

Stroke order: 一 二 十 テ 正 正 武 武

半	Notes: Adjective (半, bàn, half, semi~)
bàn half	

丶 丷 䒑 half 半

半 半 半 半 半 半 半 半 半

半	半	半	半	半	半	半	半	半	半
bàn half	bàn half	bàn half	bàn half	bàn half	bàn half	bàn half	bàn half	bàn half	bàn half
半	半	半	半	半	半	半	半	半	半
bàn half	bàn half	bàn half	bàn half	bàn half	bàn half	bàn half	bàn half	bàn half	bàn half

[Type text]

候

hòu — time

Notes: Verb

(候, hòu, wait)

(候, hòu, time, situation)

Stroke order: 丿 亻 亻 伊 伊 伊 伊 候 候 候

必	Notes: Adverb (必, bì, must)
bì must	

丿 心 心 必 必

必 必 必 必 必 必 必 必 必

城

Notes: Common Noun

(城, chéng, city)

chéng / city

一 十 土 扩 圹 坂 城 城 城

城 chéng city

父	Notes: Common Noun
fù father	(父, **fù**, **father**)
	(父, **fǔ**, **old man**)

丶 ハ ⁄ 父

父 父 父 父 父 父 父 父 父

父	父	父	父	父	父	父	父	父	父
fù	fù	fù	fù	fù	fù	fù	fù	fù	fù
father	father	father	father	father	father	father	father	father	father
父	父	父	父	父	父	父	父	父	父
fù	fù	fù	fù	fù	fù	fù	fù	fù	fù
father	father	father	father	father	father	father	father	father	father

强

qiáng — strong

Notes: Adjective

(强, **qiáng**, **strong**)

(强, **qiǎng**, **strive**)

(强, **jiàng**, **stubborn, unbending**)

Stroke order: 丁 ㇆ 弓 弓' 弘 弘 弘 弘 㢸 强 强

步	Notes: Verb (步, **bù**, **step**)
bù	
step	

丨 卜 止 止 牛 步 步

步 步 步 步 步 步 步 步 步

步	步	步	步	步	步	步	步	步	步
bù	bù	bù	bù	bù	bù	bù	bù	bù	bù
step	step	step	step	step	step	step	step	step	step
步	步	步	步	步	步	步	步	步	步
bù	bù	bù	bù	bù	bù	bù	bù	bù	bù
step	step	step	step	step	step	step	step	step	step

完	Notes: Verb (完, **wán**, **finish**, **complete**)
wán finish	

丶 丶 宀 宁 宇 完

完 完 完 完 完 完 完 完 完

完	完	完	完	完	完	完	完	完	完
wán finish	wán finish	wán finish	wán finish	wán finish	wán finish	wán finish	wán finish	wán finish	wán finish
完	完	完	完	完	完	完	完	完	完
wán finish	wán finish	wán finish	wán finish	wán finish	wán finish	wán finish	wán finish	wán finish	wán finish

完	完	完	完	完	完	完	完	完	
完	完	完	完	完	完	完	完	完	
完	完	完	完	完	完	完	完	完	
完	完	完	完	完	完	完	完	完	
完	完	完	完	完	完	完	完	完	
完	完	完	完	完	完	完	完	完	
完	完	完	完	完	完	完	完	完	
完	完	完	完	完	完	完	完	完	

[Type text]

革

gé
leather

Notes: Common Noun

(革, **gé**, **leather**)

(革, **jí**, **about to die of illness**)

一 十 卄 丱 芊 芇 甚 莒 革

深

shēn — deep

Notes: Adjective

(深, shēn, deep)

Stroke order: 丶 丶 氵 氵 氵 氵 氵 深 深 深

即

jí
namely

Notes: Adverb

(即, **jí**, **namely**, **that is**, **even if**)

フ ⁊ ∃ 𠬝 艮 即 即

即 即 即 即 即 即 即 即 即

即	即	即	即	即	即	即	即	即	即
jí	jí	jí	jí	jí	jí	jí	jí	jí	jí
namely	namely	namely	namely	namely	namely	namely	namely	namely	namely
即	即	即	即	即	即	即	即	即	即
jí	jí	jí	jí	jí	jí	jí	jí	jí	jí
namely	namely	namely	namely	namely	namely	namely	namely	namely	namely

求	Notes: Verb (求, qiú, seek, ask)
qiú seek	

一 十 寸 寸 求 求 求

求 求 求 求 求 求 求 求 求

求(qiú, seek) practice grid

Notes: Common Noun

(品, **pǐn**, **product**)

pǐn — product

转 zhuǎn turn	Notes: Verb (转, **zhuǎn**, **turn**, **transfer**) (转, **zhuàn**, **rotate**) (转, **zhuǎi**, **to flaunt one's speech**)

一 𠂇 车 车 轩 轩 转 转

转 转 转 转 转 转 转 转 转

量

liàng — amount

Notes: Verb

(量, liáng, to measure)

(量, liàng, amount, measure word)

Stroke order: 丨 冂 冃 曰 旦 旦 昌 昌 冒 量 量 量

空	Notes: Adjective (空, **kōng**, empty, sky) (空, **kòng**, leave empty, free time)
kōng	
empty	

丶 丷 宀 宀 宂 空 空 空

空 空 空 空 空 空 空 空 空

空	空	空	空	空	空	空	空	空	空
kōng	kōng	kōng	kōng	kōng	kōng	kōng	kōng	kōng	kōng
empty	empty	empty	empty	empty	empty	empty	empty	empty	empty
空	空	空	空	空	空	空	空	空	空
kōng	kōng	kōng	kōng	kōng	kōng	kōng	kōng	kōng	kōng
empty	empty	empty	empty	empty	empty	empty	empty	empty	empty

[Type text]

甚	Notes: Adjective (甚, **shèn**, **very**)
shèn	
very	

一 十 廿 䒑 甘 甚 其 其 甚

甚 甚 甚 甚 甚 甚 甚 甚 甚

甚	甚	甚	甚	甚	甚	甚	甚	甚	甚
shèn	shèn	shèn	shèn	shèn	shèn	shèn	shèn	shèn	shèn
very	very	very	very	very	very	very	very	very	very
甚	甚	甚	甚	甚	甚	甚	甚	甚	甚
shèn	shèn	shèn	shèn	shèn	shèn	shèn	shèn	shèn	shèn
very	very	very	very	very	very	very	very	very	very

Notes: Common Noun

(众, zhòng, crowd)

(众, zhòng, many)

zhòng
crowd

丿 亻 个 仒 众 众

众 众 众 众 众 众 众 众 众

众	众	众	众	众	众	众	众	众	众
zhòng	zhòng	zhòng	zhòng	zhòng	zhòng	zhòng	zhòng	zhòng	zhòng
crowd	crowd	crowd	crowd	crowd	crowd	crowd	crowd	crowd	crowd
众	众	众	众	众	众	众	众	众	众
zhòng	zhòng	zhòng	zhòng	zhòng	zhòng	zhòng	zhòng	zhòng	zhòng
crowd	crowd	crowd	crowd	crowd	crowd	crowd	crowd	crowd	crowd

[Type text]

技

jì — method

Notes: Common Noun

(技, **jì**, **technique**, **method**)

Stroke order: 一 十 扌 扩 扩 拢 技

轻

Notes: Common Noun

(轻, **qīng**, **light**)

qīng / light

程 chéng — level

Notes: Adjective

(程, chéng, level, degree, extent)

Stroke order: 丿 一 千 千 禾 和 种 秆 秆 程 程 程

告

gào
tell

Notes: Verb

(告, gào, tell)

丿 ⺧ ⺧ 生 告 告 告

告 告 告 告 告 告 告 告 告

告	告	告	告	告	告	告	告	告	告
gào	gào	gào	gào	gào	gào	gào	gào	gào	gào
tell	tell	tell	tell	tell	tell	tell	tell	tell	tell
告	告	告	告	告	告	告	告	告	告
gào	gào	gào	gào	gào	gào	gào	gào	gào	gào
tell	tell	tell	tell	tell	tell	tell	tell	tell	tell
告	告	告	告	告	告	告	告	告	
告	告	告	告	告	告	告	告	告	
告	告	告	告	告	告	告	告	告	
告	告	告	告	告	告	告	告	告	
告	告	告	告	告	告	告	告	告	
告	告	告	告	告	告	告	告	告	
告	告	告	告	告	告	告	告	告	
告	告	告	告	告	告	告	告	告	

[Type text]

江 jiāng

Notes: Common Noun

(江, **jiāng**, **river**)

语	Notes: Verb
	(语, yù, tell)
yǔ	(语, yǔ, language)
tell	

丶 讠 讠 讠 讠 讠 语 语

语 语 语 语 语 语 语 语 语

语	语	语	语	语	语	语	语	语	语
yǔ	yǔ	yǔ	yǔ	yǔ	yǔ	yǔ	yǔ	yǔ	yǔ
tell	tell	tell	tell	tell	tell	tell	tell	tell	tell
语	语	语	语	语	语	语	语	语	语
yǔ	yǔ	yǔ	yǔ	yǔ	yǔ	yǔ	yǔ	yǔ	yǔ
tell	tell	tell	tell	tell	tell	tell	tell	tell	tell

英	Notes: Adjective (英, yīng, brave, outstanding person)
yīng	
brave	

一 艹 艹 艹 艼 苎 茊 英 英

英 英 英 英 英 英 英 英 英

英	英	英	英	英	英	英	英	英	英
yīng	yīng	yīng	yīng	yīng	yīng	yīng	yīng	yīng	yīng
brave	brave	brave	brave	brave	brave	brave	brave	brave	brave
英	英	英	英	英	英	英	英	英	英
yīng	yīng	yīng	yīng	yīng	yīng	yīng	yīng	yīng	yīng
brave	brave	brave	brave	brave	brave	brave	brave	brave	brave

英	英	英	英	英		英	英		
英	英	英	英	英		英	英		
英	英	英	英	英		英	英		
英	英	英	英	英		英	英		
英	英	英	英	英		英	英		
英	英	英	英	英		英	英		
英	英	英	英	英		英	英		
英	英	英	英	英		英	英		

基	Notes: Adjective (基, jī, basic, fundamental, essential)
jī	
basic	

一 十 卄 卄 廿 甘 其 其 其 基 基

基 基 基 基 基 基 基 基 基

基	基	基	基	基	基	基	基	基	基
jī	jī	jī	jī	jī	jī	jī	jī	jī	jī
basic	basic	basic	basic	basic	basic	basic	basic	basic	basic
基	基	基	基	基	基	基	基	基	基
jī	jī	jī	jī	jī	jī	jī	jī	jī	jī
basic	basic	basic	basic	basic	basic	basic	basic	basic	basic

派	Notes: Verb
pài send	(派, **pài**, **send**) (派, **pài**, **faction**) (派, **pā**, **passport, identification**)

丶 丶 氵 厂 厂 沪 沂 派 派 派

派 派 派 派 派 派 派 派 派

派	派	派	派	派	派	派	派	派	派
pài	pài	pài	pài	pài	pài	pài	pài	pài	pài
send	send	send	send	send	send	send	send	send	send
派	派	派	派	派	派	派	派	派	派
pài	pài	pài	pài	pài	pài	pài	pài	pài	pài
send	send	send	send	send	send	send	send	send	send

满

mǎn
full

Notes: Common Noun

(满, mǎn, full, satisfied, contented)

	Notes: Common Noun
式 shì model	式, shì, model, standard)
	(式, shì, mood, mode)
	(式, shì, aspect, tense, voice)
	(式, shì, acting as suffix -ation)

一 二 丁 工 式 式

式 式 式 式 式 式 式 式 式

式	式	式	式	式	式	式	式	式	式
shì	shì	shì	shì	shì	shì	shì	shì	shì	shì
model	model	model	model	model	model	model	model	model	model
式	式	式	式	式	式	式	式	式	式
shì	shì	shì	shì	shì	shì	shì	shì	shì	shì
model	model	model	model	model	model	model	model	model	model

李

lǐ — plum

Notes: Common Noun

(李, **lǐ**, **plum**)

(李, **Lǐ**, **surname Lǐ**)

Stroke order: 一 十 才 木 杏 李 李

息

xī — breath

Notes: Verb

(息, xī, breath)

(息, xī, stop, cease)

Stroke order: 丶 丿 宀 冂 臼 自 自 息 息 息

写	Notes: Verb (写, **xiě**, **write**) (写, **xiě**, **describe**, **depict**)
xiě	
write	

丶 ㇇ 冖 写 写

写 写 写 写 写 写 写 写 写

写	写	写	写	写	写	写	写	写	写
xiě	xiě	xiě	xiě	xiě	xiě	xiě	xiě	xiě	xiě
write	write	write	write	write	write	write	write	write	write
写	写	写	写	写	写	写	写	写	写
xiě	xiě	xiě	xiě	xiě	xiě	xiě	xiě	xiě	xiě
write	write	write	write	write	write	write	write	write	write

呢

ne

Notes: Grammatical Particle

(呢, **ne**, sentence final particle)

(呢, **ní**, woolen cloth)

丨 冂 口 口⁻ 口' 口⁻ 呢 呢

识	Notes: Verb (识, **shí**, **know**) (识, **zhì**, **remember**) (识, **zhì**, **mark, sign, record**)
shí	
know	

丶 讠 讠 识 识 识 识

识 识 识 识 识 识 识 识 识

识	识	识	识	识	识	识	识	识	识
shí	shí	shí	shí	shí	shí	shí	shí	shí	shí
know	know	know	know	know	know	know	know	know	know
识	识	识	识	识	识	识	识	识	识
shí	shí	shí	shí	shí	shí	shí	shí	shí	shí
know	know	know	know	know	know	know	know	know	know

极

jí — extreme

Notes: Adjective

(极, jí, extreme)

(极, jí, pole)

一 十 才 木 朳 朳 极 极

	Notes: Verb (令, lìng, make, cause) (令, lǐng, ream) (令, lǐng, classifier for paper)
lìng	
make	

黄

huáng
yellow

Notes: Qualitative Adjective

(黄, **huáng**, **yellow**)

一 十 卄 卅 芇 芇 芇 苩 苗 黄 黄

德

dé — virtue

Notes: Common Noun

(德, **dé**, **virtue**)

Stroke order: 丿 彳 彳 彳 徏 徏 徝 徝 徳 德 德 德 德

收

shōu — gather

Notes: Verb

(收, **shōu**, **gather**)

Stroke order: 丨 丩 屮 屮 收 收

脸

Notes: Common Noun

(脸, **liǎn**, **face**)

liǎn / face

丿 几 月 月 肸 胪 胎 脸 脸 脸 脸

钱

qián
money

Notes: Common Noun

(钱, qián, money, copper coin)

Stroke order: 丿 𠂉 丰 𠂉 年 钅 钅 钱 钱 钱

党

dǎng / clique

Notes: Common Noun

(党, **dǎng, political party, clique**)

Stroke order: 丨 丬 丷 ⺌ 𭕄 ⺍ 屵 ⺌ 党 党

党	党	党	党	党	党	党	党	党	党
dǎng	dǎng	dǎng	dǎng	dǎng	dǎng	dǎng	dǎng	dǎng	dǎng
clique	clique	clique	clique	clique	clique	clique	clique	clique	clique
党	党	党	党	党	党	党	党	党	党
dǎng	dǎng	dǎng	dǎng	dǎng	dǎng	dǎng	dǎng	dǎng	dǎng
clique	clique	clique	clique	clique	clique	clique	clique	clique	clique

倒

dǎo / clique

Notes: Verb

(倒, **dǎo**, fall, fall down, topple, drop, collapse)

(倒, **dào**, invert, move backwards, back, in reverse order, place upside down, contrary to expectations)

(倒, **dào**, pour)

Stroke order: 丿 亻 亻 乍 乍 乍 佫 倅 倒 倒

倒 倒 倒 倒 倒 倒 倒 倒 倒

倒	倒	倒	倒	倒	倒	倒	倒	倒	倒
dǎo	dǎo	dǎo	dǎo	dǎo	dǎo	dǎo	dǎo	dǎo	dǎo
clique	fall	fall	fall	fall	fall	fall	fall	fall	fall
倒	倒	倒	倒	倒	倒	倒	倒	倒	倒
dǎo	dǎo	dǎo	dǎo	dǎo	dǎo	dǎo	dǎo	dǎo	dǎo
fall	fall	fall	fall	fall	fall	fall	fall	fall	fall

未	Notes: Adverb (未, wèi, have not, did not, have not yet) (未, wèi, 8th of the 12 Earthly Branches)
wèi	
did not	

一 二 十 才 未

未 未 未 未 未 未 未 未 未

持

chí
hold

Notes: Verb

(持, chí, hold)

一 十 扌 扌 疒 扩 挂 挂 持 持

持 持 持 持 持 持 持 持 持

取	Notes: Verb (取, qǔ, take, get, fetch)
qǔ take	

一 丆 丌 开 开 耳 取 取

设

Notes: Verb

(设, shè, set up)

shè — set up

丶 讠 讴 讴 设 设

始	Notes: Verb (始, shǐ, begin, start)
shǐ begin	

亅 乇 女 女 女 女 始 始

始 始 始 始 始 始 始 始

版

bǎn — plate

Notes: Verb

(版, bǎn, printing, to print)

(版, bǎn, plate, edition)

丿 丨 片 片 片 片 版 版

双	Notes: Adjective (双, **shuāng**, **pair**, **twin**, **double**)
shuāng / pair	

フ 又 夘 双

双 双 双 双 双 双 双 双 双

双	双	双	双	双	双	双	双	双	双
shuāng	shuāng	shuāng	shuāng	shuāng	shuāng	shuāng	shuāng	shuāng	shuāng
pair	pair	pair	pair	pair	pair	pair	pair	pair	pair
双	双	双	双	双	双	双	双	双	双
shuāng	shuāng	shuāng	shuāng	shuāng	shuāng	shuāng	shuāng	shuāng	shuāng
pair	pair	pair	pair	pair	pair	pair	pair	pair	pair

历	Notes: Common Noun (历, lì, history)
lì history	

一 厂 历 历

历 历 历 历 历 历 历 历 历

历	历	历	历	历	历	历	历	历	历
lì	lì	lì	lì	lì	lì	lì	lì	lì	lì
history	history	history	history	history	history	history	history	history	history
历	历	历	历	历	历	历	历	历	历
lì	lì	lì	lì	lì	lì	lì	lì	lì	lì
history	history	history	history	history	history	history	history	history	history

越

yuè — the more

Notes: Adjective

(越, yuè, the more...)

Stroke order: 一 十 土 キ キ キ 走 走 起 越 越 越

史 shǐ history	Notes: Common Noun (史, **shǐ**, **history**) (史, **Shǐ**, **surname Shǐ**)

丨 冂 口 史 史

史 史 史 史 史 史 史 史 史

史	史	史	史	史	史	史	史	史	史
shǐ	shǐ	shǐ	shǐ	shǐ	shǐ	shǐ	shǐ	shǐ	shǐ
history	history	history	history	history	history	history	history	history	history
史	史	史	史	史	史	史	史	史	史
shǐ	shǐ	shǐ	shǐ	shǐ	shǐ	shǐ	shǐ	shǐ	shǐ
history	history	history	history	history	history	history	history	history	history

商

shāng — discuss

Notes: Verb

(商, shāng, discuss)

(商, shāng, business)

Stroke order: 丶 亠 产 产 产 产 商 商 商

片	Notes: Verb (片, **piàn**, slice) (片, **piān**, film)
piàn / slice	

丿 丿' 𠂆 片

片 片 片 片 片 片 片 片 片

容

róng — contain

Notes: Verb

(容, **róng**, **contain**)

Stroke order: 丶 丷 宀 宀 穴 灾 灾 容 容 容

研	Notes: Verb (研, **yán**, **grind**)
yán	
grind	

一 ㄏ ㄏ 石 石 矴 矴 矴 研

研 研 研 研 研 研 研 研 研

研	研	研	研	研	研	研	研	研	研
yán	yán	yán	yán	yán	yán	yán	yán	yán	yán
grind	grind	grind	grind	grind	grind	grind	grind	grind	grind
研	研	研	研	研	研	研	研	研	研
yán	yán	yán	yán	yán	yán	yán	yán	yán	yán
grind	grind	grind	grind	grind	grind	grind	grind	grind	grind
研	研	研	研	研	研	研	研	研	
研	研	研	研	研	研	研	研	研	
研	研	研	研	研	研	研	研	研	
研	研	研	研	研	研	研	研	研	
研	研	研	研	研	研	研	研	研	
研	研	研	研	研	研	研	研	研	
研	研	研	研	研	研	研	研	研	
研	研	研	研	研	研	研	研	研	

[Type text]

像

xiàng
alike

Notes: Verb

(像, xiàng, resemble, similar to, like, alike)

找	Notes: Verb (找, zhǎo, look for, seek)
zhǎo	
seek	

一 十 扌 扌 找 找 找

找 找 找 找 找 找 找 找 找

找	找	找	找	找	找	找	找	找	找
zhǎo	zhǎo	zhǎo	zhǎo	zhǎo	zhǎo	zhǎo	zhǎo	zhǎo	zhǎo
seek	seek	seek	seek	seek	seek	seek	seek	seek	seek
找	找	找	找	找	找	找	找	找	找
zhǎo	zhǎo	zhǎo	zhǎo	zhǎo	zhǎo	zhǎo	zhǎo	zhǎo	zhǎo
seek	seek	seek	seek	seek	seek	seek	seek	seek	seek

友

yǒu — friend

Notes: Common Noun

(友, **yǒu**, **friend**)

Stroke order: 一 ナ 方 友

孩

hái — child

(孩, **hái**, **child**)

Notes: Common Noun

Stroke order: 乛 了 孑 孑 孑 孑 孩 孩 孩

Notes: Common Noun

(站, zhàn, stand)

zhàn
stand

丶 亠 丶 立 立 立 立 站 站

站 站 站 站 站 站 站 站 站

站	站	站	站	站	站	站	站	站	站
zhàn	zhàn	zhàn	zhàn	zhàn	zhàn	zhàn	zhàn	zhàn	zhàn
stand	stand	stand	stand	stand	stand	stand	stand	stand	stand
站	站	站	站	站	站	站	站	站	站
zhàn	zhàn	zhàn	zhàn	zhàn	zhàn	zhàn	zhàn	zhàn	zhàn
stand	stand	stand	stand	stand	stand	stand	stand	stand	stand

[Type text]

改

gǎi — change

Notes: Verb

(改, gǎi, change, transform, amend, revise, correct, put right)

Stroke order: 乛 コ 己 改 改 改 改

议

yì — suggest

Notes: Verb

(议, yì, **criticize**, **suggest**)

Stroke order: 丶 讠 讠 议 议

形	Notes: Verb (形, xíng, form, take shape)
xíng form	

一 二 干 开 开 形 形

形 形 形 形 形 形 形 形 形

形	形	形	形	形	形	形	形	形	形
xíng form	xíng form	xíng form	xíng form	xíng form	xíng form	xíng form	xíng form	xíng form	xíng form
形	形	形	形	形	形	形	形	形	形
xíng form	xíng form	xíng form	xíng form	xíng form	xíng form	xíng form	xíng form	xíng form	xíng form
形	形	形	形	形		形	形	形	
形	形	形	形	形		形	形	形	
形	形	形	形	形		形	形		
形	形	形	形	形		形	形		
形	形	形	形	形		形	形	形	
形	形	形	形	形		形	形		
形	形	形	形	形		形	形		
形	形	形	形	形		形	形		

委	Notes: Verb (委, wěi, entrust, designate)
wěi	
entrust	

一 二 千 千 禾 禾 委 委

早	Notes: Adjective (早, **zǎo**, **early**) (早, **zǎo**, **morning**)
zǎo early	

丨 冂 日 日 旦 早

早 早 早 早 早 早 早 早 早

早	早	早	早	早	早	早	早	早	早
zǎo	zǎo	zǎo	zǎo	zǎo	zǎo	zǎo	zǎo	zǎo	zǎo
early	early	early	early	early	early	early	early	early	early
早	早	早	早	早	早	早	早	早	早
zǎo	zǎo	zǎo	zǎo	zǎo	zǎo	zǎo	zǎo	zǎo	zǎo
early	early	early	early	early	early	early	early	early	early

房	Notes: Common Noun (房, **fáng**, room)
fáng	
room	

丶 亠 亠 户 户 户 房 房

房 房 房 房 房 房 房 房 房

房	房	房	房	房	房	房	房	房	房
fáng	fáng	fáng	fáng	fáng	fáng	fáng	fáng	fáng	fáng
room	room	room	room	room	room	room	room	room	room
房	房	房	房	房	房	房	房	房	房
fáng	fáng	fáng	fáng	fáng	fáng	fáng	fáng	fáng	fáng
room	room	room	room	room	room	room	room	room	room

音	Notes: Common Noun (音, **yīn**, **sound**)
yīn / sound	

丶 亠 亡 立 产 产 音 音 音

音 音 音 音 音 音 音 音 音

音	音	音	音	音	音	音	音	音	音
yīn	yīn	yīn	yīn	yīn	yīn	yīn	yīn	yīn	yīn
sound	sound	sound	sound	sound	sound	sound	sound	sound	sound
音	音	音	音	音	音	音	音	音	音
yīn	yīn	yīn	yīn	yīn	yīn	yīn	yīn	yīn	yīn
sound	sound	sound	sound	sound	sound	sound	sound	sound	sound
音	音	音	音	音		音	音		
音	音	音	音	音		音	音		
音	音	音	音	音		音	音		
音	音	音	音	音		音	音		
音	音	音	音	音		音	音		
音	音	音	音	音		音	音		
音	音	音	音	音		音	音		
音	音	音	音	音		音	音		

[Type text]

火	Notes: Common Noun (火, **huǒ**, **fire**)
huǒ	
fire	

丶 丷 少 火

火 火 火 火 火 火 火 火 火

火	火	火	火	火	火	火	火	火	火
huǒ	huǒ	huǒ	huǒ	huǒ	huǒ	huǒ	huǒ	huǒ	huǒ
fire	fire	fire	fire	fire	fire	fire	fire	fire	fire
火	火	火	火	火	火	火	火	火	火
huǒ	huǒ	huǒ	huǒ	huǒ	huǒ	huǒ	huǒ	huǒ	huǒ
fire	fire	fire	fire	fire	fire	fire	fire	fire	fire
火	火	火	火	火	火	火	火	火	
火	火	火	火	火	火	火	火	火	
火	火	火	火	火	火	火	火	火	
火	火	火	火	火	火	火	火	火	
火	火	火	火	火	火	火	火	火	
火	火	火	火	火	火	火	火	火	
火	火	火	火	火	火	火	火	火	
火	火	火	火	火	火	火	火	火	

[Type text]

际 jì border

Notes: Common Noun

(际, jì, border, boundary)

阝 阝 阝 阝 阝 际 际

则

zé
rule

Notes: Common Noun

(则, **zé**, **rule**, **regulation**)

丨 冂 贝 贝 则

则 则 则 则 则 则 则 则 则

首

Notes: Common Noun

(首, shǒu, head)

Notes: Adjective

(单, dān, alone, single, sheet)

(单, chán, chief of the Xiongnu tribe)

(单, Shàn surname Shàn)

dān
alone

丶 丷 广 丷 ㄩ 肖 甴 单

据	Notes: Verb (据, jù, seize, occupy) (据, jù, according to, on the grounds of) (据, jù, depend on)
jù	
seize	

一 † † † 扌 扩 护 护 押 挹 据 据

据 据 据 据 据 据 据 据 据

据	据	据	据	据	据	据	据	据	据
jù	jù	jù	jù	jù	jù	jù	jù	jù	jù
seize	seize	seize	seize	seize	seize	seize	seize	seize	seize
据	据	据	据	据	据	据	据	据	据
jù	jù	jù	jù	jù	jù	jù	jù	jù	jù
seize	seize	seize	seize	seize	seize	seize	seize	seize	seize

影

Notes: Common Noun

(影, yǐng, shadow, image)

yǐng — image

| 失 shī lose | Notes: Verb
(失, **shī**, **lose**) |

丿 𠂉 ⊢ 失 失

失 失 失 失 失 失 失 失 失

失	失	失	失	失	失	失	失	失	失
shī	shī	shī	shī	shī	shī	shī	shī	shī	shī
lose	lose	lose	lose	lose	lose	lose	lose	lose	lose
失	失	失	失	失	失	失	失	失	失
shī	shī	shī	shī	shī	shī	shī	shī	shī	shī
lose	lose	lose	lose	lose	lose	lose	lose	lose	lose

拿

ná — hold

Notes: Verb

(**拿**, **ná**, **hold**)

Stroke order: 丿 人 𠆢 𠆢 合 合 合 拿 拿 拿

网

Notes: Common Noun

(网, wǎng, net)

wǎng / net

Stroke order: 丨 冂 冂 区 网 网

香	Notes: Adjective (香, **xiāng**, **fragrant**, **aroma**) (香, **xiāng**, **perfume**)
xiāng fragrant	

一 二 千 千 禾 禾 香 香 香

香 香 香 香 香 香 香 香 香

似	Notes: Adjective (似, sì, similar)
sì similar	

丿 亻 亻ㄨ 伇 似 似

似 似 似 似 似 似 似 似 似

似	似	似	似	似	似	似	似	似	似
sì	sì	sì	sì	sì	sì	sì	sì	sì	sì
similar	similar	similar	similar	similar	similar	similar	similar	similar	similar
似	似	似	似	似	似	似	似	似	似
sì	sì	sì	sì	sì	sì	sì	sì	sì	sì
similar	similar	similar	similar	similar	similar	similar	similar	similar	similar

斯

sī — thus

Notes: Adverb

(斯, sī, thus)

Stroke order: 一 十 十 艹 艹 甘 其 其 其 斯 斯 斯

专	Notes: Adjective (专, zhuān, special)
zhuān special	

一　二　专　专

专 zhuān special

石	Notes: Common Noun (石, **shí, stone, rock**) (石, **dàn, unit of grain**)
shí stone	

一 ア ア 石 石

石 石 石 石 石 石 石 石 石

石	石	石	石	石	石	石	石	石	石
shí	shí	shí	shí	shí	shí	shí	shí	shí	shí
stone	stone	stone	stone	stone	stone	stone	stone	stone	stone
石	石	石	石	石	石	石	石	石	石
shí	shí	shí	shí	shí	shí	shí	shí	shí	shí
stone	stone	stone	stone	stone	stone	stone	stone	stone	stone
石	石	石	石	石		石	石	石	
石	石	石	石	石		石	石		
石	石	石	石	石		石	石		
石	石	石	石	石		石	石		
石	石	石	石	石		石	石		
石	石	石	石	石		石	石		
石	石	石	石	石		石	石		
石	石	石	石	石		石	石		

[Type text]

若	Notes: Adverb (若, **ruò**, **seem, as if**)
ruò	
seem	

一 艹 艹 艹 艹 若 若

若 若 若 若 若 若 若 若

若	若	若	若	若	若	若	若	若	若
ruò	ruò	ruò	ruò	ruò	ruò	ruò	ruò	ruò	ruò
seem	seem	seem	seem	seem	seem	seem	seem	seem	seem
若	若	若	若	若	若	若	若	若	若
ruò	ruò	ruò	ruò	ruò	ruò	ruò	ruò	ruò	ruò
seem	seem	seem	seem	seem	seem	seem	seem	seem	seem
若	若	若	若	若	若	若	若	若	
若	若	若	若	若	若	若	若	若	
若	若	若	若	若	若	若	若	若	
若	若	若	若	若	若	若	若	若	
若	若	若	若	若	若	若	若	若	
若	若	若	若	若	若	若	若	若	
若	若	若	若	若	若	若	若	若	

兵

bīng soldier

Notes: Common Noun

(兵, **bīng**, **soldier**)

Stroke order: 丿 丆 斤 斤 斤 丘 兵 兵

弟	Notes: Common Noun (弟, **dì, younger brother**) (弟, **respect for one's older brother**)
dì brother	

丶 丷 丷 ⺌ ⺍ 弟 弟

弟 弟 弟 弟 弟 弟 弟 弟 弟

谁

Notes: Interrogative Pronoun

(谁, **shuí**, **who**)

(谁, **shéi**, **who**)

shéi / who

丶 讠 讠 讠 讠 讠 讠 诈 谁 谁

谁 谁 谁 谁 谁 谁 谁 谁 谁

校	Notes: Common Noun
xiào	(校, xiào, school)
school	(校, jiào, proofread)

一 十 十 才 木 木` 朴 杧 栌 柼 校

校 校 校 校 校 校 校 校 校

校 校 校 校 校 校 校 校 校 校
xiào xiào xiào xiào xiào xiào xiào xiào xiào xiào
school school school school school school school school school school

校 校 校 校 校 校 校 校 校 校
xiào xiào xiào xiào xiào xiào xiào xiào xiào xiào
school school school school school school school school school school

读

dú
read

Notes: Verb

(读, **dú**, read)

(读, **dòu**, pause in reading)

丶 亠 讠 计 访 诗 诗 读 读 读

志

zhì — will

Notes: Common Noun

(志, **zhì**, **will, aspiration, ideal, ambition**)

(志, **zhì**, **be devoted to**)

(志, **zhì**, **records, annals**)

一 十 士 士 志 志 志

志 志 志 志 志 志 志 志 志

志	志	志	志	志	志	志	志	志	志
zhì	zhì	zhì	zhì	zhì	zhì	zhì	zhì	zhì	zhì
will	will	will	will	will	will	will	will	will	will
志	志	志	志	志	志	志	志	志	志
zhì	zhì	zhì	zhì	zhì	zhì	zhì	zhì	zhì	zhì
will	will	will	will	will	will	will	will	will	will

飞	Notes: Verb (飞, fēi, fly)
fēi	
fly	

观	Notes: Verb
guān	(观, **guān**, **view, contemplation**)
view	(观, **guān**, **view, look at, watch, observe**)
	(观, **guàn**, **temple**)

丁 又 刃 邓 观 观

观 观 观 观 观 观 观 观 观

观	观	观	观	观	观	观	观	观	观
guān view	guān view	guān view	guān view	guān view	guān view	guān view	guān view	guān view	guān view
观	观	观	观	观	观	观	观	观	观
guān view	guān view	guān view	guān view	guān view	guān view	guān view	guān view	guān view	guān view
观	观	观	观	观	观	观	观	观	观
观	观	观	观	观	观	观	观	观	观
观	观	观	观	观	观	观	观	观	观
观	观	观	观	观	观	观	观	观	观
观	观	观	观	观	观	观	观	观	观
观	观	观	观	观	观	观	观	观	观
观	观	观	观	观	观	观	观	观	观
观	观	观	观	观	观	观	观	观	观

[Type text]

争	Notes: Verb (争, zhēng, contend, dispute)
zhēng contend	

丿 ク 勹 匀 乌 争

争 争 争 争 争 争 争 争 争

争	争	争	争	争	争	争	争	争	争
zhēng	zhēng	zhēng	zhēng	zhēng	zhēng	zhēng	zhēng	zhēng	zhēng
contend	contend	contend	contend	contend	contend	contend	contend	contend	contend
争	争	争	争	争	争	争	争	争	争
zhēng	zhēng	zhēng	zhēng	zhēng	zhēng	zhēng	zhēng	zhēng	zhēng
contend	contend	contend	contend	contend	contend	contend	contend	contend	contend

究

jiū study

Notes: Verb

(究, **jiū**, **study**, **research**)

Stroke order: 丶 丶 宀 宀 穴 宊 究

包

bāo — bag

Notes: Common Noun

(包, **bāo**, **bag**)

(包, **bāo**, **wrap**)

Stroke order: 丿 勹 勺 匀 包

组

zǔ
group

Notes: Verb

(组, zǔ, organize, group)

造

Notes: Verb

(造, **zào**, **create**)

zào — create

丿 𠂉 匕 生 牛 告 告 告 造 造

落	Notes: Verb
	(落, luò, fall)
	(落, là, be missing)
	(落, lào, fade)
luò fall	(落, luō absolutely nothing left, open, spacious and desolate)

一 艹 艹 艹 艹 艹 艹 莎 莎 落 落 落

落 落 落 落 落 落 落 落 落

落	落	落	落	落	落	落	落	落	落
luò	luò	luò	luò	luò	luò	luò	luò	luò	luò
fall	fall	fall	fall	fall	fall	fall	fall	fall	fall
落	落	落	落	落	落	落	落	落	落
luò	luò	luò	luò	luò	luò	luò	luò	luò	luò
fall	fall	fall	fall	fall	fall	fall	fall	fall	fall

视

shì
look

Notes: Verb

(视, shì, look)

Stroke order: 丶 冫 礻 礻 礻 视 视 视

济

jì — ferry

Notes: Verb

(济, **jì, cross a river, to ferry**)

(济, **jì, aid**)

(济, **jì, frugal**)

Stroke order: 丶 丶 氵 冫 沪 汐 泲 济 济

喜	Notes: Adjective (喜, xǐ, happy, happiness)
xǐ happy	

一 十 士 吉 吉 吉 吉 吉 壴 喜 喜 喜

喜 喜 喜 喜 喜 喜 喜 喜 喜

喜	喜	喜	喜	喜	喜	喜	喜	喜	喜
xǐ	xǐ	xǐ	xǐ	xǐ	xǐ	xǐ	xǐ	xǐ	xǐ
happy	happy	happy	happy	happy	happy	happy	happy	happy	happy
喜	喜	喜	喜	喜	喜	喜	喜	喜	喜
xǐ	xǐ	xǐ	xǐ	xǐ	xǐ	xǐ	xǐ	xǐ	xǐ
happy	happy	happy	happy	happy	happy	happy	happy	happy	happy

离

lí — leave

Notes: Verb

(离, lí, leave, part from, be away from)

(离, lí, separate, defy, go against)

Stroke order: 丶 亠 ナ 文 玄 卤 产 肉 离 离

虽

suī
although

Notes: Adverb

(虽, **suī**, **although**)

Stroke order: 丨 冂 口 曰 吊 吕 吊 虽 虽

虽 虽 虽 虽 虽 虽 虽 虽 虽

虽	虽	虽	虽	虽	虽	虽	虽	虽	虽
suī	suī	suī	suī	suī	suī	suī	suī	suī	suī
although	although	although	although	although	although	although	although	although	although
虽	虽	虽	虽	虽	虽	虽	虽	虽	虽
suī	suī	suī	suī	suī	suī	suī	suī	suī	suī
although	although	although	although	although	although	although	although	although	although

坐 zuò sit	Notes: Verb (坐, zuò, seat, sit, sit down) (坐, zuò, travel by car / plane, etc.) (坐, zuò, put a kettle, or similar, on the fire) (坐, zuò, classifier for bridges, buildings)

丿 人 サ 从 丛 华 坐

坐 坐 坐 坐 坐 坐 坐 坐 坐

坐	坐	坐	坐	坐	坐	坐	坐	坐	坐
zuò	zuò	zuò	zuò	zuò	zuò	zuò	zuò	zuò	zuò
sit	sit	sit	sit	sit	sit	sit	sit	sit	sit
坐	坐	坐	坐	坐	坐	坐	坐	坐	坐
zuò	zuò	zuò	zuò	zuò	zuò	zuò	zuò	zuò	zuò
sit	sit	sit	sit	sit	sit	sit	sit	sit	sit

集

jí
gather

(集, jí, gather, collect)

Notes: Verb

Stroke order: 丿 亻 彳 广 广 广 忄 隹 隹 隹 隼 集 集

编	Notes: Verb (编, biān, weave, organize)
biān weave	

丿 ㇀ 纟 纟 纩 纩 纩 纩 纺 绢 编 编

编 编 编 编 编 编 编 编 编

宝

bǎo — treasure

Notes: Common Noun

(宝, bǎo, treasure)

Stroke order: 丶 丶 宀 宀 宀 宇 宝 宝

谈

Notes: Verb

(谈, tán, talk)

tán — talk

丶 讠 讠 讠 ⺭ 访 谈 谈 谈 谈

谈 谈 谈 谈 谈 谈 谈 谈 谈

谈	谈	谈	谈	谈	谈	谈	谈	谈	谈
tán	tán	tán	tán	tán	tán	tán	tán	tán	tán
talk	talk	talk	talk	talk	talk	talk	talk	talk	talk
谈	谈	谈	谈	谈	谈	谈	谈	谈	谈
tán	tán	tán	tán	tán	tán	tán	tán	tán	tán
talk	talk	talk	talk	talk	talk	talk	talk	talk	talk

Notes: Common Noun

(府, fǔ, government, officials)

府
fǔ
talk

丶 亠 广 广 庁 庁 府 府

拉	Notes: Verb
	(拉, lā, pull, drag, haul)
	(拉, lǎ, half)
	(拉, lá, slit)
lā	(拉, là)
pull	

一 十 扌 扌 扩 扩 拉 拉

拉 拉 拉 拉 拉 拉 拉 拉 拉

拉	拉	拉	拉	拉	拉	拉	拉	拉	拉
lā	lā	lā	lā	lā	lā	lā	lā	lā	lā
pull	pull	pull	pull	pull	pull	pull	pull	pull	pull
拉	拉	拉	拉	拉	拉	拉	拉	拉	拉
lā	lā	lā	lā	lā	lā	lā	lā	lā	lā
pull	pull	pull	pull	pull	pull	pull	pull	pull	pull

	Notes: Qualitative Adjective (黑, **hēi**, **black**)
黑	
hēi	
black	

丨 冂 冂 冃 罒 甲 甲 里 黒 黑 黑 黑

黑 黑 黑 黑 黑 黑 黑 黑 黑

黑	黑	黑	黑	黑	黑	黑	黑	黑	黑
hēi	hēi	hēi	hēi	hēi	hēi	hēi	hēi	hēi	hēi
black	black	black	black	black	black	black	black	black	black
黑	黑	黑	黑	黑	黑	黑	黑	黑	黑
hēi	hēi	hēi	hēi	hēi	hēi	hēi	hēi	hēi	hēi
black	black	black	black	black	black	black	black	black	black

黑	黑	黑	黑	黑		黑	黑		
黑	黑	黑	黑	黑		黑	黑		
黑	黑	黑	黑	黑		黑	黑		
黑	黑	黑	黑	黑		黑	黑		
黑	黑	黑	黑	黑		黑	黑		
黑	黑	黑	黑	黑		黑	黑		
黑	黑	黑	黑	黑		黑	黑		
黑	黑	黑	黑	黑		黑	黑		

且	Notes: Adverb
qiě / still	(且, **qiě, for the time being**)
	(且, **jū, only used for personal names**)
	(且, **jū, moreover, still, further**)

丨 冂 冃 且 且

随

suí — follow

Notes: Verb

(随, **suí**, **follow**)

Stroke order: 了 阝 阝⁻ 阝ナ 阝′ 阝冇 阝有 阝有 阝有 随

格	Notes: Verb
	(格, gé, check)
	(格, gē, the sound of laughter, clucking of a hen)
gé	(格, gé, pattern, standard)
check	

一 十 才 才 木 朩 朳 枚 柊 格 格

尽

jìn — use up

Notes: Verb

(尽, jìn, use up)

(尽, jǐn, to the maximum extent)

Stroke order: 一 コ 尸 尺 尺 尽

尽 尽 尽 尽 尽 尽 尽 尽 尽

尽	尽	尽	尽	尽	尽	尽	尽	尽	尽
jìn	jìn	jìn	jìn	jìn	jìn	jìn	jìn	jìn	jìn
use up	use up	use up	use up	use up	use up	use up	use up	use up	use up
尽	尽	尽	尽	尽	尽	尽	尽	尽	尽
jìn	jìn	jìn	jìn	jìn	jìn	jìn	jìn	jìn	jìn
use up	use up	use up	use up	use up	use up	use up	use up	use up	use up

剑

Notes: Common Noun

(剑, **jiàn**, **sword**)

jiàn — sword

丿 亻 亼 仒 仒 仒 亽 金 剑 剑

jiàn	jiàn	jiàn	jiàn	jiàn	jiàn	jiàn	jiàn	jiàn	jiàn
sword	sword	sword	sword	sword	sword	sword	sword	sword	sword

jiàn	jiàn	jiàn	jiàn	jiàn	jiàn	jiàn	jiàn	jiàn	jiàn
sword	sword	sword	sword	sword	sword	sword	sword	sword	sword

讲

jiǎng — speak

Notes: Verb

(讲, **jiǎng**, **speak**, **explain**, **discuss**, **stress**)

丶 讠 讠 计 讲 讲

布	Notes: Verb (布, **bù**, **spread**) (布, **bù**, **cloth**)
bù	
cloth	

一 ナ 冇 右 布

杀	Notes: Verb (杀, shā, kill, fight, weaken, reduce, burn)
shā kill	

丿 乂 ㇇ 辛 杀 杀

杀 杀 杀 杀 杀 杀 杀 杀 杀

杀	杀	杀	杀	杀	杀	杀	杀	杀	杀
shā kill	shā kill	shā kill	shā kill	shā kill	shā kill	shā kill	shā kill	shā kill	shā kill
杀	杀	杀	杀	杀	杀	杀	杀	杀	杀
shā kill	shā kill	shā kill	shā kill	shā kill	shā kill	shā kill	shā kill	shā kill	shā kill

微 wēi tiny

Notes: Adjective

(微, wēi, tiny, micro)

怕

pà — fear

Notes: Verb

(怕, pà, to fear)

Stroke order: 丶 丷 忄 忄' 忄' 怕 怕 怕

母

mǔ — mother

Notes: Common Noun

(母, mǔ, mother)

调

diào
shift

Notes: Verb

(调, tiáo, adjust, shift)

(调, diào, a tone)

丶 亠 讠 讥 讥 调 调 调 调 调

调 调 调 调 调 调 调 调 调

调	调	调	调	调	调	调	调	调	调
diào shift	diào shift	diào shift	diào shift	diào shift	diào shift	diào shift	diào shift	diào shift	diào shift
调	调	调	调	调	调	调	调	调	调
diào shift	diào shift	diào shift	diào shift	diào shift	diào shift	diào shift	diào shift	diào shift	diào shift
调	调	调	调	调	调	调	调	调	调
调	调	调	调	调	调	调	调	调	调
调	调	调	调	调	调	调	调	调	调
调	调	调	调	调	调	调	调	调	调
调	调	调	调	调	调	调	调	调	调
调	调	调	调	调	调	调	调	调	调
调	调	调	调	调	调	调	调	调	调
调	调	调	调	调	调	调	调	调	调

[Type text]

局

jú — office

Notes: Common Noun

(局, jú, bureau, office, department)

(局, jú, situation, condition, state)

Stroke order: 乛 コ 尸 尸 局 局 局

根	Notes: Common Noun (根, gēn, essence, foundation, basic) (根, gēn, utterly)
gēn basic	

一 十 才 木 木 朩 杞 杞 根 根

céng / before

Notes: Temporal Adverb

(曾, **céng, in the past, once, before**)

(曾, **zēng, great-**) of a relative.

(曾, **cēng, to get a scolding**)

准

zhǔn
allow

Notes: Verb

(准, zhǔn, allow)

(准, zhǔn, certainly, precise)

段	Notes: Common Noun (段, **duàn**, **section**, **paragraph**)
duàn section	

丶 ſ 斤 斤 斤 斤 段 段 段

段 段 段 段 段 段 段 段 段

段	段	段	段	段	段	段	段	段	段
duàn	duàn	duàn	duàn	duàn	duàn	duàn	duàn	duàn	duàn
section	section	section	section	section	section	section	section	section	section
段	段	段	段	段	段	段	段	段	段
duàn	duàn	duàn	duàn	duàn	duàn	duàn	duàn	duàn	duàn
section	section	section	section	section	section	section	section	section	section

终	Notes: Common Noun (终, zhōng, end)
zhōng end	

终 character stroke practice sheet with pinyin "zhōng" and meaning "end".

乐	Notes: Verb (乐, lè, enjoy) (乐, lè, be glad, pleasure) (乐, yuè, music)
lè enjoy	

一 乍 乐 乐 乐

乐 乐 乐 乐 乐 乐 乐 乐 乐

切

qiē — to cut

Notes: Verb

(切, **qiē**, **to cut**)

(切, **qiè**, correspond to)

Stroke order: 一 七 切 切

级 jí grade	Notes: Verb (级, jí, to grade) (级, jí, a level of achievement)

丿 幺 纟 纠 级 级

级 级 级 级 级 级 级 级

级	级	级	级	级	级	级	级	级	级
jí	jí	jí	jí	jí	jí	jí	jí	jí	jí
grade	grade	grade	grade	grade	grade	grade	grade	grade	grade
级	级	级	级	级	级	级	级	级	级
jí	jí	jí	jí	jí	jí	jí	jí	jí	jí
grade	grade	grade	grade	grade	grade	grade	grade	grade	grade

克	Notes: Verb
	(克, **kēi**, **scold**)
jí	(克, **kè**, **overcome**)
scold	

一 十 ナ 古 古 卢 克

克 克 克 克 克 克 克 克 克

克	克	克	克	克	克	克	克	克	克
kè	kè	kè	kè	kè	kè	kè	kè	kè	kè
scold	scold	scold	scold	scold	scold	scold	scold	scold	scold
克	克	克	克	克	克	克	克	克	克
kè	kè	kè	kè	kè	kè	kè	kè	kè	kè
scold	scold	scold	scold	scold	scold	scold	scold	scold	scold

精

jīng — sharp

Notes: Attributive Adjective

(精, jīng, sharp, clever, shrewd)

(精, jīng, refined, perfect, excellent)

(精, jīng, meticulous, precise)

(精, jīng, skilled, conversant, proficient)

Stroke order: 丶 丷 ᅭ 半 半 米 米⁻ 米⁻ 米ᵗ 米ᵗ 精 精 精

哪

nǎ — which

Notes: Interrogative Pronoun

(哪, nǎ, which)

(哪, něi, before classifier)

(哪, na, used in orders and exclamations)

guān — official

Notes: Common Noun

(官, guān, government official, officeholder)

(官, guān, official)

(官, Guān, surname Guān)

示 shì show	Notes: Verb (示, shì, show, indicate)

一 二 亍 示 示

示 示 示 示 示 示 示 示 示

示	示	示	示	示	示	示	示	示	示
shì	shì	shì	shì	shì	shì	shì	shì	shì	shì
show	show	show	show	show	show	show	show	show	show
示	示	示	示	示	示	示	示	示	示
shì	shì	shì	shì	shì	shì	shì	shì	shì	shì
show	show	show	show	show	show	show	show	show	show

| 冲 chōng rush | Notes: Verb
(冲, chōng, charge, rush, dash, clash, collide)
(冲, chòng, towards)
(冲, chòng, vigorously, bluntly, candidly)
(冲, chōng, pour boiling water on, rinse, flush) |

丶 冫 冫 冫¬ 冫口 冲

冲 冲 冲 冲 冲 冲 冲 冲 冲

冲	冲	冲	冲	冲	冲	冲	冲	冲	冲
chōng rush	chōng rush	chōng rush	chōng rush	chōng rush	chōng rush	chōng rush	chōng rush	chōng rush	chōng rush
冲	冲	冲	冲	冲	冲	冲	冲	冲	冲
chōng rush	chōng rush	chōng rush	chōng rush	chōng rush	chōng rush	chōng rush	chōng rush	chōng rush	chōng rush

竟	Notes: Verb (竟, jìng, finish)
jìng	
finish	

丶 亠 产 产 产 产 音 音 竟 竟

竟 竟 竟 竟 竟 竟 竟 竟 竟

竟	竟	竟	竟	竟	竟	竟	竟	竟	竟
jìng	jìng	jìng	jìng	jìng	jìng	jìng	jìng	jìng	jìng
finish	finish	finish	finish	finish	finish	finish	finish	finish	finish
竟	竟	竟	竟	竟	竟	竟	竟	竟	竟
jìng	jìng	jìng	jìng	jìng	jìng	jìng	jìng	jìng	jìng
finish	finish	finish	finish	finish	finish	finish	finish	finish	finish
竟	竟	竟	竟	竟	竟	竟	竟	竟	竟
竟	竟	竟	竟	竟	竟	竟	竟	竟	竟
竟	竟	竟	竟	竟	竟	竟	竟	竟	竟
竟	竟	竟	竟	竟	竟	竟	竟	竟	竟
竟	竟	竟	竟	竟	竟	竟	竟	竟	竟
竟	竟	竟	竟	竟	竟	竟	竟	竟	竟
竟	竟	竟	竟	竟	竟	竟	竟	竟	竟
竟	竟	竟	竟	竟	竟	竟	竟	竟	竟

[Type text]

乎	Notes: Grammatical Affix
hū	(乎, hū, suffix forming adverbs)
	(乎, hū, expressing interrogation, surmise, surprise, admiration)
	(乎, hū, used for forming co-verbs, to, at, with, than)

男	Notes: Common Noun (男, **nán**, **male**)
nán	
male	

丨 冂 冂 闩 田 甲 男 男

男 男 男 男 男 男 男 男 男

男	男	男	男	男	男	男	男	男	男
nán	nán	nán	nán	nán	nán	nán	nán	nán	nán
nearly	male	male	male	male	male	male	male	male	male
男	男	男	男	男	男	男	男	男	男
nán	nán	nán	nán	nán	nán	nán	nán	nán	nán
male	male	male	male	male	male	male	male	male	male
男	男	男	男	男	男	男	男	男	男
男	男	男	男	男	男	男	男	男	男
男	男	男	男	男	男	男	男	男	男
男	男	男	男	男	男	男	男	男	男
男	男	男	男	男	男	男	男	男	男
男	男	男	男	男	男	男	男	男	男
男	男	男	男	男	男	男	男	男	男
男	男	男	男	男	男	男	男	男	

[Type text]

举	Notes: Verb (举, jǔ, lift, raise, hold up)
jǔ lift	

丶 丷 丷 䒑 严 兴 兴 誉 举

举 举 举 举 举 举 举 举 举

举	举	举	举	举	举	举	举	举	举
jǔ nearly	jǔ lift	jǔ lift	jǔ lift	jǔ lift	jǔ lift	jǔ lift	jǔ lift	jǔ lift	jǔ lift
举	举	举	举	举	举	举	举	举	举
jǔ lift	jǔ lift	jǔ lift	jǔ lift	jǔ lift	jǔ lift	jǔ lift	jǔ lift	jǔ lift	jǔ lift

[Type text]

客	Notes: Common Noun (客, **kè visitor, guest, traveler, passenger**)
kè visitor	

丶 丷 宀 穴 㝯 安 字 客 客

客 客 客 客 客 客 客 客 客

客	客	客	客	客	客	客	客	客	客
kè nearly	kè visitor	kè visitor	kè visitor	kè visitor	kè visitor	kè visitor	kè visitor	kè visitor	kè visitor
客	客	客	客	客	客	客	客	客	客
kè visitor	kè visitor	kè visitor	kè visitor	kè visitor	kè visitor	kè visitor	kè visitor	kè visitor	kè visitor
客	客	客	客	客	客	客	客	客	
客	客	客	客	客	客	客	客	客	
客	客	客	客	客	客	客	客	客	
客	客	客	客	客	客	客	客	客	
客	客	客	客	客	客	客	客	客	
客	客	客	客	客	客	客	客	客	
客	客	客	客	客	客	客	客	客	
客	客	客	客	客	客	客	客	客	

[Type text]

证	Notes: Verb (证, zhèng, prove, testify, demonstrate)
zhèng	
prove	

丶 讠 讠 订 讧 评 证

证 证 证 证 证 证 证 证 证

证	证	证	证	证	证	证	证	证	证
zhèng	zhèng	zhèng	zhèng	zhèng	zhèng	zhèng	zhèng	zhèng	zhèng
prove	prove	prove	prove	prove	prove	prove	prove	prove	prove
证	证	证	证	证	证	证	证	证	证
zhèng	zhèng	zhèng	zhèng	zhèng	zhèng	zhèng	zhèng	zhèng	zhèng
prove	prove	prove	prove	prove	prove	prove	prove	prove	prove

苦

kǔ
bitter

Notes:

(苦, **kǔ**, **bitter**)

一 十 艹 芒 芊 芊 苦 苦

Notes:

Notes:

Notes:

Kangxi Radicals

Introduction

The functional building blocks, the alphabet as such, of the written Chinese language known as (汉字, **Hànzì**, **Hanzi**) are the 214 Kangxi Radicals. A Radical is a visual representation, a written image that represents a thought or meaning but variable phonetic information. It may not help to pronounce or verbally ***put forth*** the spoken character but rather may give the character obvious flavour or meaning, or it may not. The Radical can be used alone or in combination to assemble a character.

All characters have one spoken syllable; hence, they are ***monosyllabic***. The character list dates from the year 1615. They were compiled in a dictionary called (字汇, **Zìhuì**, **Zihui**). This allowed for collection, indexing and compilation of characters in an organized fashion. In 1716, a dictionary, the (康熙字典, **Kāngxī Zìdiǎn**, **Kangxi dictionary**) was created organizing the characters using the Radicals as organizational section headers. This dictionary was commissioned by Emperor Kangxi (**1654-1722**) of China's Qing Dynasty. This dictionary has 47,035 characters. Chinese dictionaries are organized not phonetically, but by the Radical then the number of additional strokes in each character. Since then no new Radicals or characters have been added but many words have been.

Modern words are created by creating descriptive character strings. ***Cell phone*** for example is an obvious modern word and is described by ancient characters. The characters are (电, **diàn**, **lightening**) and (话, **huà**, **talk**) forming (电话, **diànhuà**, **lightening talk**) roughly, *electric talk*. This makes utilization for a ***foreigner***

[Type text]

difficult, as he has to reference a lexicon of unfamiliarity. To get to the train station you must ask for the (火车站, **huǒchēzhàn**, **fire cart stand**).

Learning to write Chinese characters is best achieved by mastering the fundamental graphic components, the Kangxi Radicals. Then you can learn which strokes and Radicals are used in particular characters and how they are combined. This allows for efficient memorization and production of Hanzi. This is much easier than learning to write each character as a sequence of memorized strokes. For example, one can remember how to write (義 **yì**, **right conduct**) by knowing that it consists of the character for (羊, **yáng**, **sheep**) above (我, **wǒ**, **me**).

There are a total of some 50,000 Chinese characters. A far smaller number, some 4,000 to 6,000, are in daily use. All characters no matter how complex can be decomposed into radicals and constituent strokes.

A character may have typically one to three Radicals in its composition. Some of the Radicals are pictographic and visually project meaning. (女, **nǚ**, **female**) has a crossed leg, booty sticking out the back look and is easy to remember as it has visually anchoring clues. The picture however does not give any suggestion to pronunciation and this is what differs from a roman type alphabet. It can stand alone as a Radical forming a character, (女, **nǚ**, **female**), or can be part of a multi-Radical character. The character for (好, **hǎo**, **good**) is the Radical (女, **nǚ**, **female**) plus the Radical for (子, **zǐ**, **child**). However, it is not pronounced **nǚzǐ**. Neither Radical gives phonetic clues. You can draw inference that it is good for a female to have a child. Hence, the character makes some sense visually and adds flavour to the interpretation. However, (女, **nǚ**, **female**) is used as part of many characters that do not have a feminine flavour.

[Type text]

(要, **yào**, **want**) combines the Radical for (西, **xī**, **west**), with the Radical of (女, **nǚ**, **female**) under it. Neither (西, **xī**, **west**), nor (女, **nǚ**, **female**), lend phonetic clues or meaning to the character (要, **yào**, **want**) If you want to make up a little story about a Chinese man looking *west* and he *want* to find a *female*, more power to you if it helps you remember. However, remember, you will have about 50,000 little stories to make up to remember all the characters.

Radicals and Their Variants

In writing Hanzi, many Radicals are distorted or changed in form in order to fit into a character with other Radicals or characters. They may be narrowed, shortened, or may have different shapes entirely. Changes in shape, rather than simple distortion, may result in a reduction in the number of strokes used to write it. In some cases, these written forms may have several variants. The actual shape of the component when it is used in a character can depend on its placement with respect to the other elements in the character.

Although there are 214 Radicals, some of them have numerous variants that are only generally recognizable once the parent Radical is compared to it. Some variants are very common and some are very obscure. As with all facets of learning Hanyu and Hanzi, it is best to build on the most commonly occurring components and then to add the less common variants. In this book variants are marked with a (**V**), simplified Radicals with an (**S**) and Traditional Radicals with a (**T**).

The tables in this book list the most common variants. Given the huge historic number of characters, you may never see many of the variants in common usage.

Examples

1) (刀, **dāo**, **knife**) can be represented in its full form with the Radical in these positions, appearing on the top, bottom, left and right within a character.

切 刋 分 办 刅 召 刍

A common variant is (刂, **dāo**, **knife**).

削 刂 刐 刊 刉 切 刑

A less common variant is (⺈, **dāo**, **knife**).

叼 书 汈 芀

2) (人, **rén**, **person**) can be represented in its full form with the Radical in these positions.

天 似 亾 坐 从 以 贝 囚 仄

(亻, **rén**, **standing person**) appears on the left side of characters.

似 亿 他 你 仁 仔 仟 仕 仉

(人, **rén**, **person**) become can also appear on the top of characters.

亽 全 弇 会 仝 亼 仓 个

3) (R#61, 心, **xīn**, **heart**) the character, is the same as Radical.

必 志 忘 忠 忐 忒 癹 惢 㣺

For characters with (#61', 忄, **xīn**, **standing heart**) the Radical always appears on the left side of the character.

快 怖 怪 悟 忆 忛 忏 忓 忔

[Type text]

4) (手, shǒu, hand) appears in varied positions, top, bottom, left and right.

 釆 夅 挛 拿 彛 劤 杕

(扌, shǒu, hand) appears on the left side of characters.

 扎 打 拖 打 扐 扑 扒

(才, shǒu, hand)

 团 财 材 闭 财 斋

(手, shǒu, hand)

 毛 拜 掰

(广, shǒu, hand)

 在 存

(㐄, shǒu, hand)

 发

5) (水, shuǐ, water) occurs on the top, bottom, left and right of characters.

 水 氽 沓 烋 永 丞 丞 承

(氵, shuǐ, standing water) appears on the left of characters. An alternate name for this Radical is (三点水, sān diǎn shuǐ, three dot water)

 氵 汀 汁 汇 汈 清

(氺, shuǐ, water) is a less common variant. There are very few Radicals forming characters with this Radical. Examples: (录, lù, to record), (黍, tiǎn, to shame)

[Type text]

In learning (汉字, **Hànzì, Hanzi**) it is imperative to compare the precise meaning of the individual characters to the Pinyin to the literal translation. This learning strategy will allow you to see how the Radicals flavour the characters and how the characters are compiled to make sentences. A methodical learning of the Radicals is essential to learn the language. What seems tedious at first and counterproductive to learning will give you the most important tools to (汉字, **Hànzì, Hanzi**). A close analogy would be to try to learn English without knowing the alphabet. After you grind away at learning the Radicals, the language will suddenly open up to you. You will no longer need to remember 13 strokes for (想, **xiǎng, think, desire**) to write the character but only need to remember the individual Radicals that compose it, (木, **mù, tree**) *beside* (目, **mù, eye**) *over* (心, **xīn, heart**) *equal* (想, **xiǎng, think**).

This reduces your memory load from 13 to 3 visual images. Again, if you want to make up a little memory aid story about a *tree* with an *eye* on the top standing on a *heart* equal *think* that only leaves 49,998 more little stories. However, if you can remember the Hanzi character for (相, **xiāng, mutually**), you only need to remember two visual images. *Mutually* or *each other* over *heart* equals *think*.

It is not a matter of this language being complicated or not, it is only *how complicated* you want to make it. However, 2 billion people cannot be wrong. To further complicate the story, each Radical has a name, a category and an assigned number. In addition, the Radical name may be different and more complex than the character name when the Radical stands alone as a character.

Convention dictates that the (汉字, **Hànzì, Hanzi**) characters roughly fit into a square. This leads the Radicals to morph to fit the space allowed. They may elongate, widen, deepen or narrow to fit the space. Some Radicals even change in

[Type text]

form from the right side to the left side to the top to bottom of a character. Throughout this book are examples of Radicals in characters and they are represented by the various physical mutations as they change position in a character.

There will come a time when you have no choice but to buy a very large amount of paper, I would recommend a case of 10 reams, a box of soft tipped fine marker pens, a cushion for your butt, and start to start copying out the Radicals, writing their name in Pinyin, their assigned number, chanting the phonetic and the semantic translation.

Learning Hanzi is more akin to art class than English class. The amount of practice you will need will depend on your innate ability and the complexity of the character. The Radicals are conveniently indexed by order of increasing complexity. You can build on the initial simple Radicals and strokes, and progress through the list. Please look forward to the Work Book and find characters you can overwrite with a plastic sheet or velum paper. There is no other way. This is the way that billions of Chinese students have done it over thousands of years. This is not like learning French, German, Italian or Spanish, with an alphabet with which you are familiar. This is more like learning to draw thousands of pictures and remembering their names, meaning, pronunciation and intonation.

The workbook is a workbook to learn stroke order and to write Hanzi. The characters are not chosen for their general utility. I have tried to find a progressive selection of characters that will build your writing skills. You will not find any two references that give the exact same stroke orders for the Kangxi Radicals. The goal is to make a visual representation and get the meaning of the character communicated. Hanzi is an art form. This must not be forgotten as the Western

[Type text]

world rushes to digitalize and standardize the stroke order of characters and Radicals.

Once you arrive in China you will see scripts on signboards that the native Chinese struggle to interpret. Just as we print and write our language, there is a free form artistic **grass script** that will defy your most imaginative interpretation. Also there remains much Traditional Hanzi on old signs and in villages.

The correct stroke choice is that which you have to draw to reproduce or create a character. It varies from font to font and author to author. Further ahead in this book is a detailed chapter on the various strokes of Hanzi. As an example, there are many sources that say the 1st stroke for (月, **yuè**, **moon**) is (撇, **Piě**, ノ). **Piě** stroke is a near 45 degree angle right to left descending stroke. The correct stroke has little curvature. It is obvious on inspection that the first stroke in 月 is not entirely curved but is (竖撇, **Shù Piě**, **SP**, 丿). **SP** is vertical line with a finishing curve to the left.

There are countless examples of these variations. There is no **solution**. Once written with a brush and ink, Hanzi is an artistic expression. If the message of the character is preserved, it is difficult to assign **right** or **wrong** to an individual's efforts.

As another example, here are some of the various expressions of the Radical #45 (**R #45**, 屮, **chè**, **sprout**). 屮, 屮, 屮, 屮. Each example of this character in different fonts introduces questions as to which named strokes are most appropriate. But, the visual meaning is preserved. Although there are tens of thousands of characters, the meaning is readily preserved in these examples even though the strokes are not standardized.

[Type text]

List of the 214 Kangxi Radicals

The following is a list of all 214 Kangxi Radicals categorized under the number of strokes along with some examples of characters containing these Radicals. The accompanying numbers are the officially assigned numbers. Further on in this book are the rules of writing the Radicals. Stroke order, stroke direction and stroke choice become very important. Common variants of each character are displayed such as (**R#64**, 手, **shǒu, hand**) and (**R#64'**, 扌, **standing hand, shǒu**). Some of the Radicals have both Traditional (**T**) and Simplified (**S**) forms. The written official Chinese language, (汉字, **Hànzì, Hanzi**), when broken down to its constituent components, is a combination of the Radicals plus or minus additional strokes.

Knowing how to draw each character stroke and Radical ultimately simplifies learning to write characters. The characters no longer look like a confusing collection of lines but become a small collection of Radicals. There is no way to master this other than repetitive copying and recitation of the name with the correct tone. If you do not do this, you will find that your ability to learn (汉字, **Hànzì, Hanzi**) will dead-end when you reach the limits of your usual memory for volume and complexity. It is easy to remember how to draw characters with up to four or five strokes. Beyond that, you need a systematic approach. There is no need to belabour learning theory in this book.

However, the volume and complexity of learning to write (汉字, **Hànzì, Hanzi**) and (汉语, **Hànyǔ, Hanyu**) is such that you need to recruit every learning tool possible. Native English speakers are not used to a non-phonetic based language with no recognizable alphabet. There are few clues to recognize previously unseen

[Type text]

words or characters. You will need lots of paper, many pens and lots of time and patience. Once you can draw every Radical, you can draw every character.

There are numerous variants of many of the Radicals. This book attempts to compile the most common Radicals used in the PRC. These Radicals are shared to a degree by China, Japan and Korea and are often referred to as the CJK Radicals.

There are several defined sets of organized Radicals ranging in number from 187 to 540 Radicals, plus their variants. There is no *correct* collection. Traditional Chinese sets and Radicals are predictably quantitatively greater in number and complexity than Simplified Radicals. The Radical set chosen for this book is the Chinese Japanese Korean (**CJK**) Radicals from the Kangxi dictionary published in 1716. The original set was of course all Traditional Chinese Radicals and characters.

This set uses the original number of Radicals with simplified variants substituted. I have also added the historic Traditional Radicals in the work sheets for comparison. China currently uses a simplified set with 187 Radicals. Although China created and embraced simplification, there is still Traditional Chinese Radicals and characters throughout China. I was once entrenched in not learning any Traditional characters. This changed when I came across very old historic sites with poems, stories and explanations set into stone, bronze and pottery.

China will set the stage for Asia for usage of Simplified characters and spoken Standard Mandarin as the Lingua Franca of Asia. I encourage you to concentrate on Simplified Radicals but to gradually assimilate some Traditional Radicals and characters.

[Type text]

1 Stroke

- 1. 一 (one) (yī) - 丁 七 丈 三
- 2. 丨 (line) (gǔn) - 中 丰 串 十
- 3. 丶 (dot) (zhǔ) - 丸 丹 主 丼
- 4. 丿 (slash) (piě) - 乂 乃 久 乎
- 5. 乙 (second) (yǐ) - 乞 乾 挖 氹
- 5'. 乚 (second) (yǐ) - 也 乳 亂 说
- 6. 亅 (hook) (jué) - 了 予 丁 乎

2 Strokes

- 7. 二 (two) (èr) - 于 五 井 些
- 8. 亠 (lid) (tóu) - 亡 交 亥 京
- 9. 人 (human) (rén) - 今 介 从 令
- 9'. 亻 (standing human) (rén) - 仁 仕 他 休
- 10. 儿 (legs) (ér) - 兄 兆 先 光
- 11. 入 (enter) (rù) - 氽 籴 痊 拴
- 12. 八 (eight) (bā) - 公 共 兵 具
- 13. 冂 (down box) (jiǒng) - 冉 再 同 囘
- 14. 冖 (cover) (mì) - 冗 冠 冢 冥
- 15. 冫 (ice) (bīng) - 冰 冶 冷 凍
- 16. 几 (table) (jī) - 凡 凭 凰 凳
- 17. 凵 (open box) (qǔ) - 凶 凸 凹 出
- 18. 刀 (knife) (dāo) - 刃 分 切 券

- 18'. 刂 (standing knife) (dāo) - 刘 刊 刑 列
- 19. 力 (power) (lì) - 功 劣 努 励
- 20. 勹 (wrap) (bāo) - 勺 匀 勾 包
- 21. 匕 (spoon) (bǐ) - 北 匙 老 能
- 22. 匚 (right open box) (fāng) - 匠 匡 匣 匪
- 23. 匸 (hiding enclosure) (xǐ) - 匹 医 匛 匿
- 24. 十 (ten) (shí) - 千 午 南 博
- 25. 卜 (divination) (bǔ) - 卞 占 卡 卦
- 26. 卩 (seal) (jié) - 卯 印 危 却
- 27. 厂 (cliff) (hàn) - 厄 厘 厚 原
- 28. 厶 (private) (sī) - 厷 去 叀 參
- 29. 又 (again) (yòu) - 叉 友 双 受

3 Strokes

- 30. 口 (mouth) (kǒu) - 史 名 君 吟
- 31. 囗 (enclosure) (wéi) - 囚 因 困 国
- 32. 土 (earth) (tǔ) - 地 均 坊 城
- 33. 士 (scholar) (shì) - 壬 壻 喜 声
- 34. 夂 (go) (zhǐ) - 夅 夆 逢 缝
- 35. 夊 (go slowly) (suī) - 夋 复 夎 夏
- 36. 夕 (evening) (xī) - 外 名 多 夜
- 37. 大 (big) (dà) - 天 太 夫 契
- 38. 女 (woman) (nǚ) - 好 妊 妹 姓

- 39. 子 (child) (zǐ) - 孔 字 孝 孟
- 40. 宀 (roof) (mián) - 宅 宇 宗 官
- 41. 寸 (inch) (cùn) - 寺 封 射 时
- 42. 小 (small) (xiǎo) - 少 尖 尔 尚
- 43. 尢 (lame) (wāng) - 允 尤 尬 尪
- 44. 尸 (corpse) (shī) - 尺 尻 尾 局
- 45. 屮 (sprout) (chè) - 屯 纯 出 沌
- 46. 山 (mountain) (shān) - 屹 岳 峰 屿
- 47. 川 (river) (chuān) - 州 训 顺 酬
- 48. 工 (work) (gōng) - 左 巧 巫 差
- 49. 己 已 巳 (oneself) (jǐ) - 巴 卮 巷 巽
- 50. 巾 (turban) (jīn) - 市 布 帆 怖
- 51. 干 (dry) (gān) - 平 开 并 平
- 52. 幺 (tiny) (yāo) - 幻 幼 幻 幼
- 53. 广 (dotted cliff) (yǎn) - 床 底 店 府
- 54. 廴 (long stride) (yǐn) - 延 廷 建 廻
- 55. 廾 (two hands) (gǒng) - 弁 异 弃 弄
- 56. 弋 (shoot) (yì) - 式 弒 弍 式
- 57. 弓 (bow) (gōng) - 引 弟 弦 弱
- 58. 彑 (snout) (jì) - 互 彖 彘 彝
- 58. 彐 (snout) (jì) - 事 当 档 铛
- 59. 彡 (bristle) (shān) - 形 彦 彩 彬

[Type text]

- 60. 彳 (step) (chì) - 役 往 待 律

4 Strokes

- 61. 心 (heart) (xīn) - 必 志 忘 忠
- 61'. 忄 (standing heart) (xīn) - 忙 快 怖 怪
- 62. 戈 (halberd) (gē) - 戊 戎 成 我
- 63. 戶 (door) (hù) - 房 所 扁 扇
- 64. 手 (hand) (shǒu) - 拜 拳 掌 掣
- 64'. 扌 (standing hand) (shǒu) - 打 批 技 抱
- 65. 支 (branch) (zhī) - 竧 敆 䠯 技
- 66. 攴 攵 (rap) (pū) - 改 放 政 故
- 67. 文 (script) (wén) - 孝 斌 斐 斑
- 68. 斗 (dipper) (dǒu) - 料 斛 斜 斟
- 69. 斤 (axe) (jīn) - 斥 斧 斬 新
- 70. 方 (square) (fāng) - 於 施 旁 旅
- 71. 旡 (not) (wú) - 既 旤 慨 暨
- 71. 无 (not) (wú) - 芜 庑 抚 芜
- 72. 日 (sun) (rì) - 旦 旱 明 星
- 73. 曰 (say) (yuē) - 晉 曷 書 曹
- 74. 月 (moon) (yuè) - 朏 朖 期 朦
- 75. 木 (tree) (mù) - 末 本 杉 林
- 76. 欠 (yawn) (qiàn) - 次 欣 欲 歌
- 77. 止 (stop) (zhǐ) - 此 步 武 歪

[Type text]

- 78. 歹 (death) (dǎi) - 死 殉 殊 殘
- 78. 歺 (death) (dǎi)- 妑 餐 璨 瀿
- 79. 殳 (weapon) (shū) - 段 殷 殺 殿
- 80. 毋 (do not) (wú) - 毐 每 盉 冊
- 80. 母 (do not) (wú) - 每 馳 毒 毒
- 81. 比 (compare) (bǐ) - 毕 毖 毘 毚
- 82. 毛 (fur) (máo) - 毫 毽 毯 毳
- 83. 氏 (clan) (shì) - 氐 民 㐄 氓
- 84. 气 (steam) (qì) - 氛 氙 氣 氤
- 85. 水 (water) (shuǐ) - 汞 泉 淼 漿
- 85'. 氵 (standing water) (shuǐ) - 河 泣 洋 海
- 85". 氺 (water) (shuǐ) - 求 泰 滕 录
- 86. 火 (fire) (huǒ) - 灼 炊 炎 炒
- 86'. 灬 (fire) (huǒ) - 烈 烹 焦 然
- 87. 爪 (claw) (zhuǎ) - 爬 笊 抓 朳
- 87. 爫 (claw) (zhuǎ) - 采 爭 爯 爰
- 88. 父 (father) (fù) - 爸 爹 爺 交
- 89. 爻 (double crosses) (yáo) - 爼 爾 希 网
- 90. 爿 (bed) (qiáng) - 牀 牁 牂 牒
- 90. 丬 (bed) (qiáng) - 将 状 壮 妆
- 91. 片 (slice) (piàn) - 版 牋 牌 牒
- 92. 牙 (fang) (yá) - 牚 穿 呀 芽

- 93. 牛 (cow) (niú) - 牧 物 牲 犀
- 94. 犬 (dog) (quǎn) - 狀 猋 猒 獸
- 94'. 犭 (standing dog) - 犯 狂 狗 狩

5 Strokes

- 95. 玄 (profound) (xuán) - 玅 玆 率 旒
- 96. 玉 (jade) (yù) - 瑩 瑬 瑿 璧
- 96'. 王 (jade) (yù) - 珍 珠 現 球
- 97. 瓜 (melon) (guā) - 㼌 㼝 瓠 瓢
- 98. 瓦 (earthenware) (wǎ) - 瓮 瓷 甄 甌
- 99. 甘 (sweet) (gān) - 甙 甚 甜 甝
- 100. 生 (life) (shēng) - 甥 產 甥 甦
- 101. 用 (use) (yòng) - 甩 甫 甬 甭
- 102. 田 (field) (tián) - 男 界 留 畦
- 103. 疋 (bolt of cloth) (pǐ) - 疌 疎 疏 疑
- 104. 疒 (sickness) (chuáng) - 疼 疾 病 痴
- 105. 癶 (dotted tent) (bō) - 癸 癸 發 登
- 106. 白 (white) (bái) - 的 皆 皇 皎
- 107. 皮 (skin) (pí) - 皰 皺 皽 皾
- 108. 皿 (dish) (mǐn) - 盂 盆 盒 盛
- 109. 目 (eye) (mù) - 盲 看 眺 眼
- 110. 矛 (halberd) (máo) - 矜 矝 矞 矠
- 111. 矢 (arrow) (shǐ) - 矣 知 矩 短

- 112. 石 (stone) (shí) - 砂 砥 砲 硬
- 113. 示 (spirit) (shì) - 祟 票 祭 禁
- 113'. 礻 (standing spirit) (shì) - 礼 社 祈 祝
- 114. 禸 (track) (róu) - 禹 禺 离 离
- 115. 禾 (grain) (hé) - 秋 税 稔 稻
- 116. 穴 (cave) (xué) - 究 空 穿 突
- 117. 立 (stand) (lì) - 站 竝 章 竣

6 Strokes

- 118. 竹 (bamboo) (zhú) - 竿 笏 算 箱
- 119. 米 (rice) (mǐ) - 粒 粗 粟 精
- 120. 糸 (silk) (mì) - 系 紊 素 索
- 120'. 纟 (standing silk) (mì) - 紅 納 紙 細
- 121. 缶 (jar) (fǒu) - 缸 缺 罅 罐
- 122. 网 (net) (wǎng) - 罾
- 122'. 罒 (net) (wǎng) - 罠 罪 置 罰
- 123. 羊 (sheep) (yáng) - 着 美 群 羯
- 124. 羽 (feather) (yǔ) - 翁 翌 習 翔
- 125. 老 (old) (lǎo) - 耄 耆 耋 姥
- 125'. 耂 (old) (lǎo) - 考 者 耆
- 126. 而 (and) (ér) - 耍 耏 耐 耑
- 127. 耒 (plow) (lěi) - 耕 耗 耘 耙
- 128. 耳 (ear) (ěr) - 耽 聰 聲 聽

- 129. 聿 (brush) (yù) - 殯 肄 肅 肇
- 130. 肉 (meat) (ròu) - 胥 胾 腐 臠
- 130. 月 (standing meat) (ròu) - 肌 肝 肥 肱
- 131. 臣 (minister) (chén) - 臤 臥 臦 臧
- 132. 自 (self) (zì) - 乸 臬 臭 鼻
- 133. 至 (arrive) (zhì) - 致 侄 铚 臻
- 134. 臼 (mortar) (jiù) - 臾 舁 舂 與
- 135. 舌 (tongue) (shé) - 舍 舐 舒 舔
- 136. 舛 (oppose) (chuǎn) - 舜 舞 桀 嶙
- 137. 舟 (boat) (zhōu) - 航 舫 般 船
- 138. 艮 (stopping) (gèn) - 艱 很 恨 狠
- 139. 色 (color) (sè) - 艴 艳 艷 绝
- 140. 艸 (grass) (cǎo) - 芔 芻 芔 芔
- 140'. 艹 (grass) (cǎo) – 花 茶 草 菓 獎
- 141. 虍 (tiger) (hǔ) – 虎 虐 處 號
- 142. 虫 (insect) (chóng) – 蛇 蛙 蜜 蝶
- 143. 血 (blood) (xiě) – 衄 衅 衆 衇
- 144. 行 (walk enclosure) (xíng) – 衕 術 街 衝
- 145. 衣 (clothes) (yī) – 表 衰 袋 裔
- 145'. 衤 (standing clothes) (yī) – 袂 袖 裸 裙
- 146. 襾 覀 西 (west) (yà) – 覀 覉 覂 覆

- 146. 襾 (west) (yà) – 覀 覆 覇 覈
- 146. 西 (west) (yà) – 洒 牺 晒 栖

7 Strokes

- 147. 见 (see) (jiàn) – 现 觉 观 视
- 148. 角 (horn) (jiǎo) – 觜 确 嘴 触
- 149. 言 (speech) (yán) – 詈 誓 馨 警
- 149'. 讠 (standing speech) (yán) – 证 记 认 训
- 150. 谷 (valley) (gǔ) – 容 裕 浴 峪
- 151. 豆 (bean) (dòu) – 豈 豉 豌 短
- 152. 豕 (pig) (shǐ) – 豚 象 豢 家
- 153. 豸 (badger) (zhì) – 豹 豺 貂 貌
- 154. 贝 (shell) (bèi) – 员 则 责 负
- 155. 赤 (red) (chì) – 赦 赧 赫 郝
- 156. 走 (run) (zǒu) – 赴 起 超 越
- 157. 足 (foot) (zú) – 距 跨 跪 路
- 158. 身 (body) (shēn) – 躬 躟 躺 射
- 159. 车 (car) (chē) – 军 转 连 较
- 160. 辛 (bitter) (xīn) – 辜 辟 辣 新
- 161. 辰 (morning) (chén) – 辱 晨 唇 震
- 162. 辵 (walk) (chuò) – 辵 辺 辺 辺
- 162'. 辶 (walk) (chuò) – 近 返 述 道
- 163. 邑 (city) (yì) – 扈 挹 悒 邕

[Type text]

- 163'. 阝 (city) (yì) – 那 邦 邸 郁
- 164. 酉 (wine) (yǒu) – 酋 配 酒 酸
- 165. 釆 (distinguish) (biàn) – 釉 釋 悉 奧
- 166. 里 (village) (lǐ) – 重 野 量 理

8 Strokes

- 167. 金 (metal) (jīn) – 釜 鏖 鏨 鑾
- 167'. 金 (standing metal) (jīn) – 銀 銅 鋼 錫
- 167'. 钅 (standing metal) (jīn) – 钱 错 银 铁
- 168. 长 (long) (cháng) – 长 张 涨 帐
- 169. 门 (gate) (mén) – 间 们 闷 扪
- 170. 阜 (mound) (fù) – 阜 埠 頮 焯
- 170'. 阝 (standing mound) (fù) – 防 降 陰 階
- 171. 隶 (slave) (lì) – 逮 隸 康 逮
- 172. 隹 (small bird) (zhuī) – 隻 隼 雀 雄
- 173. 雨 (rain) (yǔ) – 雪 雲 零 雷
- 174. 青 靑 (blue) (qīng) – 靖 艶 靚 靛
- 175. 非 (wrong) (fēi) – 辈 靠 靡 悲

9 Strokes

- 176. 面 (face) (miàn) – 靤 靦 醼 靨
- 177. 革 (leather) (gé) – 勒 靴 鞋 鞍
- 178. 韦 (tanned leather) (wéi) – 韧 韨 韓 韙
- 179. 韭 (leek) (jiǔ) – 韮 韲 韱 韰

- 180. 音 (sound) (yīn) – 韷 韶 韸 響
- 181. 页 (face) (yè) – 项 顶 顺 预
- 182. 风 (wind) (fēng) – 疯 枫 讽 砜
- 183. 飞 (fly) (fēi) – 飞 飛 飜 飝
- 184. 食 (eat) (shí) – 養 餐 飱 饕
- 184'. 饣 (standing eat) (shí) – 饰 蚀 饵 钚
- 185. 首 (head) (shǒu) – 馗 馘 道 渞
- 186. 香 (fragrant) (xiāng) – 馛 馞 馥 馨

10 Strokes

- 187. 马 (horse) (mǎ) – 吗 妈 骂 玛
- 188. 骨 (bone) (gǔ) – 骰 骸 髀 髓
- 189. 高 (tall) (gāo) – 髚 髜 髝 髞
- 190. 髟 (hair) (biāo) – 髦 髮 髯 鬆
- 191. 鬥 (fight) (dòu) – 鬧 鬨 鬩 鬪
- 192. 鬯 (sacrificial wine) (chàng) – 鬱 鬻 鬽 秬
- 193. 鬲 (cauldron) (lì) – 鬳 鬴 鬶 鬷
- 194. 鬼 (ghost) (guǐ) – 魁 魂 魃 魅

11 Strokes

- 195. 鱼 (fish) (yú) – 渔 藓 鲁 廯
- 196. 鸟 (bird) (niǎo) – 莺 袅 岛 鸡
- 197. 卤 (alkaline) (lǔ) – 龄 鹼 鹹 鹾
- 198. 鹿 (deer) (lù) – 麋 麒 麓 麗

[Type text]

- 199. 麦 (wheat) (mài) – 唛 麸 麵 陵
- 200. 麻 (hemp) (má) – 摩 魔 靡 磨

12 Strokes

- 201. 黄 (yellow) (huáng) – 尣 黇 黉 穔
- 202. 黍 (millet) (shǔ) – 黎 黏 黐 漆
- 203. 黑 (black) (hēi) – 嘿 潶 黔 熏
- 204. 黹 (needlework) (zhǐ) – 黺 黻 黼 黻

13 Strokes

- 205. 黾 (amphibian) (mǐn) – 鼋 鼍 鳌 鼈
- 206. 鼎 (tripod) (dǐng) – 鼐 鼑 鼎 鼒
- 207. 鼓 (drum) (gǔ) – 鼙 鼖 鼘 鼞
- 208. 鼠 (rat) (shǔ) – 鼰 鼩 鼬 鼯

14 Strokes

- 209. 鼻 (nose) (bí) – 濞 劓 齈 鼾
- 210. 齐 (uniformly) (qí) – 剂 济 挤 侪

15 Strokes

- *211.* 齿 (tooth) (chǐ) - 啮 龀 龅 龈

16 Strokes

- 212. 龙 (dragon) (lóng) – 笼 拢 陇 珑
- 213. 龟 (tortoise) (guī) – 阄 龟

17 Strokes

- 214 龠 (flute) (yuè) – 龡 龢 龣 龥

Written Variants

Orthography

The nature of Chinese characters makes it very easy to produce an allograph for any character. There have been many efforts at orthographical standardization throughout history. The widespread usage of the characters in different nations that do not see *eye to eye* has prevented any one system from becoming universally adopted. Consequently, the standard stroke order of any given character in Chinese usage may differ subtly from its standard shape in Japanese or Korean usage, even where no simplification has taken place. With inherent individuality in hand writing, there is significant difference between individuals. Even type fonts create a great number of variations.

Usually each Hanzi character takes up the same amount of space due to their block-like square nature. This is more true for electronic fonts than free hand writing. Some introductory books typically practice writing with a grid as a guide. In addition to strictness for the space that a character takes up, Hanzi characters are written with very precise rules. The three most important rules are the strokes employed, stroke placement, and the order in which they are written, stroke order. Most words can be written with just one stroke order. Some words also have variant stroke orders. This may occasionally result in different stroke counts. Certain characters are also written with different stroke orders in different countries.

Common Typefaces

There are two common typeface groups. These typefaces are based on the regular script for Chinese characters, which are akin to serif and sans serif fonts in the West.

[Type text]

The popular set for body text is a family of serif fonts called Song typeface (宋体), also known as Minchō (明朝) in Japan, and Ming typeface (明體) in Taiwan and Hong Kong. This typeface is similar to Western serif fonts such as Times New Roman in both appearance and function. These two fonts give strong clues to named stroke and stroke direction.

The other common group of fonts are called the black typeface, (黑体) in Chinese, and Gothic typeface. This group is characterized by straight lines of even thickness for each stroke, akin to sans-serif styles such as Arial and Helvetica in Western typography. This group of fonts, first introduced on newspaper headlines, is commonly used on headings, websites, signs and billboards.

The sans-serif style fonts take away the esthetic beauty and clues to stroke and stroke order. The lines of even thickness give the beginner writer little visual clue to stroke technique. Microsoft operating systems have numerous Asian fonts that are esthetically appealing and many more can be purchased online. I encourage you to learn to type in Pinyin and convert to Hanzi and to use a font that shows the esthetic beauty and stroke clues.

If I was to pick one font that encompasses the spirit of the artistic nature of Hanzi, I would chose (楷体, **Kai Ti**). This is embedded in the Microsoft Office 2007 Word program. This font makes clear the artistic nature and defined strokes of each character. It retains a flavour of hand printed script.

Below are examples of the characters for (汉字, **Hànzì**, **Hanzi**) written with different type faces and type fonts. You can see how the top six fonts preserve the shape and definition of the individual strokes while the bottom four do not.

[Type text]

汉字	Sim Sun
汉字	Kai Ti
汉字	MS Mincho
汉字	P Ming Li U
汉字	DF Kai-SB
汉字	Sim Hei
汉字	MS YaHei
汉字	Arial Unicode MS
汉字	Microsoft Jheng Hei

Stroke Order

(**筆順**, **bǐshùn**, **stroke order**) refers to the way in which Hanzi characters are written. A stroke is a movement of the writing instrument. In modern times, this is most commonly a pen, pencil or writing brush. Historically, a (**毛笔**, **máobǐ**, **hair-brush**) was held vertically in the right hand and dipped in ink and the strokes were made. *Stroke Order* can refer both to the numerical order in which the strokes of a given character are written and to the direction in which the writing instrument must move in producing a particular stroke.

A common misconception is that Chinese characters were originally engraved into wood. In fact, Chinese characters are believed to have originally been brush-written on perishable materials such as bamboo or on wood slats. These would then be bound together like Venetian blinds and rolled for storage. Examples of such books have been found dating to the late Zhou dynasty. (**周朝**, **Zhōu Cháo**, **1122 BC to 256 BC**)

History has shown that it would take over a thousand years for uniform, defined forms for each character to appear. Now, as then, each character comprises a number of strokes, which must be written in a prescribed order.

The number of strokes per character for most characters is usually between one and thirty. However, the number of strokes in some obscure characters may reach as many as seventy strokes. In the twentieth century, simplification of Hanzi characters took place in mainland China. This greatly reduced the number of strokes in some characters. The basic rules of stroke order, however, remained the same.

Basic and Compound Strokes

There are six basic strokes, eight classic strokes and an overall total of about 55 distinct named strokes recognized in Chinese characters. Many of these are compound strokes, that is, sequential single strokes comprising more than one movement of the writing instrument. There are also variants of some strokes that can be named. In addition, with the advent of electronic fonts and digitalization of the written Chinese language, each named font type has its own variation of the written characters.

All of the simple strokes have more than one name in Chinese literature. This book uses the most current and common names. Many of the compound strokes have no agreed-upon name. They are thus named by an acronym compilation of their strokes. Digitalization of the fonts has taken much of the shape and *character* out of the strokes.

Each single stroke includes all the motions necessary to produce a given part of a character before lifting the writing instrument from the writing surface. Thus, a single setting down of the brush may use more than one *stroke* and may produce complex lines.

The character above for *eternity* has eight strokes, two of which, the second and third, are compound strokes. These are considered the eight *classic strokes*. All of the six *basic strokes* are used in this character.

[Type text]

Development of Stroke Order Rules

This is an outline of the character (永, yǒng, forever) This character, meaning *eternity*, contains 8 stroke shapes in 5 sequential strokes, 3 basic and 2 compound strokes, and is often used for practice by beginning calligraphers.

The rules for stroke order facilitate vertical character writing, to maximize ease of writing and reading and to further aid in producing uniform characters. A person who has learned the rules of stroke order can infer the stroke order of most characters. This eases the process of learning to write.

Many experienced writers may ignore or forget the normalized stroke order characters, or develop idiosyncratic ways of writing.

The author encourages using the exact stroke order as prescribed by rules. This eases and hastens learning. It also produces a more visually appealing character.

The Eight Principles of Yong (永字八法, **yǒngzì bā fǎ**, **Yong character 8 rules**) often uses the single character (永, yǒng, eternity) meaning *eternity*, to teach the eight most basic strokes. These rules will be presented graphically starting on page 289. I encourage you to photocopy the page 366 and get a brush and some ink and get to it. This is what billions of Chinese have done over thousands of years.

[Type text]

Modern Stroke Order

The Chinese government began to reform the Hanzi character set in 1956. They also reformed the number of strokes and the stroke order of some characters. An obvious notable innovation of this reformed stroke order was the conception of a horizontal writing stroke order. This facilitates horizontal writing. The history of written Chinese had included right to left, top to bottom and now left to right.

Basic Rules of Stroke Order

(左, **zuǒ**, **left**)　　　　　　　(左-右, **zuǒ-yòu**, **left to right**)

(右, **yòu**, **right**)　　　　　　(上-下, **shàng-xià**, **upper- lower**)

(上, **shàng**, **upper**)　　　　　(字, **zì**, **character**)

(中, **zhōng**, **middle**)　　　　(筆順, **bǐshùn**, **stroke order**)

(下, **xià**, **lower**)　　　　　　(文, **wén**, **language**)

1. Left to Right on Horizontal Strokes 一

The first character to learn is the number one, (一, **yī**, **one**), which is written with a single horizontal line. This character has one simple stroke, which is written from left (左, **zuǒ**, **left**) to right (右, **yòu**, **right**). The name of the horizontal character stroke is (横, **héng**, **H**, **horizontal character stroke**). Throughout this book, it will be abbreviated as **H**.

2. Left to Right and Top to Bottom on Multiple Horizontal Strokes 二

As a rule, characters are written from the top to the bottom, (上, **shàng**, **upper**) to (下, **xià**, **lower**). If the components of the character are horizontally stacked and the

[Type text]

lowermost is towards the left (左, **zuǒ**, **left**), yet under the upper strokes, the top to bottom priority is preserved.

The character for *two* has two strokes. (二, **èr**, **two**) In this case, both are written from (左, **zuǒ**, **left**) to (右, **yòu**, **right**) hence **héng, héng** or **H, H**. The top stroke is written first, hence (上, **shàng**, **upper**) to (下, **xià**, **lower**). The character for three has three strokes, (三, **sān**, **three**), hence, **héng, héng, héng**, or **H, H, H**. Hence each stroke is written from left to right, 左-右, starting of course with the uppermost stroke, (上, **shàng**, **upper**), then next (中, **zhōng**, **middle**), then the lower most stroke (下, **xià**, **under**). The structures thus take the form of the first three examples below.

1st ― $\quad\begin{matrix}1^{st}\\2^{nd}\end{matrix}$ 二 $\quad\begin{matrix}1^{st}\\2^{nd}\\3^{rd}\end{matrix}$ 三

The Chinese character for *person*, (人, **rén**, **person**), has two strokes. The first stroke is the compound accelerating curve downward to the left (弯撇, **Wān Piě**, **downwards left double curved stroke**). The second stroke is the down swooping stroke on the right side thickening at the base (捺, **nà**, **downwards-right curved stroke**). This preserves the stroke order of (上-下, **shàng-xià**, **upper-lower**) and the (左-右, **zuǒ-yòu**, **left to right**) stroke order.

This rule applies also to characters that are formed more complexly. Take for example, (相, **xiāng**, **each other**). The polymorphic character can be divided into

[Type text]

two separate characters. (木, **mù**, **tree**) and (目, **mù**, **eye**). The leftmost side of the character, (木, **mù**, **tree**) is written first. The right side (目, **mù**, **eye**) is written second.

1ˢᵗ 2ⁿᵈ

There are some exceptions to this rule, mainly occurring when the right side of a character has an underscore originating from the left character. Take for example the character (这, **zhè**, **this**) In this case, the right side is written first, followed by the left side, and finally the lower underscore stroke. This can be further seen in the characters, (迷, **mí**, **bewilder**) and (过, **guò**, **to live**). In a multi component character such as (谜, **mí**, **riddle**), there are three components. The left component is first, the right component (米, **mǐ**, **rice**) is second and the middle component (**R#162'**, 辶, **chuò**, **walk**) underlining the right component goes last. When there are upper and lower components, the upper components are written first, then the lower components, as in (旦, **dàn**, **dawn**) which is composed of the character for *day* or *sun*,(日, **rì**, **day**) plus (一, **yī**, **one**).

3. Top to Bottom on Single Vertical Strokes |

The general rule for single vertical strokes is that they are written from top to bottom. The name of the stroke is (竖, **shù**, **vertical down character stroke**).

4. Left to Right and Top to Bottom in Multiple Vertical Strokes. 川

In a simple character such as (川, **chuān**, **river**), the rules of stroke are readily apparent in the top to bottom and left to right order. Again, the rules are preserved, all three strokes are written top to bottom. The name of the first vertical character stroke is (竖撇, 丿, **shùpiě**, **SP**, **vertical down stroke left curve**). Hence, the order

[Type text]

is **shùpiě**, **shù**, **shù** or **SP**, **S**, **S**. The left side vertical down stroke has a short left curve finish on it (撇, ノ, **piě**, **downwards-left curved character stroke**). The stroke order is thus numerically,

1ˢᵗ 2ⁿᵈ 3ʳᵈ

There is not a fixed consensus on compound stroke naming. The names I will use will be functional and may not agree with other sources but will adequately describe the stroke.

(儿, **ér**, **son**) is another example. This is formed from two compound strokes, (竖撇, ノ, **shùpiě**, **SP**, **vertical stroke left curve**) then the right side stroke is (竖折弯鉤, ㄴ, **shùzhéwāngōu**, **SZWG**, **vertical down stroke, break, hook**).

5. Top Left Side Vertical Stroke meets Top Left Side Horizontal Stroke.

There is not a simple unifying rule to clarify what happens on the top left part of a character or Radical. Ultimately one needs to simply memorize the Radicals that deal with this. The first category of the Radicals that fit into this designation can be divided into groups that have similar patterns. The first group are Radicals in which **S** and **HZ** meet together.

丨 ⼌

For these closed box Radicals the stroke order is the same. The left side **S** is always first. This is observed in (口, **kǒu**, **mouth**), (囗, **wéi**, **enclosure**), (日, **rì**, **sun**), (曰, **yuē**, **speak**), (田, **tián**, **field**), (目, **mù**, **eye**) and (**R#108** 皿, **mǐn**, **dish**). All other characters that contain these Radicals within another Radical or character follow the initial stroke order **S-HZ**.

[Type text]

The second category of Radicals that fit into this designation are the Radicals in which **S** and **HZG** meet. For (**R#13**, 冂, **jiǒng**, **down box**) the stroke order is **S-HZG**.

丨 冂

However, for (**R#26**, 卩, **jié seal**) the stroke order becomes **HZG-S**. You can see that it is the scale that differs, for **R#26**, **S** is proportionately longer.

⇁ 卩

The third category are Radicals in which **SP / WP** and **HZWG** meet. For the Radical (**R#16**, 几, **jī**, **table**) the stroke order is **SP-HZWG**.

丿 几

The fourth category are Radicals in which **WP** and **HZG** meet or intersect. For (**R#18**, 刀, **dāo**, **knife**) the stroke order is **HZG-WP**. This stroke order is also preserved for (**R#19**, 力, **lì**, **power**) in which the stroke order is also **HZG-WP**.

⇁ 刀 and ⇁ 力

The fifth category of Radicals are those in which **SZ** and **H** meet. For both Radical (**R#22**, 匚, **fāng**, **right open box**) and (**R#23**, 匸, **xǐ**, **hiding enclosure**) the stroke order is **H-SZ** or **H-SW**. For Radical (**R#131**, 臣, **chén**, **minister**) **H** is written first, the other strokes are written and **SZ** is written last. This follows a pattern in which characters based on **R#22** and **R#23** have **H** written first.

[Type text]

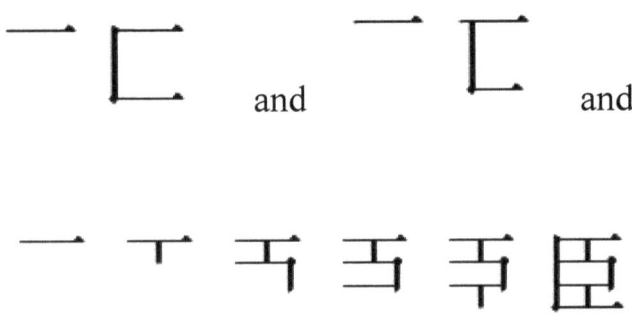

一 丁 于 亐 弓 臣

The sixth category are Radicals in which **SP** and **HZG** meet. The lone representative in this category is Radical (**R#74**, 月, **yuè**, **moon**). The stroke order is **SP-HZG**.

丿 月

The seventh category are Radicals in which **SP** and **HZ** meet. The lone representative is Radical (**R#44**, 尸, **shī**, **corpse**). The stroke order is **HZ-(x)-SP**.

㇇ ㇈ 尸

The eighth category are Radicals and characters in which **SZ** and **HZG** meet. The lone Radical in this category is Radical (**R#80**, 毋/母, **wú**, **do not**). The stroke order is **SZ-HZG**.

㇗ 毋

The ninth category are characters and Radicals in which **H** and **S** meet. Radical (**R#99**, 甘, **gān**, **sweet**) and (**R#128**, 耳, **ěr**, **ear**) represent this category. The stroke order for both is **H-S**. A variant of **H-S** is (年, **nián**, **year**).

一 十 and 一 丅

The tenth category are characters and Radicals in which **ST** and **HZ** meet. The representative Radical is (**R#138**, 艮, **gèn**, **stopping**). In this Radical **HZ** comes before **ST**.

⼁ ⼂ ⺕ 㠯

The eleventh category are characters and Radicals in which **SP** and **HG** meet. Radical (**R#107**, 皮, **pí**, **skin**) is the lone member of this category. The stroke order is **HG-SP**.

一 厂 广 皮 皮

The twelfth category are Radicals in which **H** and **SP** meet. This is seen in Radicals (**R#27**, 厂, **hàn**, **cliff**) and (**R#104**, 疒, **chuáng**, **sickness**). In both of these Radicals **H** precedes **SP**.

一 厂   and   丶 亠 广 广 疒

6. Horizontal before Vertical 十

When **S** and **H** strokes cross, horizontal strokes are written before vertical strokes. The character for (十, **shí**, **ten**), has two strokes. The left to right horizontal stroke (横, **héng**, **H**, **horizontal stroke**) is written first. The top to bottom vertical stroke (竖, **shù**, **S**, **vertical down stroke**) is written second. Hence, the stroke order is **héng-shù** or **H-S**.

[Type text]

7. Bottom Horizontal Stroke Last 王

In situations where a horizontal stroke is on the bottom of a character and it is not crossed by the vertical stroke, but intersects with it, the vertical stroke is drawn before the last horizontal **H** stroke. Example, (王, **wáng**, **king**), the stroke order is **héng**, **héng**, **shù**, **héng** or **H**, **H**, **S**, **H**. This allows for a neater finish in which the horizontal stroke can neatly intersect the vertical line. This dates from the use of a hair brush and ink in which the descending hand would obscure the neat intersection of a horizontal line being drawn first. Further examples are (土, **tǔ**, **earth**), (工, **gōng**, **work**) and (主, **zhǔ**, **master**)

8. Vertical Cutting Strokes Last 中

Vertical strokes that cut through a character are written after the horizontal strokes that they cut through, as in (中, **zhōng**, **centre**). This rule applies when the vertical line starts above the top horizontal line and finishes below the bottom horizontal line. (中, **zhōng**, **center**) is such an example. The box is completed and then the vertical line is drawn through it.

9. Horizontal Cutting Strokes Last 母

Horizontal strokes that cut through a character are written last, as in 母 and 海. The usual strokes to cut through are **H** and **T**. Example (母, **mǔ**, **female**)

[Type text]

10. Right to Left down Sloping before Left to Right down Sloping 文

Right-to-left diagonals (丿) are written before left-to-right diagonals (㇏) such as in (文, **wén**, **language**), (这, **zhè**, **this**) and (友, **yǒu**, **friend**). The crossing strokes are typically **P, N** or **CD**.

11. Centre Verticals before Left and Right Strokes. 永

In characters that show a left to right symmetry with a central dividing vertical stroke, the central stroke is written first. Vertical centre strokes are written before vertical or diagonal outside strokes, left outside strokes are written before right outside strokes (水, **shuǐ**, **water**), (永, **yǒng**, **eternity**), (小, **xiǎo**, **small**).

12. Box Rules, Left Vertical First, Outside before Inside 回

All closed boxes are constructed the same. The left vertical edge is drawn first with the vertical downward stroke **S**. The top horizontal and right vertical strokes are written in one continuous stroke using (**HZ, héngzhé**). This is the left to right horizontal stroke with a down dropping vertical stroke. The box is left open at this time if it has contents inside. All inside contents are then finished. The bottom horizontal left to right box-closing stroke **H** is written last. If there is a box within a box, the inner box is closed first. Example, (回, **huí**, **turn around**). An easy order to remember is *make three sided down box*, *fill box*, *close box*.

This rule applies also to top enclosing characters that have no bottom stroke, such as 同 and 月. The outer structure is finished first, then the inside contents are added.

[Type text]

13. Bottom Enclosure Last (R#17, qǔ, 凵, Open Box)

Bottom box enclosures, (**R#17, qǔ, 凵, open box**) are always written last. The contents of the box are written first. Then the box encloses the contents. Examples are (**画, huà, draw**), (**涵, hán, contain**), (**凶, xiōng, fierce**). The box is made in two strokes, **SZ-S**. This follows the rule of underlining strokes being placed last.

14. Down Box Rules 冂

(**R#13, jiǒng, 冂, down box**) is made with **S-HZG**. If there is a Radical, stroke or character over top of (**R#13, jiǒng, 冂, down box**), as in (**再, zài, again**), it is made first. Next, (**R#13, jiǒng, 冂, down box**) is formed. Strokes dropping from above and entering the box, in this situation, **S**, are made after the open Down Box is formed. Strokes inside the box are made after the box is formed, (**同, tóng, same**).

15. Ride Side Open Box Rules 匚, 匚

(**R#22, fāng, 匚, right open box**) as a Radical, is formed with the strokes **H-SZ**. However, the stroke order is **H** plus whatever is under **H**, then **SZ** when a character is made. This follows the general rule of underlining and enclosing strokes occurring last. (**匠, jiàng, craftsman**) (**匡, kuāng, correct**) (**匣, xiá, box**).

(**R#23, xǐ, 匚, hiding enclosure**) as a Radical, is formed with the strokes **H-SW**. Again, any Radical or character is made under **H** then the enclosing-underlining stroke **SW** occurs last. This follows the general rule of underlining and enclosing strokes occurring last. (**匹, pī, mate**) (**医, yī, to treat**)

[Type text]

16. Bottom Underlining Strokes Last 这

Bottom underlining strokes are always written last. If the left hand Radical of a character has a bottom underlining stroke, it is written last. Examples are Radical (**R#162'**, 辶, **chuò**, **walk**) and (这, **zhè**, **this**). This construction can even occur in the middle of a character composed of three radicals side by side. (谜, **mí**, **riddle**).

17. Dots and Minor Strokes Last 戈

Minor strokes are usually written last, as the small *dot* (点, **diǎn**, **dot**) in the following. (玉, **yù**, **jade**) In a character such as (国, **guó**, **country**), the **Box Rules** are preserved and the (玉, **yù**, **jade**) character is finished first then the box is closed. It must be remembered that **R#8**, (亠, **tóu**, **lid**) is a Radical and as it occurs at the top of a character (点, **diǎn**, **dot**) comes first.

18. 提, Tí, Stroke Rule ✓

(提, **Tí**, ✓) when it crosses another stroke is drawn after the stroke it crosses. Examples are (孑, **jié**, **alone**), (扌, **shǒu**, **hand**), (我, **wǒ**, **me**)

19. Not Withstanding Rule

There are apparent exceptions to many rules. However the apparent exceptions are often misinterpretations through choice of fonts or characters that have so many strokes that in a small sized font you cannot see the definition of the individual

[Type text]

strokes. (**R#67**, 文, **wén**, **script**) appear to offend rule #17, **Dots and Minor Strokes Last**. It does follow the rule however of completion of radicals within a character and the first stroke (点, **diǎn**, **dot**) is part of the Radical (**R#8**, 亠, **tóu**, **lid**).

R#97, 瓜, **guā**, **melon** may appear to have a stroke selection of **H-P** or **H-WP** for the first two strokes. However, the first two strokes are not the **Radical R#27**, 厂, **hàn**, **cliff** but rather **PP-WP**. Despite trying four different fonts, 瓜 瓜 瓜 瓜, the proper strokes cannot be seen until you increase the size of the character.

瓜

(**R#26**, 卩, **jié**, **seal**) is another example of an apparent exception. On casual inspection it may look like **HZ-H-S**. The stroke order is in fact **HZG-S**. If one was to follow rule # 14. **Down Box Rules**, it would be easy to assume that **S** is the first stroke. Again, font selection demonstrates the correct strokes. 卩 卩 卩 卩 In fact, some fonts make it look like Radical (**R# 13**, 冂, **jiǒng**, **down box**) 卩 卩 卩.

Hanzi characters are built up from basic strokes. The simplest characters have only one stroke while the more complex ones can have more than 60 strokes. You will find in the workbook below some Hanzi characters and the most common basic strokes in Hanzi. The strokes must be written in the right order and in the right direction. It is important to follow those rules. If you always write a character the same way you will develop a memorized pattern for how to write it. The character will also look much more symmetrical and be reproducible if you follow the rules. Proportions are very important so you have to have it in mind when you write.

[Type text]

Often a stroke can be altered to look more aesthetically pleasing in a character. If you look at the character for (学, **xué**, **study**), you find a character with a group of two (点, **diǎn**, **dot**) strokes on top and one **DP**. The two to the left are written angled from left to right while the last one is written angled from right to left. This is made to make the character more visually appealing.

学 学 学 学 学 学 学

The same occurs if you have many (横, 一, **héng**, **H**, **horizontal stroke**) in a character such as in the character (三, **sān**, **three**). In this example it is three **héng** and they are all different sizes.

However, in characters such as (士, **shì**, **scholar**) and (土, **tǔ**, **dirt**) the proportion of stroke length does have meaning. The upper (横, 一, **héng**, **H**,) stroke of (士, **shì**, **scholar**) is longer that the base **héng**. In the character (土, **tǔ**, **dirt**), the top most **héng** is shorter and this is what defines the difference between the two characters.

Certain strokes such as (折, **zhé**, **break**) and (钩, **gōu**, **left down hook**) never occur alone, but are components in compound strokes. Thus, they are not in themselves individual strokes. (折, **zhé**, **break**) is often described as a right angle turn but it often is not as in (也, **yě**, **also**) which has the compound character stroke (**横折鈎**, **Héng Zhé Gōu**, 𠃌) also seen as right-angled as in (刀, **Dāo**, **knife**). Other named components give *character* to names strokes by modifying their curvature or slope.

[Type text]

The Six Single Strokes

横, **Héng**, **H**, **Horizontal**, 一, is a horizontal or near horizontal stroke. It is drawn from the left to the right. As you can see with the character (三, **sān**, **three**) and angled in (七, **qī**, **seven**).

竖, **Shù**, **S**, **Line**, ｜, is a vertical or near vertical top to bottom stroke. You can clearly see this is the character (中, **zhōng**, **middle**). However, in the character (五, **wǔ**, **five**) it is it is leaning to the right.

提, **Tí**, **T**, **Flick**, ⁄, is a left to right *flick* stroke at an upward and variable angle. It is drawn from the left to the right. As you can see in the example (玫, **méi**, **rose**) it rises slightly from the left to the right.

捺, **Nà**, **N**, **Press Down**, ⟍, is a left to right falling arc stroke at a 45 degree angle. It has a small concavity. In many electronic fonts it appears as a line and loses the brush stroke character.

撇, **Piě**, **P**, **Slash**, ⁄, is a right to left falling slash stroke at a 45 degree angle. It has a small concavity. In many electronic fonts it appears as a line and loses the brush stroke character.

点, **Diǎn**, **D**, **Dot**, ⟍, is a *dot* falling from the left to the right with a convexity. In many electronic fonts it appears as a line with no tear drop like character.

[Type text]

Stroke Variations and Additives

鉤, **Gōu**, **G**, **Hook**, ⌐ ⌐, is a *hook* that is added to 6 other strokes to create the compound strokes; **HG**, **SG**, **PG**, **WG**, **XG**, **BXG**. It is not a named stroke by its self.

折, **Zhé**, **Z**, **Break**, ⌐ indicates a right angle or near angle change in direction. It is not a stroke but is used to describe the transition from (横, 一, **Héng**, **H**) to (横折, **Héng Zhé**, **HZ**, ⌐).

折, **Zhé**, **Z**, **Break**, ∟ indicates a right angle or near angle change in direction. It is not a stroke but is used as a descriptive to describe the transition from (竖, **Shù**, **S**) to (竖折, **Shù Zhé**, **SZ**).

短撇, **Duǎn Piě**, **DP**, **Short Slash**, ノ is a short variant of 撇, **Piě**. In this book, in a character with multiple variants of the stroke (撇, **Piě**, ノ), the shorter will be called **DP**.

平撇, **Píng Piě**, **PP**, **Flat Slash**, is a flattened stroke seen on the top of characters. It is a flattened version of 撇, **Piě**. It can be mistaken for (横, **Héng**) with some fonts.

右点, **Yòu Diǎn**, **YD**, **Right Dot**, is the most common variation of (点, **Diǎn**, **Dot**). It is not commonly referred to as (右点, **Yòu Diǎn**) but simply as (点, **Diǎn**, **Dot**).

[Type text]

左点, **Zuǒ Diǎn**, **ZD**, **Left Dot**, is a right to left falling concave dot. It is a mirror image inverse reflection of the right handed (右点, **Yòu Diǎn**, **right dot**).

长点, **Cháng Diǎn**, **CD**, **Long Dot** is the long dot seen as a long convex arc. It occurs in characters such as (这, **zhè**, **this**). As characters are scaled up **D** loses its dot shape and becomes **CD**

扁斜, **Biǎn Xié**, **BX**, is a curve flattening trait seen in one stroke (扁斜鉤, **Biǎn Xié Gōu**, ⌣). (扁, **biǎn**, **flat**) and (斜, **xié**, **slanting**) combine to form this trait.

直提, **Zhí Tí**, **ZT** is an upright version of (提, **Tí**).

点提, **Diǎn Tí**, **DT**, retains brush stroke character and is an alternative 提, **Tí**. It is formed by making (右点, **Yòu Diǎn**, **right dot**) then an uprising **T**.

短撇长点, **Duǎn Piě Cháng Diǎn**, **DPCD** is the same character stroke as (撇点, **Piě Diǎn**, **PD**). This alternate name is offered to provide a better sense of proportion.

弯, **Wān**, **W**, is a right to left falling slightly concave stroke.

Compound Strokes

竪鈎, **Shù Gōu**, **SG**, 亅 is a vertical down stroke with a hook to the left.

點捺, **Diǎn Nà**, **DN** is seen only in the character (入, **rù**, **to enter**) and its derivatives. It can be mistaken for (提捺, **Tí Nà**).

平捺, **Píng Nà**, **PN** is a left to right flattened falling stroke. It is a flattened version of 捺, Nà. It is seen as the underlining stroke in characters as above.

提捺, **Tí Nà**, **TN** can be confused with 点捺, **Diǎn Nà** as in (入, **rù**, enter).

提平捺, **Tí Píng Nà**, **TPN** occurs as an under stroke as demonstrated. 㕯

橫折, **Héng Zhé**, **HZ** is a right angle or near right angle turn from (橫, **Héng**, **H**, **Horizontal**)

横撇, **Héng Piě**, **HP** exists as a compound stroke and can be confused with **H-P**.

横鈎, **Héng Gōu**, **HG** is often seen at the top of a character as **Diǎn - Héng Gōu**, ⁃.

竖折, **Shù Zhé**, **SZ** has a right angle turn and can be confused with 竖弯, **Shù Wān** which has a curved transition versus a right angle transition.

竖弯, **Shù Wān**, **SW** has a smooth turn and can be mistaken for (竖折, **Shù Zhé**, **SZ**).

竖提, **Shù Tí**, **ST**. The (提, **Tí**, **T**, **Flick**, ⸝) component can be proportionally different lengths compared to (竖, **Shù**, **S**, **Line**, ｜) component.

竖折, **Shù Piě**, **SP** is a vertical down stroke with a 45 degree tail to the left.

弯撇, **Wān Piě**, **WP** differs from (竖撇, **Shù Piě**) in the non-vertical initial stroke. Characters described as (撇, **Piě**, **P**) often are in fact (弯撇, **Wān Piě**, **WP**).

[Type text]

撇折, **Piě Zhé**, **PZ**, the (折, **Zhé**, **Z**) stroke is horizontal and longer than the stroke (提, **Tí**, **T**) in (竖提, **Shù Tí**, **ST**). ㇊ vs ㇏.

撇點, **Piě Diǎn**, **PD**

撇鈎, **Piě Gōu**, **PG** is a very rare stroke.

弯鈎, **Wān Gōu**, **WG** is characterized by the top portion of the stroke being to the left of the apex of the curve that occurs in the vertical plane.

斜鈎, **Xié Gōu**, **XG**

扁斜鈎, **Biǎn Xié Gōu**, **BXG** is the flattened character stroke (斜鈎, **Xié Gōu**, **XG**) as seen in (心, **xīn**, **heart**) versus the stroke in (心, **xīn**, **heart**).

竖弯左, **Shù Wān Zuǒ**, **SWZ** differs from the compound stroke (竖折, **Shù Piě**, **SP**) in that the tail is not as acutely deviating from the vertical.

竖折折, **Shù Zhé Zhé**, **SZZ**

竖折撇, **Shù Zhé Piě**, **SZP**

竖折鉤, **Shù Zhé Gōu**, **SZG**

竖折弯鉤, **Shù Zhé Wān Gōu**, **SZWG** is a brush stroke variant of (竖折鉤, **Shù Zhé Gōu**, **SZG**).

横撇弯, **Héng Piě Wān**, **HPW**

横折折, **Héng Zhé Zhé**, **HZZ**

横折弯, **Héng Zhé Wān**, **HZW** differs from the compound stroke (横折折, **Héng Zhé Zhé**, **HZZ**) in that the transition from vertical to horizontal is curved versus a right angle.

[Type text]

横折提, **Héng Zhé Tí**, **HZT**

┐ 横折鉤, **Héng Zhé Gōu**, **HZG**

┐ 横折弯鉤, **Héng Zhé Wān Gōu**, **HZWG** is a brush stroke variant of (横折鉤, **Héng Zhé Gōu**, **HZG**).

乚 横斜鉤, **Héng Xié Gōu**, **HXG**

㇉ 横折折折, **Héng Zhé Zhé Zhé**, **HZZZ**

㇋ 横折折撇, **Héng Zhé Zhé Piě**, **HZZP**

 横折折弯鉤, **Héng Zhé Zhé Wān Gōu**, **HZZWG** is a variant of (**R#5**, 乙, **yǐ**, **second**).

横撇弯鈎, **Héng Piě Wān Gōu, HPWG**

竖折折鈎, **Shù Zhé Zhé Gōu, SZZG**

竖折折弯鈎, **Shù Zhé Zhé Wān Gōu, SZZWG** is a brush stroke variant of (竖折折鈎, **Shù Zhé Zhé Gōu, SZZG**).

横撇折弯鈎, **Héng Piě Zhé Wān Gōu, HPZWG** as a Radical is (**R#5**, 乙, **yǐ, second**). This stroke is often called **HZWG**.

横折折弯鈎, **Héng Zhé Zhé Wān Gōu, HZZWG**

圈, **Quān, Q** is an extraordinarily rare stroke.

[Type text]

Exercise for Individual Strokes

This is the introduction to practical stroke and character writing in this book. Using the templates provided you can directly trace over the strokes. Alternately you can photocopy or use a clear acetate sheet and a wipe-off marker. Equally important is to recite the Pinyin word and tone. In the appendix you will find a section on pronunciation and tone.

Pick groups of five to ten sheets to practice by doing one character on each sheet and then going to the next. If you simply write over an entire page while watching television you may find that you flip the page over and do not remember any of it.

Once you have mastered the simple strokes and stroke additives, then it is time to move on to compound strokes. Try and stick to logical groups of strokes rather than randomly picking appealing strokes. For example, learn all the compound strokes that start with (横, **héng**, **H**, **horizontal**, 一) then move on to all the compound strokes with (竖, **shù**, **S**, **vertical line**, 丨).

The first 15 work sheets are the most important as the entire written language is built upon compounding and compiling these most basic units. Like all learning, set reasonable objectives. As your skills develop, you will see that more complex characters require balancing the proportions of different radicals to make the result esthetically pleasing.

Radicals are compilations of one or more strokes. The higher you go through the numbered Radical list the more the Radical is a composite of previous Radicals and additional strokes.

[Type text]

横	Notes: (横, héng, H, horizontal, 一)
héng H	

一	一	一	一	一	一	一	一	一	一
héng H	héng H	héng H	héng H	héng H	héng H	héng H	héng H	héng H	héng H
一	一	一	一	一	一	一	一	一	一
héng H	héng H	héng H	héng H	héng H	héng H	héng H	héng H	héng H	héng H
一	一	一							
一	一	一							
一	一	一							
一	一	一							
一	一	一							
一	一	一							
一	一	一							
一	一	一							

竖

shù
S

Notes:

(竖, shù, S, vertical line, 丨)

提

Notes:

(提, tí, T, flick, ✓)

tí / T

撇

piě / P

Notes:
(撇, piě, P, slash, ノ)

捺

nà
N

Notes:

(捺, nà, N, press down, ㇏)

点
diǎn
D

Notes:

(点, diǎn, D, dot, 丶)

鉤	Notes: (鉤, **gōu**, **G**, **hook**) is added as an accessory to other strokes.
gōu **G**	

zhé
Z

Notes:

(折, **Zhé**, **Z**, **break**, ㄱㄴ) indicates a right angle or near right angle change in direction. It is not a stroke but is used as a descriptive to describe the transition from one linear stroke to another.

短	撇	Notes:
duǎn	piě	(**短撇**, **duǎn piě**, **DP**) The difference between this stroke and (**撇**, **piě**, **P**, **slash**, ノ) is only in scale proportionate to the character. In this book **DP** will be marked when it is ½ or less of the character height or unmatched to **N**.
D	P	

píng	piě
P	P

Notes:

(平撇, **píng piě**, **PP**, **flat slash**) is a flattened version of (撇, **piě**) seen on the top of characters. It can be mistaken for (横, **héng**, **H**) with some fonts.

右	点	Notes:
yòu	diǎn	(右点, **yòu diǎn**, **right dot**, **YD**) is the most common variation of (点, **diǎn**, **dot**). It is not commonly referred to as (右点, **yòu diǎn**) but simply as (点, **diǎn**, **D**).
Y	D	

A practice sheet for writing the 右点 (yòu diǎn) stroke.

zuǒ	diǎn	Notes:
	点	(左点, **zuǒ diǎn**, **left dot**, **ZD**) is a right to left falling concave dot.
Z	**D**	

ZD	ZD	ZD	ZD	ZD	ZD	ZD	ZD	ZD	ZD
ZD	ZD	ZD	ZD	ZD	ZD	ZD	ZD	ZD	ZD

[Type text]

cháng	diǎn
C	D

Notes:

(长点, **cháng diǎn**, **long dot**, **CD**) is a elongated version of the (右点, **yòu diǎn**, **right dot**, **D**)

直	提	Notes:
zhí	tí	(直提, **zhí tí**, **ZT**) is an upright version of the stroke (提, **Tí**, **T**).
Z	**T**	

点	提	Notes:
diǎn	tí	(点提, **diǎn tí**, **DT**) retains brush stroke character and is an alternate (提, **Tí**).
D	**T**	

短	撇	长	点	Notes:
duǎn	piě	cháng	diǎn	
D	P	C	D	

〈 〈 〈 〈 〈 〈 〈 〈 〈

〈	〈	〈	〈	〈	〈	〈	〈	〈	〈
DPCD	DPCD	DPCD	DPCD	DPCD	DPCD	DPCD	DPCD	DPCD	DPCD
〈	〈	〈	〈	〈	〈	〈	〈	〈	〈
DPCD	DPCD	DPCD	DPCD	DPCD	DPCD	DPCD	DPCD	DPCD	DPCD

竖鈎

(竖鈎, shù gōu, SG, 亅)

shù — S
gōu — G

竖	撇	Notes:
shù	piě	(竖撇, **shù piě**, **SP**, ﻝ) has an initial vertical component to the stroke.
S	P	

ﻝ	ﻝ	ﻝ	ﻝ	ﻝ	ﻝ	ﻝ	ﻝ		
ﻝ	ﻝ	ﻝ	ﻝ	ﻝ	ﻝ	ﻝ	ﻝ	ﻝ	ﻝ
SP	SP	SP	SP	SP	SP	SP	SP	SP	SP
ﻝ	ﻝ	ﻝ	ﻝ	ﻝ	ﻝ	ﻝ	ﻝ	ﻝ	ﻝ
SP	SP	SP	SP	SP	SP	SP	SP	SP	SP
ﻝ	ﻝ	ﻝ	ﻝ	ﻝ					
ﻝ	ﻝ	ﻝ	ﻝ	ﻝ					
ﻝ	ﻝ	ﻝ	ﻝ	ﻝ					
ﻝ	ﻝ	ﻝ	ﻝ	ﻝ					
ﻝ	ﻝ	ﻝ	ﻝ	ﻝ					
ﻝ	ﻝ	ﻝ	ﻝ	ﻝ					
ﻝ	ﻝ	ﻝ	ﻝ	ﻝ					
ﻝ	ﻝ	ﻝ	ﻝ	ﻝ					

平	捺	Notes:
píng	nà	(平捺, píng nà, PN) is a left to right flattened falling stroke. It is a flattened version of (捺, nà). It is seen as the underlining stroke in characters.
P	N	

⌣ ⌣ ⌣ ⌣ ⌣ ⌣ ⌣ ⌣ ⌣ ⌣

⌣	⌣	⌣	⌣	⌣	⌣	⌣	⌣	⌣	⌣
PN	PN	PN	PN	PN	PN	PN	PN	PN	PN
⌣	⌣	⌣	⌣	⌣	⌣	⌣	⌣	⌣	⌣
PN	PN	PN	PN	PN	PN	PN	PN	PN	PN
⌣	⌣	⌣	⌣	⌣	⌣	⌣	⌣	⌣	⌣
⌣	⌣	⌣	⌣	⌣	⌣	⌣	⌣	⌣	⌣
⌣	⌣	⌣	⌣	⌣	⌣	⌣	⌣	⌣	⌣
⌣	⌣	⌣	⌣	⌣	⌣	⌣	⌣	⌣	⌣
⌣	⌣	⌣	⌣	⌣	⌣	⌣	⌣	⌣	⌣
⌣	⌣	⌣	⌣	⌣	⌣	⌣	⌣	⌣	⌣
⌣	⌣	⌣	⌣	⌣	⌣	⌣	⌣	⌣	⌣
⌣	⌣	⌣	⌣	⌣	⌣	⌣	⌣	⌣	⌣

提	捺	Notes: (提捺, **Tí Nà**, **TN**) is a rare stroke.
tí	nà	
T	N	

提	平	捺	Notes: (提平捺, **Tí Píng Nà**, **TPN**) occurs as an under stroke as demonstrated. 心
tí	píng	nà	
T	P	N	

点	捺	Notes:
diǎn	nà	(點捺, **diǎn nà**, **DN**) is a very rare stroke.
D	N	

横	折	Notes:
héng	zhé	(横折, **Héng Zhé**, **HZ** is a right angle or near right angle turn from (横, **Héng**, **H**, **Horizontal**)
H	Z	

横	撇	Notes: (横撇, Héng Piě, HP)
héng H	piě P	

フ フ フ フ フ フ フ フ フ フ

フ	フ	フ	フ	フ	フ	フ	フ	フ	フ
HP	HP	HP	HP	HP	HP	HP	HP	HP	HP

フ	フ	フ	フ	フ	フ	フ	フ	フ	フ
HP	HP	HP	HP	HP	HP	HP	HP	HP	HP

フ	フ	フ	フ	フ	フ	フ	フ	フ	フ
フ	フ	フ	フ	フ	フ	フ	フ	フ	フ
フ	フ	フ	フ	フ	フ	フ	フ	フ	フ
フ	フ	フ	フ	フ	フ	フ	フ	フ	フ
フ	フ	フ	フ	フ	フ	フ	フ	フ	フ
フ	フ	フ	フ	フ	フ	フ	フ	フ	フ
フ	フ	フ	フ	フ	フ	フ	フ	フ	フ
フ	フ	フ	フ	フ	フ	フ	フ	フ	フ
フ	フ	フ	フ	フ	フ	フ	フ	フ	フ

[Type text]

橫	鉤	Notes:
héng	gōu	(橫鉤, Héng Gōu, HG) is often seen at the top of a character as Diǎn - Héng Gōu, ⁀.
H	G	

竖	折	Notes:
shù	zhé	(竖折, **Shù Zhé**, **SZ**) has a right angle turn and can be confused with 竖弯, **Shù Wān** which has a curved transition versus a right angle transition.
S	Z	

Practice rows: SZ

竖	弯	Notes:
shù	**wān**	(竖弯, **shù wān**, **SW**) has a curved transition from the vertical stroke versus **SZ** which is a right angle.
S	**W**	

Practice grid for the stroke 竖弯 (SW).

竖提

shù (S) **tí** (T)

(竖提, Shù Tí, ST)

Notes:

撇折

piě P | **zhé** Z

Notes:
(撇折, Piě Zhé, PZ)

撇 点

piě P | **diǎn** D

(撇點, Piě Diǎn, PD)

撇	鈎	Notes: (撇鈎, **Piě Gōu**, **PG**) is a very rare stroke.
piě	gōu	
P	**G**	

wān	gōu
W	G

Notes:

(弯鉤, **Wān Gōu**, **WG**) is characterized by the top portion of the stroke being to the left of the apex of the curve that occurs in the vertical plane.

弯	撇	Notes:
wān	piě	(弯撇, **wān piě**, **WP**) differs from a similar stroke (竖撇, **shù piě**, **SP**, ノ) in that the initial stroke is non vertical. They are both used interchangeably in many characters without changing meaning.
W	**P**	

斜	鉤	Notes: (斜鉤, Xié Gōu, XG)
xié	gōu	
X	G	

扁	斜	鈎	Notes:
biǎn	xié	gōu	(扁斜鈎, biǎn xié gōu, ⌣) is seen in (心, xīn, heart).
B	X	G	

竖	弯	左	Notes:
shù	wān	zuǒ	(竖弯左, **Shù Wān Zuǒ**) differs from (竖折, **Shù Piě**, **SP**) in that the tail is not as bent from the vertical.
S	W	Z	

竖	折	折	Notes: (竖折折, Shù Zhé Zhé, SZZ)
shù	zhé	zhé	
S	Z	Z	

竖	折	撇	Notes: (竖折撇, Shù Zhé Piě, SZP)
shù	zhé	piě	
S	Z	P	

竖	折	鉤	Notes:
shù	zhé	gōu	(竖折鉤, **Shù Zhé Gōu, SZG**)
S	Z	G	

竖	折	弯	鉤	Notes: SZWG
shù	zhé	wān	gōu	
S	Z	W	G	

横 折 折

Notes:

(横折折, Héng Zhé Zhé, HZZ)

héng	zhé	zhé
H	Z	Z

横	折	弯	Notes: (横折弯, **Héng Zhé Wān**, **HZW**)
héng H	zhé Z	wān W	

横	折	提	Notes: (横折提, Héng Zhé Tí, HZT)
héng	zhé	tí	
H	Z	T	

橫 折 鉤

héng — H
zhé — Z
gōu — G

Notes:
(橫折鉤, Héng Zhé Gōu, HZG)

橫	斜	鉤	Notes: (橫斜鉤, Héng Xié Gōu, HXG)
héng H	xié X	gōu G	

HXG practice sheet

横	折	折	折	Notes: HZZZ
héng H	zhé Z	zhé Z	zhé Z	

横	折	折	撇	Notes: HZZP
héng H	zhé Z	zhé Z	piě P	

HZZP HZZP HZZP HZZP HZZP HZZP HZZP HZZP HZZP HZZP

HZZP HZZP HZZP HZZP HZZP HZZP HZZP HZZP HZZP HZZP

横	折	弯	鈎	Notes: HZWG
héng	zhé	wān	gōu	
H	Z	W	G	

横	撇	弯	鉤	Note: HPWG
héng	piě	wān	gōu	
H	P	W	G	

ㄋ ㄋ ㄋ ㄋ ㄋ ㄋ ㄋ ㄋ ㄋ

ㄋ	ㄋ	ㄋ	ㄋ	ㄋ	ㄋ	ㄋ	ㄋ	ㄋ	ㄋ
HPWG	HPWG	HPWG	HPWG	HPWG	HPWG	HPWG	HPWG	HPWG	HPWG
ㄋ	ㄋ	ㄋ	ㄋ	ㄋ	ㄋ	ㄋ	ㄋ	ㄋ	ㄋ
HPWG	HPWG	HPWG	HPWG	HPWG	HPWG	HPWG	HPWG	HPWG	HPWG

[Type text]

竖折折鉤

shù	zhé	zhé	gōu	
S	Z	Z	G	SZZG

Notes: SZZG

竖	折	折	弯	鉤
shù	zhé	zhé	wān	gōu
S	Z	Z	W	G

ㄅ ㄅ ㄅ ㄅ ㄅ ㄅ ㄅ ㄅ ㄅ

ㄅ	ㄅ	ㄅ	ㄅ	ㄅ	ㄅ	ㄅ	ㄅ	ㄅ	ㄅ
SZZWG	SZZWG	SZZWG	SZZWG	SZZWG	SZZWG	SZZWG	SZZWG	SZZWG	SZZWG
ㄅ	ㄅ	ㄅ	ㄅ	ㄅ	ㄅ	ㄅ	ㄅ	ㄅ	ㄅ
SZZWG	SZZWG	SZZWG	SZZWG	SZZWG	SZZWG	SZZWG	SZZWG	SZZWG	SZZWG

[Type text]

横	撇	折	弯	鉤
héng	piě	zhé	wān	gōu
H	P	Z	W	G

乙 乙 乙 乙 乙 乙 乙 乙

乙	乙	乙	乙	乙	乙	乙	乙	乙	乙
HPZWG	HPZWG	HPZWG	HPZWG	HPZWG	HPZWG	HPZWG	HPZWG	HPZWG	HPZWG
乙	乙	乙	乙	乙	乙	乙	乙	乙	乙
HPZWG	HPZWG	HPZWG	HPZWG	HPZWG	HPZWG	HPZWG	HPZWG	HPZWG	HPZWG

橫	折	折	彎	鉤
héng	zhé	zhé	wān	gōu
H	Z	Z	W	G

HZZWG

圈

quān
circle

Notes:

(圈, **quān**, **Q**) This is a very rare stroke. It is not seen in Chinese character sets.

Eight Principles of Yong

Yǒng

(永字八法, **Yǒngzì Bā Fǎ**, **Eternity Character Eight Method**)
There is a stream of explanation in classical Chinese literature that explains how to write the eight strokes common in Chinese characters. These strokes are all found in the one character (永, **yǒng**, **eternity**). It was believed that the frequent practice of these principles as a beginner calligrapher could ensure beauty in one's writing.

The direction and shape of these strokes originate from the use of a brush with soft hair bristles and black ink. The brush was held vertical between the first three fingers. Calligraphy is the art of drawing characters. Much can be learned from buying a bottle of ink and a brush. However, buy a large sheet of plastic to put under your work. I spent about two dollars in China for a large bottle of ink and a brush and did about $1,000.00 damage when I spilled it. There is a hotel owner in **Yuping** who is very angry. The ink will also penetrate most cheap paper so you may want to get a sheet of cardboard to put under your paper or a blotter sheet. If you can find a **Hero 99** pen or a refillable **Emporer Dragon 801**, they are excellent as they have a soft tapered synthetic tip. Also available but harder to find are fountain type pens with ink cartridges and similar soft tips that deform with pressure. They are mess free and the cartridges are inexpensive. Your Chinese friends may tell you to practice with a pencil. Forget it, they can alter the colour and the shape of the stroke by varying the pressure on the pencil or pen by moving it several thousandths of an inch. They have been doing it since they were infants, they have written millions of characters and they have better dexterity than you have.

1) (右点, **Yòu Diǎn, right dot**), the short downwards left to right convex stroke, is formed by drawing the brush toward the writer left to right in a downward arc. On the shortest strokes, it will look like a teardrop shape in which the brush is pushed into the page. The convex shape is hard to achieve with short strokes. On smaller characters, you simply push the brush down and pull it toward yourself with no draw of the tip.

2) (横, **Héng, horizontal**), the horizontal stroke is a varied stroke. The thickness is maintained by moving the wrist horizontally with no downward deflection. You will often see an ending flourish on various type fonts. This is a reflection of the history of **Hanzi** in which stamps

were carved in wood and the small notch at the end of the stroke kept the wooden block from splitting with repeated use.

3) (竖, **Shù**, **vertical**), the vertical down stroke, is a straight draw toward the writer. The thickness is varied by down pressure that comes at the beginning of the stroke. Any variations in down pressure result in uneven thickness of the line.

4) (鉤, **Gōu**, **hook**), the hook, exists as an addition to several strokes. It is formed by a flick of the writing instrument. The tip of the brush must be raised to get a sharp point. The direction of the stroke varies with the primary stroke it is attached to, either down or to the left.

5) (提, **Tí**, **to lift**), the left to right rising tapering stroke. This stroke is formed by a rising flick with a lift of the brush. This achieves the taper on the right tail of the stroke.

6) (弯, **Wān**, **bent**), describes a smooth curve. Although it is seen to exist standing alone in this classic character description, it is seldom seen in modern Hanzi. It is most often used to describe a curved transition.

7) (撇, **Piě**, **throw away**), the downwards right to left curved stroke is formed by drawing the brush initially down and to the left in a near flat rising arc at 45 degrees. A lift of the brush gives a tapered tail.

8) (捺, **Nà**, **press down firmly**), the downwards left to right up curved stroke is formed by drawing the brush toward and to the right of the writer. The brush follows a small flat rising arc to create a concave shape by pushing the brush away from the writer as it travels.

[Type text]

Guide to Pronunciation

If you become obsessed with the perfect pronunciation, grammar and tone of Standard Mandarin, your efforts will be in vain. You will be the only one in China and the world speaking it. A native English speaker from Hamilton, Ontario, where perfect English is spoken, can understand a man from England, Scotland, Australia, Newfoundland, East India and Nigeria. As long as you get close with Mandarin, an authentic Chinese friend can fine tune you. You will find that in China the pronunciation varies as much as the food and geography of China does. In fact you will find that as soon as you write a Hanzi character or speak Mandarin an enthusiastic smiling throng of proud Chinese will descend upon you to assist you. One of the more distressing things I have discovered is the inconsistency in different published books about the pronunciation of Pinyin.

Pinyin vowels are pronounced similarly to vowels in Roman alphabet languages and most consonants are similar to English. A pitfall for native English speakers is, however, the unusual pronunciation of *x*, *q*, *c*, *zh*, *sh* and *z* and sometimes *i* and the unvoiced portion of the pronunciation of *d*, *b*, *g*, and *j*. This will be detailed below.

The pronunciation of Pinyin is broken into Initials and Finals. Initials are initial consonants or vowels in a phoneme, while Finals are all possible combinations of consonants and vowels that form the ending of the word, hence the term **Finals**.

What Defines a Chinese Word?

Words used to describe English grammar do not entirely work for Chinese grammar. A word in Hanzi / Hanyu is not necessarily one character. Some characters do not have a distinct meaning and must be bound to one or more other characters to give them meaning. These are described as **Bound Morphemes**.

[Type text]

Morpheme

In English, a morpheme is the smallest unit of meaning. For example, the *s* added to a noun to make it plural is a morpheme. It has meaning and is indivisible. If a Chinese character does not have meaning, it is not a morpheme. However, Chinese language is all characters. There are no *s* equivalents to add to a character. Adding another stroke to a character creates a different character. A morpheme in Chinese grammar is thus enough characters to give meaning and cannot be broken down to give a different meaning. But it can be more than one character.

With this definition, many characters stand alone as having meaning and are thus morphemes and also words. Some words then are minimally two characters. A Chinese word is one or more characters combined to have meaning.

Phoneme

Pinyin is a system of assigning sounds or phonemes written with the Roman English alphabet to assign a standardized sound to each character. The sounds however are not unique. Each character has a unique appearance, defined by the placement of strokes that are used to make it. Each Pinyin sound word is assigned to many characters. It is more like assigning part numbers to inventory than it is a language. Because Pinyin does not have uniqueness of meaning, it is not a language; you cannot effectively communicate in Pinyin. You can use it to study the pronunciation of Chinese characters.

The compilation of phonemes of Pinyin parallels the words of Hanzi. If two characters are put together to create a Chinese word, then two Pinyin phonemes are put together to create a Pinyin sound word. If four characters are put together to create a Chinese word, then the four corresponding sound words are put together to create a Pinyin sound word. However, as Chinese characters are currently written, there are no space breaks between characters. Reading the Pinyin can help you determine which Chinese characters are compiled together to create multi-character words.

It is always important to remember the mathematical difficulty of writing a sentence using Pinyin. If you have 4 sound words that each are assigned to 10 different characters, you have 10,000 possible character combinations. If you think that you can write in Hanyu Pinyin as a language I assure you I can write a sentence in which it is necessary to use a computer to plot the multitude of different translations. This is why you will read about the difference in written versus spoken grammar and sentence construction. The choice of words used to speak is much less than the choice of words used to write due to the confusion of homophones.

Homophones

A homophone is a sound that is unique yet has more than one meaning. In English, eight-ate, great-grate and lie-lye are all paired homophones. Each pairing sounds the same but has different meanings. There are about 70,000 Chinese characters. Yet there are only about 1500 unique sounds to represent them. This means that one sound can represent many characters, dozens sometimes. This has many implications. Mandarin is a spoken representation of Chinese characters. It is spoken differently than it is written. Writing gives much greater opportunity to use a broad range of characters that spoken would be confused with others. One does not have to worry about chose of words when writing.

Speaking is another matter. Every spoken sound has different meanings. The context of the conversation and what has been spoken before gives great assistance to the listener. Of necessity, the vocabulary of speaking is limited. It is possible to say something that written would be easy to understand but spoken would be indecipherable.

The advantage of this is that you can learn to communicate with a very small number of spoken words in Mandarin. The difficulty is understanding someone who has a greater vocabulary. The mythical Standard Mandarin is precise but you can create grammatically correct sentences that just are not commonly used. This is why the most common expression in China may be;

请写下来
Qǐng xiě xiàlái.
Please write down.

Initials

(声母, **shēng mǔ**, **initial sound**)

Pronunciation of Initials

Initials are the consonants that form the beginning of Hanyu Pinyin words. Fine tuning can only occur in a region specific context. The ***she b00 sh**e* (是不是, **shì bù shì**, **is not is**) of Beijing becomes ***see buh see*** of Chengdu. While you are trying to get a Mandarin speaker to slow down you have to gauge their neutral tone, make adjustments for ethnic and geographic phonetic drift and figure out the dozens of meanings for each identical sounding word, good luck.

Just as an Englishman, an Australian and a Scotsman can understand each other, even though their accents vary, you will be able to adjust and understand various accents in Hanyu, eventually, maybe. In many books, you will find the Initial and Finals grouped according to where your tongue is in your mouth and whether you are leaking air up your nose. I encourage you to group the Initials as to how it makes most sense to you.

[Type text]

Pinyin	Explanation
b	As in English, un-aspirated *p*, as in *spit*, examples *b*ig, *b*ad, *b*one.
p	As in English, aspirated *p*, as in *pi*, examples *p*it, *p*athetic, *p*ortrait.
m	As in English, examples *m*an, *m*aw, *m*ow, *m*aul.
f	As in English, examples *f*ind, *f*eel, *f*ord.
d	As in English, examples *d*ig, *d*uffle, *d*oubt.
t	As in English, examples *t*ime, *t*empo, *t*art.
n	As in English, examples *n*o, *n*ight, *n*ever.
l	As in English, examples *l*eft, *l*ime, *l*over.
g	As in English, examples *g*ay, *g*ive, *g*ore.
k	As in English, examples *k*ill, *k*ick, *k*iss.
h	As in English, if followed by an *a*, otherwise, like the *ch* in *loch*.
j	As in English, almost, this exact sound is not used in English, the closest match is the *j* in *ajar*, examples *j*ing, *j*ittery, *J*esus.

q   Like the *ch* in *church*, examples *ch*urch, *ch*ess, *ch*est.

x   Like the *sh* in *shy*, examples *sh*ower, *sh*ade, *sh*iver.

zh   As in English, with no aspiration, the tongue is curled back on the roof of the mouth, retroflexed. Examples fu*dge*, ju*dge*, gru*dge*.

ch   As in English as in *chin*, but with the tongue curled back on the roof of the mouth. Very similar to the *tu* of *nurture* but strongly aspirated.

sh   As in English, as in *shinbone*, but with the tongue curled back on the roof of the mouth, retroflexed, very similar to under*sh*irt.

r   As in English as in *rank*, but with the lips spread and with the tongue curled back on the roof of the mouth, retroflexed. Examples, *pleasure*, *treasure*.

z   As in the English, examples, su*ds*, bu*ds*, du*ds*.

c   As in English *cats*, examples ma*ts*, ba*ts*, ra*ts*.

s   As in English, examples *s*un, *s*ow, *s*ung, *s*ong.

w   As in English, examples *w*ay, *w*hy, *w*ind.

y   As in English, examples *y*es, *y*ellow, *y*et. Exception *yi* as *ēē*.

[Type text]

The only two-consonant Initials are *zh*, *sh* and *ch*. There are 11 Pinyin with no Initial consonant. They are *a*, *ai*, *ao*, *an*, *ang*, *o*, *ou*, *e*, *ei*, *en*, and *er*. Please note that none of these start with *i*, *u*, or *ü*. There are special and unnecessary rules for these.

In this table above I have put 23 Initials. Many books would disagree with this and would not include *w* and *y*. Some books say there are 21 Initials and a *zero* Initial. The *zero* Initial is put in front of phonemes that begin with an *i*, *u* or *ü*. So you are to pretend that there is a silent and invisible letter in front of the phoneme because some anal linguist cannot stand the thought of a consonant and vowel having the same sound.

The almighty and great reference Li and Thompson (1981) says that there are 22 Initials yet their table shows 21 so they must attribute an invisible and silent consonant in absentia. Hopefully one day someone will logically reference the great and mighty (大毛猴子, **Dà Máo Hóuzi**, **Big Hairy Monkey**) and point out that there are 23.

[Type text]

Finals

(韵母, **yùn mǔ**, **final sound**)

Pronunciation of Finals

Finals are the vowels and vowel consonant combinations that are the ending of Pinyin phonemes. Several of these sounds do not correspond directly to sounds in English. If you agonize over a perfect pronunciation, you will find it varies immensely in China. The assumption is that you speak a neutral tone English such as would be spoken in the province of Ontario in Canada. If you have a highland Scottish brogue, are a Hungarian who speaks English as a second language, or are from East India, good luck with your background accent.

The only parts of *Finals* that are purely consonants in standard Hanyu are *n* and *ng*. (儿化, **érhuà**, **erhua**) is a phonetic regional window dressing with no meaning so I will avoid it here. The *Finals* take the form of;

single Vowel only (V),

two vowels (VV),

three vowels (VVV),

one vowel and a consonant (VC),

one vowel and two consonants (VCC),

two vowels and a consonant (VVC),

and two vowels and two consonants (VVCC).

In all these situations the single (C) is the letter *n* and the (CC) is always *ng*.

This is important to know as many *words* in Pinyin are composed from more than one character and the Pinyin is thus compiled together similarly. Knowing which

[Type text]

combinations cannot go together helps you know where the break in a phoneme string or word is.

To find a given final, remove the initial consonant. For *zh*, *ch*, *sh*, both letters should be removed. They are the only Initial consonants spelled with two letters.

Many books show Finals beginning with *i as* a standalone Pinyin beginning with *y*. Example, *-ian* as *yan*. I do not see the utility of this confusion. This language is already confusing enough. These statements result from the conversion of older styles of Romanization such as Wade Gillis. The rule is simple, the Pinyin *y* is silent before the Pinyin *i*. In all other situations it is pronounced as the English letter *y*. When you see a character represented with *yan* there is no value to trying to remember it as really being represented as *–ian* with the letter *y* acting as a silent place holder.

Many books show Finals beginning with *u* as a standalone Pinyin beginning with *w*. Example, *-ua* as *wa*. The rule is simple, the Pinyin *u* is pronounced *w* when the Final stands alone. Same argument as above.

Many books show Finals beginning with *ü as* a standalone Pinyin beginning with *y*. Example, *- ün* as *yun*. Same argument as above.

Pinyin is not a language; it is a system that assigns a sound to each Chinese character.

This is the reason that many books do not show *w* and *y* as Initial consonants. This language is already confusing enough. There are in fact very few Pinyin that begin with a vowel as an Initial. The 11 combinations are *a*, *ai*, *ao*, *an*, *ang*, *o*, *ou*, *e*, *ei*, *en*, and *er*. I see little reason to learn complex rules about stand alone Finals as they never stand alone. Learn the combined sounds of the Initials and Finals and forget the *i-y*, *u-w* and, *ü-y*.

[Type text]

Learning from a chart, you will never get it right as there is no right. Race, height, age, alcohol, tobacco, many things affect your voice. There is so much variation in China that there is no perfect sounds. The other variable is that the transition from one phoneme to another affects the sound. Even within individual words the tone can have a great effect on the sound as you glide from one vowel to another.

(儿化, **érhuà**, **erhua**) adds another variable. Added to the neutral and first tone it is a continuation. Added to the second, third and fourth tone it can be an awkward addition.

Some books say that *zhi*, *chi*, *shi*, *ri*, *zi*, *ci* or *si* are pure consonant only sounds and that the *i* acts as a phonetic silent neutral place holder. Other books say that the *i* is sounded as a prolonged **zzzzzzz**. The **zzzzzzz** theory is definitely wrong. Mandarin is usually spoken so fast there are no prolonged sounds. Some lackey with a Master's degree trying to get his Ph.D. must have some Chinese undergrads wired up to an phonetic oscilloscope in a laboratory. The *i* theory is a little more credible but try making any of the pure consonant sounds and ending them just as they started.

If you take any sound and isolate it phonetically and analyze it it bears little resemblance to how it is used dynamically. I have great fun in China playing my language learning DVD's to my relatives and watch them howl with laughter as some guy sounds out each Pinyin in a slow dramatic fashion with gigantic ranges of tone. The third tone is particularly impressive under scrutiny. The phonemes are stretched to about 5 times their length and 3 times their tonal range.

Pinyin	Explanation
-i	Displayed as an *i* after: *zh*, *ch*, *sh*, *r*, *z*, *c* or *s*. The consonant is very dominant with very little sound effect from the *i*.
-i	After all other consonants it sounds as Ē.
-a	As in *father*, examples *saw*, *raw*, *law*.
-o	Occurring only in **bo**, **po**, **mo**, **wo**, and **fo**, it has a ***wahw*** like sound.
-e	Similar to the English ***uh***, but not as open, *nut*, *mutt*, *but*.
-ê	As in *bet*. This is only used in certain interjections.
-ai	As in English *eye*, *sty*, *my*, *fly*, *die*.
-ei	As in English alphabetic Ā as in *lay*, *day*, *stay*, *bay*.
-ao	As in English in *cow*.
-ou	As in English ***oh*** or the long alphabetic Ō, examples *so*, *tow*, *mow*.
-an	As in English l***awn***, *sawn*, *pawn*.

[Type text]

-en As in English *-un*, as in *fun*, *done*, *run*.

-ang As in English *angst*.

-eng As in English *–ung*, *bung*, *sung*, *stung*.

er As in English *are*. This word stands alone with no Initial.

-ia As in English alphabetic *Ē* + *awh*, **ēēē-ahhh**.

-io As in English alphabetic *Ē* + *Ō*.

-ie As in English alphabetic *Ē* + **yuh**, but is short. The *yuh* is pronounced longer and carries the main stress. **Ē-yyyuh**

-iao As in English alphabetic *Ē* + **yao**, as in English in c**ow**.

-iu As in English alphabetic *Ē* + *yoe*, as in English *knee-yoe*.

-ian As in English alphabetic *Ē* + *yawn*.

-in As in English *–ēēn*, *bean*, *seen*, *mean*.

-iang As in English alphabetic *Ē* + **yawn-ggg**.

-ing As in English *ing*, examples are s*ing*, br*ing*, and st*ing*.

[Type text]

-u   As in English *ewe*, examples are *stew*, *do*, *crew*, *moo*.

-ua   As in English *w* plus the *a* in f*a*ther, examples *wa*sh, *po*sh.

-uo   As in English *woe* or *wah*, *wo*re, *wo*rn.

-uai As in English *why*.

-ui   As in English *way*.

-uan As in English *wan*der, l*awn*, s*awn*.

-un   As in English *un*, f*un*, *d*one, s*un*.

-uang As in English *wăng*.

-ong Starts with the vowel sound in b'**oo**k and ends with the nasal sound in si**ng**, ŏŏ**ng**.

-ü   As in German *ü*ber or French *lu*ne.

-ue   As ü + ê; the *ü* is short and light as in **üüuh**

-üan As ü + *on*.

-ün   As ü + n.

-iong As Ē + ŏŏng.

[Type text]

Explanations and Exceptions to General Rules

1) *ü* is written as *u* after *j*, *q*, *x*, and *y*. *ü* is written as *u* when there is no ambiguity such as *j-u*, *q-u*, and *x-u*. These combinations of Initials and Finals do not phonetically exist. It is written as *ü* when there are corresponding Initial- *ü* syllables such as *lü* and *nü*) In such situations where there are corresponding *ü* syllables, it is often replaced with *v* on computer created correspondence, making it easier to type on a standard keyboard.

2) *uo* is written as *o* after *b*, *p*, *m*, *w*, or *f*. Hanyu Pinyin that are actually pronounced as *buo*, *puo*, *muo*, *wuo*, and *fuo* are given a separate written representation as *bo*, *po*, *mo*, *wo*, and *fo*. The pronunciation remains as *buo*, *puo*, *muo*, and *fuo*.

3) The Finals that would be phonetically arranged as, *iou*, *uei*, and *uen* are simplified as *iu*, *ui*, and *un*. This allows the following phonetic changes.

   -iu is pronounced as in English alphabetic $\bar{E}$ plus *ewe*. As in English *knee-yoe*.

   -ui is pronounced as in English *way*.

   -ün as **ü + n** similar to phonetic *nyun*.

[Type text]

Tones

To counter the effect of having so few combinations of *Initials* and *Finals*, Hanyu has distinct tones to give meaning to phonemes. Each *Initial Final* combination has a total of five possible tones. This has the effect of giving five times more distinct phonemes. What appears to be a small number of phonemes is amplified. However, each Initial Final combination does not always have all five tones.

The Pinyin system also incorporates markers to represent the four tones of Hanyu. Each tone is indicated by a mark above a non-medial vowel. Many books printed in China mix type fonts. This creates vowels with tone marks rendered in a different font than the surrounding text. This a practice that tends to give such Pinyin texts a typographically awkward appearance. This style originates from the limitations of the fonts made available to type setters printing literature. These limitations are overcome with electronic type fonts.

Fifth Tone / Zero Tone / Neutral Tone

Qīngshēng
Light tone

The tone that is neutral to a voice effort is called the *Fifth Tone*, *Zero Tone* or *Neutral Tone*. It is sometimes thought of incorrectly as a lack of tone. The *Neutral Tone* is particularly difficult for non-native speakers to master correctly because of its uncharacteristically large number of contours. The level of its pitch depends almost entirely on the tone carried by the syllable preceding it. It is not possible to end one phoneme without the effect of the *Final* influencing the neutral tone initiation of the next *Initial*. In the transition from one tone to another, there is in fact four short varied tones created that are not the named tones.

The only way to get around this is when you are learning to speak Hanyu, you can speak very slowly. This allows you to finish a word completely before you start the next word. This prevents the effect of the previous Final from influencing the coming Initial. This is not an efficient way to speak as it is so slow. However, you will learn to naturally acquire an understandable tone transition.

The learning curve will occur very naturally this way.

First Tone

阴平
Yīnpíng
High-level tone

The first tone is the ***High Level Tone***. It is represented by a macron marker (¯) added to the Pinyin vowel or by adding a #1 at the end of the phoneme. To create this tone the speaker lifts his voice to a comfortable reproducible level.

Second Tone

阳平,
Yángpíng
High rising

The second tone is the ***Rising Tone***. It is denoted by an French linguistic acute accent marker (´) or by adding a **#2** at the end of the phoneme. Second tone, or rising tone is a sound that rises from mid-level tone to high. Many books describe the tone raise as being similar to a hearing impaired person saying *What*? This tone rises from the neutral position to the *First Tone* position.

[Type text]

Third Tone

上声
Shàngshēng
Up tone

The third tone is the ***Falling-Rising Tone***. It is symbolized by a grammatical marker caron (ˇ) or a **#3** added to the end of the phoneme. It has a mid-low to low descent, if at the end of a sentence or before a pause. It is then followed by a rising pitch. This tone is created by dropping the pitch from the Neutral Tone to a comfortable, reproducible and distinguishable lower tone.

Fourth Tone

去声
Qùshēng
Away tone

The fourth tone is the ***Falling Tone***. It is represented by a French grammatical grave accent (`) or by adding a **#4** at the end of the phoneme. Fourth tone or falling tone features a sharp downward accent dipping from high to low. It has a short sharp duration. Many books compare the sound to barking the command ***Stop***! This tone is created by quickly dropping the pitch from neutral tone to a tone near the depth of the downward deflection on the third tone.

Loud Tone

China has 1.5 billion people. You will seldom find yourself alone. With hundreds of people on any given bus or train conversation can get very loud. There is a tendency for cell phones to be ringing, music to be blasting and karaoke to being sung. At times like this it is very hard to discriminate tone. As a foreigner, you may

[Type text]

find the volume uncomfortably loud. The context of the situation guides the listener as to what is being said. Usually in situations like this the topic is obvious and you will adjust to determine the tones, eventually. It is also difficult to whisper in tones.

Numbers in Place of Tone Marks

I totally cut and pasted and stole this page and table from the internet. So if you did not *get it* from the above discussion, read this. Numbers are useful in typing as the conversion to tone markers is often complex and requires more than one program on your computer. In the appendix I will include a chapter on modifying your computer to make in more useful for Chinese writing. Here is the paragraph I borrowed.

Since most computer fonts do not contain the accents, a common convention is to add a digit representing the tone to the end of individual syllables. For example, *tóng* is written *tong2*. The number used for each tone is as in the table below.

If you have Office 2007 with Word 2007 you can make your computer type Pinyin with tone markers if you have the patience. You must add all the variations of Pinyin with the tone numbers into your dictionary as equivalents to the Pinyin with tone markers. The you set your document to auto correct. That way, when you type Pinyin with numbers you can auto correct to Pinyin with tone markers. You will find a document to help you with this on the included CD or at the website.

[Type text]

Tone	Tone Mark	Number added to end of syllable in place of tone mark	Example using tone mark	Example using number
First	(¯)	1	mā	ma1
Second	(´)	2	má	ma2
Third	(ˇ)	3	mǎ	ma3
Fourth	(`)	4	mà	ma4
Neutral or Fifth	No mark	*no number five or 0*	ma	ma ma5 ma0

Table above was borrowed from the internet without permission. (stolen)

[Type text]

Rules for Placing the Tone Mark

Tone markings always go above the Final. The rules for determining on which vowel the tone mark appears are as follows.

1. If there is one vowel the tone marker goes above this vowel.
2. If there is more than one vowel and the first vowel is *i*, *u*, or *ü*, then the tone mark appears on the second vowel.
3. In all other cases, the tone mark appears on the first vowel

The reasoning behind these rules is in the case of Finals of more than one vowel, the first vowel may be preserved for pronunciation of the Initial consonant. That is, in phoneme words such as (犬, **quǎn**, **dog**) the correct pronunciation is a two part syllable, similar to *chew on* not *chwan*. The tone change begins with the *ǎn* and the *qu* is preserved in the neutral tone.

There is another algorithm for determining the vowel on which the tone mark appears is as follows:

1. First, look for an *a* or an *e* If either vowel appears, it takes the tone mark. There are no possible Pinyin syllables that contain both an **a** and an **e**.
2. If there is no *a* or *e* look for an *ou*. If *ou* appears, then the *o* takes the tone mark.
3. If none of the above cases hold, then the last vowel in the syllable takes the tone mark.

[Type text]

Umlaut

An *umlaut* is placed over the letter *u* when it occurs after the initials *l* and *n* in order to represent the sound *you*. This distinguishes the *you* sound from the *ŏŏ* sound as in *boo!*

Examples:

(驴, **lü**, **donkey**)
versus
(炉, **lú**, **oven**)

Tonal markers can be added on top of the umlaut, as in *lǘ*. However, the *ü* is not used in other contexts where it represents a front high rounded vowel, namely after the letters *j*, *q*, *x* and *y*. For example, the sound of the word (鱼, *yú*, **fish**) is transcribed in Pinyin simply as *yú*, not as *yǘ*. Genuine ambiguities only happen with *nu* / *nü* and *lu* / *lü*, which are then distinguished by an umlaut diacritic marker.

Many fonts or input output methods do not support an umlaut for *ü* or cannot place tone marks on top of *ü*. Likewise, using *ü* in input methods is difficult because it is not present as a simple key on many keyboard layouts. Although a computer can be configured to type the umlaut, most do not know how to do it. For these reasons *v* is sometimes typed instead of *ü*.

Tonal Shift Patterns, or Tone Sandhi

As if learning tone is not complicated enough, there are addition rules and patterns of tone shift depending on the surrounding tones. The basis of tonal shift is that the preceding tone affects the following tone. These changes are of course not reflected in writing Chinese characters, the characters are unchanged. Neither are these changes reflected in Hanyu Pinyin. The diacritic tone markers remain unchanged. It is only the spoken presentation that changes. Many books alter the official rules to try and make it easier to understand. This is confusing, especially in books that do not provide written characters.

Sequential 1st Tone Rule

Sequential first tones are unchanged.
Example:

Sequential 2nd Tone Rule

Sequential second tones are unchanged.
Example:

Sequential 4th tone Rule

Sequential fourth tones are unchanged.
Example:

[Type text]

Sequential 3rd Tone Rule

A single syllable third tone word preceding a single syllable third tone word changes to a second tone. If there are more than two 3rd tone words of a single syllable, the rules are more complex and not clear. If the sentence has a rhetoric pause between third tones, the first third tone is preserved. This is where a clear understanding of *word* becomes important.

Example: 老鼠, **lǎoshǔ**, becomes **lao2shu4**

Example: 我很好, **wǒ hěn hǎo**, is spoken **wo2 hen2 hao3**

In a character string with a polysyllabic word composed of two characters, each with a third tone, preceding a single syllable third tone word, the first two syllables become 2nd tones, the third syllable retains the 3rd tone.

Example: 保管好, **bǎoguǎn hǎo** is spoken **bao2guan2 hao3**

If the first word is one syllable, and the second word is two syllables, the first syllable becomes a 4th tone, the second syllable becomes 2nd tone, and the last syllable stays 3rd tone.

Example: 老保管, **lǎo bǎoguǎn** is spoken **lao4 bao2guan3**

Tone Changes After the Third Tone

When a character that is assigned a 3rd tone and it is followed by a neutral, first, second or fourth tone, it usually becomes a 4th tone. This tone is oft described as a ***half-third tone*** in that it descends but does not rise. However, it does not fall as far as a full 4th tone. Variably, it may be described as a ***low flat tone***, in that it does not descend but mirrors the first tone in tone profile. You will find dialectal and regional

[Type text]

variations to these patterns. The speed of a conversation also affects these changes. There is no convention for assigning numbers or diacritic tone markers for this.

Example: 美妙, **měimiào** becomes **mei4miao4**

Rules for (一, yī, one)

(一, **yī**, **one**) has special rules which do not apply to other Chinese characters. When in front of a 4th tone syllable, (一, **yī**, **one**) becomes 2nd tone.

Example: (一定, **yīdìng**, **certainly**) becomes **yi2ding4**

When (一, **yī**, **one**) is in front of a 1st, 2nd, or 3rd tone syllable, (一, **yī**, **one**) becomes 4th tone.

Example: 1st tone (一天, **yītiān**) becomes **yi4 tian1**

Example: 2nd tone (一年, **yīnián**) becomes **yi4 nian2**

Example: 3rd tone (一起, **yīqǐ**) becomes **yi4 qi3**

When (一, **yī**, **one**) falls between two words, it becomes neutral tone.

Example: 不一样, **bù yī yáng** is spoken **bu4 yi yang2**

When used for numeric counting, and for all other situations, (一, **yī**, **one**) retains its value of 1st tone.

Rules for (不, bù, not)

(不, **bù**, **not**) has special rules which do not apply to other Chinese characters. (不, **bù**, **not**) becomes 2nd tone when followed by a 4th tone syllable.

[Type text]

Example: 不是, **bùshì** becomes **bu2shi4**

When (不, **bù**, **not**) comes between two words, it becomes neutral in tone.

Example: 是不是, **shìbùshì** becomes **shi4 bushi4**

Funny Stuff

Many books available to the learning student are written by people with numerous university degrees in language related fields. They use graphic pictures of human heads cut in cross section showing the position of the tongue inside the mouth. This is supposed to give you an idea as to how you are forming the sounds of Hanyu. If you just happen to have access to a human anatomy lab where you can look at heads cut in half, maybe this will help you, somehow. You will find it quicker and more useful if you just slosh your tongue around until the correct sound issues forth. Or buy a recording device to practice.

There is also a ton of words unique to those with Ph.D.'s that are specific to language sciences. Plosives, fricatives, labials, dental alveolars, bilabials, nasal something or another's. This is all just a barrier to learning how to speak. Toss them. Some guy even assigned numbers to the tone contours. Here they are, 55, 35, 214, 51. I have no idea what to do with them or what they mean. When I show this stuff to Chinese people they laugh heartily. The range of tones is variable on the situation. An MC in front of a crowd will make dramatic tonal ranges. An angry taxi driver will speak so fast that tone is near lost. There are many angry taxi drivers in China.

The most important hurdle to learning to speak is the acquisition of a Chinese friend. This is far better than books, tapes, MP3 players or DVD's. If you do not live in an area where there is a large Chinese population, say Antarctica, go to the local

[Type text]

Chinese restaurant, Laundromat or computer science department at a local university and put up a sign that says,

我教你英文你教我汉語

Wǒ jiāo Nǐ Yīngwén, Nǐ jiāo Wǒ Hànyǔ.
I teach you English, You teach me Han language.

汉语 拼音
Hànyǔ Pīnyīn
Hanyu Pinyin

Pinyin, more formally *Hanyu Pinyin*, is the most commonly used system to assign standardized sounds to Chinese characters. From an English speakers perspective this may sound unusual. However, The Chinese characters represent a written language, not a spoken language. In fact, over the history of the many ethnic groups and regions that eventually became China, over two hundred spoken variants of the written language emerged.

History

The formation of the People's Republic of China (**PRC**) in 1948 lead to educational reforms to increase literacy. The people of the country were largely uneducated with 80% being illiterate. 57 ethnic groups spoke over 200 languages. In 1954, the Ministry of Education of the PRC struck a Committee for the Reform of the Chinese Written Language. This committee developed a unified system of sounds so that each Chinese character could be expressed the same throughout the different ethnic groups and regions of China.

This system was named Hanyu Pinyin. The (汉, **Hàn**, **Han**) are the ethnic majority group of China. Hanyu means the Han language from (汉, **Hàn**, **Han**) and (语, **yǔ**, **language**). Pinyin is formed from (拼, **pīn**, **spell**) and (音, **yīn**, **sound**).

Together, the characters (汉语 拼音, **Hànyǔ Pīnyīn**, **Hanyu Pinyin**) identify the language of the ethnic Han majority and the phonetics used to standardize it.

The pivotal work behind Hanyu Pinyin was done by Professor Zhou Youguang. Zhou was an American working in the New York banking system. With the end of the civil war in China in 1948, he decided to return to China to help rebuild the country. He became an economics professor in Shanghai. The government assigned him to help the development of a new Romanization system.

The Cultural Revolution began in 1957. Chairman Mao oversaw the execution of millions of literate Chinese. Doctors, lawyers, teachers, and the educated were all suspect. American trained economists were high on the list, however, Zhou was spared. The switch to language and writing largely saved him from the wrath of the Cultural Revolution of Mao Zedong.

The first draft was published on February 12, 1956. The first edition of ***Hanyu Pinyin*** was approved and adopted at the Fifth Session of the 1st National People's Congress on February 11, 1958. It was introduced to primary schools as a way to teach Standard Mandarin pronunciation. This made a major impact on literacy.

Romanization versus Anglisization

The Chinese characters are not phonetically driven. That is, you cannot determine the pronunciation from looking at the character, generally. This allowed different ethnic groups that adopted the written language to assign their own sounds to the characters. With the unification of China and increased migration within the country, this caused a biblical Babel.

Many efforts were made by the West to used the Roman based alphabet to assign sounds to the Chinese characters. Several systems evolved. The goal of Hanyu Pinyin was to forever create a standardized system developed by China that made use of the previous systems such as Wade and Wade-Gillis. Thus the rules and system of Hanyu Pinyin were struck.

Romanization refers to a method in which the English speaking world takes a non-alphabetic language that is composed of non-phonetically driven symbols or logograms and assign sounds using the Roman alphabet. The phonetics of Hanyu Pinyin generally follow the phonetics of the English alphabet, with some exceptions. Hanyu Pinyin is thus Romanized yet only partially Anglisized.

Pinyin replaced older Romanization systems such as Wade-Giles which was developed in 1859; modified Wade-Gillis in 1892 and the Chinese Postal Map system of Romanization.

The International Organization for Standardization (ISO) adopted Hanyu Pinyin as the standard Romanization for modern Chinese in 1982 as ISO 7098. This was superseded by ISO 7098 in 1991. The United Nations adopted it as an official and standardized Mandarin Romanization system in 1986. It has also been accepted by the government of Singapore, the Library of Congress, the American Library Association, and many other international institutions.

Hanyu Pinyin will also be the official ISO Romanization system in the Taiwan Republic of China starting in 2009.

In 2001, the Chinese Government issued the *National Common Language Law*, providing a legal basis for applying Hanyu Pinyin.

[Type text]

Rules of Pinyin

Pinyin differs from other Romanization in several aspects. However, since we are not studying the other systems such as Wade Giles, it does not matter. This is not a history of Romanization but rather the modern state of affairs. Many books take great freedom in including their own altered rules of Pinyin, usually at the beginning of the book. Since Pinyin was fabricated recently, it was put together by committees, not history and time. Thus, there are rules. This book will follow the rules.

Use of the Apostrophe

In a situation in which two characters form one word, the two Hanyu Pinyin are joined together. However, this can create a situation in which a Hanyu Pinyin ending in a vowel and a Hanyu Pinyin beginning with a vowel appear as another single Hanyu Pinyin. The apostrophe marker ' is thus used before *a*, *o*, and *e* to separate syllables in a word where ambiguity could arise.

Examples:
(皮袄, **pí'ǎo**, **fur quilted jacket**) versus (票, **piào**, **ticket**)
(西安, *Xī'ān*, **Xian**) versus (先, *xiān*, **before**, **first**)

Word Formation

Ambiguity can exist in partitioning words. Each character is a single syllable sound. However, many words, being composed of two or more characters hence form polysyllabic Hanyu Pinyin words. Spacing between words is based on separating Hanyu Pinyin words, not single syllables. Generally, the separation is based on taking character compilations that form words and separating them as distinct Hanyu Pinyin. Simply, words, not characters, stand alone. If the world could get China to do the same with characters, that is, separating words with a space, learning and identifying compound character words would be much easier.

However, there are often ambiguities in partitioning a word due to the alphabetic structure of Hanyu Pinyin. Orthographic rules were put into effect in 1988 by the;

National Educational Commission of China
(State Education Commission)
国家教育委员会
Guójiā Jiàoyù Wěiyuánhuì

and the

National Language Commission of China
(National Language Writing Working Committee)
国家语言文字工作委员会
Guójiā Yǔyán Wénzì Gōngzuo Wěiyuánhuì

These above committee titles demonstrate the uninterrupted strings of Chinese characters, the Hanyu Pinyin words, and the literal versus common translation. Please note that in the first title, the word China does not appear in the character string but it appears in the translation. This is a good example of the randomness of some translations.

[Type text]

Single Meaning

Words that are created from Hanyu Pinyin that in combination or alone have a single meaning and are distinct recognizable combinations are written as one word and not capitalized.

Examples:

rén, 人, **person**

pǎo, 跑, **run**

hǎo, 好, **good**

hé, 和, **and**

hěn, 很, **very**

fúróng, 芙蓉, **cotton rose**

qiǎokèlì, 巧克力, **chocolate**

péngyou, 朋友, **friend**

diànhuà, 电话, **telephone**

yuèdú, 阅读, **reading**

dìzhèn, 地震, **earth quake**

niánqīng, 年轻, **young**

zhòngshì, 重视, **takes**

wǎnhuì, 晚会, **party**

qiānmíng, 签名, **signature**

shìwēi, 示威, **demonstration**

niǔzhuǎn, 扭转, **reverse**

chuánzhī, 船只, **ship**

dànshì, 但是, **but**

fēicháng, 非常, **extremely**

diànshìjī, 电视机, **television**

túshūguǎn, 图书馆, **library**

These above Hanyu Pinyin do not occur in the compiled format with the given tones for any other commonly spoken words.

[Type text]

Combined Meaning

Two And Three Character Words

Words created by combining two words or three words to have one meaning are written together.

Examples:

gāngtiě, 钢铁, **steel and iron**

wèndá, 问答, **question and answer**

hǎifēng, 海风, **sea breeze**

hóngqí, 红旗, **Red Flag**

dàhuì, 大会, **congress**

quánguó, 全国, **nation**

zhòngtián, 种田, **farms**

kāihuì, 开会, **holds a meeting**

dǎpò, 打破, **to break**

zǒulái, 走来, **walks**

húshuō, 胡说, **nonsense**

dǎnxiǎo, 胆小, **timidly**

qiūhǎitáng, 秋海棠, **begonia**

duìbuqǐ, 对不起, **sorry**

chīdexiāo, 吃得消, **able to endure**

àiniǎozhōu, 爱鸟周, **to like bird week**

Four Character Words

Words created by combining 4 or more characters are split up into constituent words with identified meaning. This rule is also used for compilations of more than 4 characters. Hanyu Pinyin words created by more than one character are separated in whole word units.

Examples:

wúfèng gāngguǎn, 无缝钢管, **seamless steel-tube**,

huánjìng bǎohù guīhuà, 环境保护规划, **environmental protection planning**,

jīngtǐguǎn gōnglǜ fàngdàqì, 晶体管功率放大器, **Transistor power amplifier**

Zhōnghuá Rénmín Gònghéguó, 中华人民共和国, **People's Republic of China**

Yánjiūshēngyuàn, 研究生院, **graduate school**

Hóngshízìhuì, 红十字会, **Red Cross**

Yúxīngcǎosù, 鱼腥草素, **cordate houttuynia element**

Gǔshēngwùxuéjiā, 古生物学家, **paleontologist**

Zhōngguó Shèhuì Kēxuéyuàn,
中国社会科学院,
China Academy Social Sciences

[Type text]

Duplicated Characters AA, AABB and ABAB

AA

When words are formed from characters that are duplicated in the form AA, they are written together.

Examples:

rénrén, 人人, **everybody**

kànkàn, 看看, **to have a look**

niánnián, 年年, **yearly**

tiāntiān, 天天, **everyday**

gègè, 个个, **each one**

dàda, 大大, **big**

shuōshuo, 说说, **to say**

hónghóng de, 红红的, **red**

ABAB

When two characters are duplicated in the form ABAB they are separated into two AB words repeated.

Examples:

yánjiū yánjiū, 研究研究, **to study, to research**,

xuěbái xuěbáide, 雪白雪白的, **snow-white**

chángshì chángshì, 尝试尝试, **attempts**

tōnghóng tōnghóngde, 通红通红的, **very red**

AABB

A hyphen is used with the schema AABB. The words are duplicated and separated with a hyphen.

Examples:

láilái-wǎngwǎng, 来来往往, **go back and forth**

qiānqiān-wànwàn, 千千万万, **numerous**

qīqī-bābā, 七七八八, **miscellaneous**

qīngqīng-chǔchǔ, 清清楚楚, **clear**

jiājiā-hùhù, 家家户户, **all families, each and every family**

shuōshuo-xiàoxiào, 说说笑笑, **chats**

wānwān-qūqū, 弯弯曲曲, **curving**

Abbreviations

For for ease of reading and understanding, the hyphen is used in certain situations. Words that are easily understood may be eliminated.

Examples:

huán-bǎo, 环保, **versus huánjìng bǎohù**, 环境保护, **environmental protection**

bā-jiǔ tiān, 八九天, **versus** 八十九天, **eighty-nine days**

rén-jī duìhuà, 人机对话, **versus** 人和机器的对话, **man-machine dialog**

lù-hǎi-kōngjūn, 陆海空军, **land-sea-air armed forces**

gōng-guān, 公关, **versus gōnggòng guānxì**, 公共关系, **public relations**

shíqī-bā suì, 十七八岁, **versus shíqī shíbā suì**, 十七十八岁, **17-18 years**

zhōng-xiǎoxué, 中小学, **versus zhōngxué-xiǎoxué**, 中学小学, **middle school-junior school**

[Type text]

Common Nouns and People Nouns

Common Nouns formed from multiple characters are written as one Hanyu Pinyin word.

Examples:

zhuōzi, 桌子, **table**

mùtou, 木头, **wood**

fùbùzhǎng, 副部长, **vice minister**

chéngwùyuán, 乘务员, **conductor**

háizimen, 孩子们, **children**

fēijīnshǔ, 非金属, **nonmetallic**

chāoshēngbō, 超声波, **ultrasonic wave**

zǒnggōngchéngshī, 总工程师, **chief engineer**

fēiyèwù rényuán, 非业务人员, **non-servicers**

fǎndàndào dǎodàn, 反弹道导弹, **antimissile missile**

chéngwùyuán, 乘务员, **train attendant**

kēxuéxìng, 科学性, **scientific nature**

yìshùjiā, 艺术家, **artist**

xiàndàihuà, 现代化, **modernization**

tuōlājīshǒu, 拖拉机手, **tractor driver**

[Type text]

Words of Position

Words of position acting as prepositions forming locative phrases are separated. Although standard Mandarin grammar is very similar to English, locative phrases are composed with the locative particle in the sentence final position.

Examples:

mén wàimiàn, 门外面, door outside, outdoors,

hé lǐmiàn, 河里面, river inside, in the river

huǒchē shàngmiàn, 火车上面, train upon, on the train

Huáng Hé yǐnán, 黄河以南, Yellow River by south, south of Yellow River

shān shàngmiàn, 山上面, mountain upon, on mountain

Yǒngdìng Hé shàng, 永定河上, Yongding river on, on Yongdong River

shù xià, 树下, tree under, under the tree

xuéxiào pángbiān, 学校旁边, school nearby

Exceptions

Words traditionally connected continue to be connected in Hanyu Pinyin.

Examples:

tiānshàng, 天上, at the sky

dìxià, 地下, floor on, on the floor

kōngzhōng, 空中, in the air

hǎiwài, 海外, sea away, overseas

[Type text]

Chinese Personal Names

Family names are separated from the given name. If the given name consists of two syllables, they should be written together. All proper person names are capitalized.

Examples:

Lú XuéFèng, 卢学凤　　　　　　**Lǔ Xùn**, 鲁迅

Lǐ Huá, 李花　　　　　　　　　**Zhāng Sān**, 张三

Name Titles

Titles names follow the Proper name. The title is separated and not capitalized.

Examples:

Wáng bùzhǎng, 王部长, **Wang minister**

Lǐ xiānshēng, 李先生, **Li Mister**

Tián zhǔrèn, 田主任, **Tian director**

Zhào tóngzhì, 赵同志, **Zhao comrade**

The honorific and respectful forms of addressing people with *Lǎo*, *Xiǎo*, *Dà* and *A* are capitalized: These forms of address come after the Proper Name.

Xiǎo Liú, 小刘, **young Liu**　　　　**Lǎo Wú**, 老吴, **senior Wu**

Dà Lǐ, 大李, **elder Li**　　　　　　**Lǎo Qián**, 老钱, **elder Qian**

A Sān, 阿三, **honourable San**

[Type text]

Exceptions are:

Kǒngzǐ, 孔子, **Master Confucius**

Bāogōng, 包公, **Bao Judge**

Xīshī, 西施, **Xishi, a historical person**

Mèngchángjūn, 孟尝君, **Mèngchángjūn, a historical person**

Geographical Names of China

Proper Noun location names are compounded together and any other designation is separated. Proper Nouns are capitalized as in English.

Examples:

Běijīng Shì, 北京市, **Beijing City**

Yālù Jiāng, 鸭绿江, **Yalu Stream**

Héběi Shěng, 河北省, **Hebei Province**

Dòngtíng Hú, 洞庭湖, **Donting Lake**

Táiwān Hǎixiá, 台湾海峡, **Taiwan Strait**

Tài Shān, 泰山, **Tai Mountain**

When a Proper Noun has additional characters that further define the location, each noun phrase is kept together as a single Hanyu Pinyin. Precision in location always works and thus locative words become entrenched into the Proper name.

Examples:

Xīliáo Hé, 西辽河, **Xiliao River**

Jǐngshān Hòujiē, 景山后街, **Jingshan Backstreet**

[Type text]

Cháoyángménnèi Nánxiǎojiē, 朝阳门内南小街, **Chaoyang Gate Inside, South Alley**

Many villages, towns and features are written as one Hanyu Pinyin with the usual capitalized geographic name joined to the location feature name.

Examples:

Wángcūn, 王村, **Wang Village**

Sāntányìnyuè, 三潭印月, **three pools reflecting the moon**

Jiǔxiānqiáo, 酒仙桥, **Jiuxian bridge**

Zhōukǒudiàn, 周口店, **Zhōukǒu store**

Non-Chinese Proper Nouns and Names

There is great creativity and confusion with the methodology in which the Chinese translate non-Chinese names into Hanyu Pinyin and Hanzi. Some Hanyu Pinyin are attempts to phonetically mirror the sounds of the non-Chinese Proper Nouns.

Examples:

Marx, 马克思, **Mǎkèsī**

Newton, 牛顿, **Niúdùn**

Washington, 华盛顿, **Huáshèngdùn**

London, 伦敦, **Lúndūn**

Others provide descriptives from a Chinese perspective.

[Type text]

Examples:

Dōngnányà, 东南亚, **east south Asia (South East Asia)**

Měiguó, 美国, **beautiful country (America)**

Dōngjīng, 东京, **east capital (Tokyo)**

Nánměi, 南美, **south beautiful (South America)**

The remainder are somewhat mystifying.

Examples:

Paris, 巴黎, **Bālí**

Akutagawa Ryunosuke, 芥川龙之介, **jiè chuān lóng zhī jiè**

Seypidin, 赛福鼎, **Sàifúdǐng**

Fēizhōu, 非洲, **evil continent (Africa)**

Déguó, 德国, **morality country (Germany)**

Verbs
Dòngcí
动词

Verbs and the characters affixed to them as grammatical particle suffixes such as (着, **zhe**), (了, **le**) and (过, **guo**) are written as one word.

(着, **zhe, durative grammatical particle**) is added to a verb to indicate and ongoing process. Functionally, it acts as *–ing* added to an English verb.

(了, **le, completed verb action particle**) is added to a verb to indicate the completion of the verb action.

[Type text]

(过, **guo**, **experiential verb particle**) is added to a verb to indicate initial exposure to an action.

Examples:

kànzhe, 看着, **seeing, looking**   **jìnxíngzhe**, 进行着, **to attempting**

kànle, 看了, **saw, looked**   **jìnxíngle**, 进行了, **attempted**

kànguo, 看过, **seeing**   **jìnxíngguo**, 进行过, **attempt**

The sentence final particle 了, **le**, indicating a new state or immediacy, is written separately.

Example:

Huǒchē dào le, 火车到了, **train arrived**

Verbs Object Compounds

Verbs and their objects are separated:

Examples:

kàn xìn, 看信, **read letter**

chī yú, 吃鱼, **eat fish**

kāi wánxiào, 开玩笑, **to be joking**

jiāoliú jīngyàn, 交流经验, **exchange experience**

In situations in which a Verb Object phrase word has numeric qualifiers, the quantitative adjectival phrase is inserted within the verb phrase following the appropriate rules.

[Type text]

Examples:

jūle gōng, 鞠了躬, **bowed body**

jūle yī gè gōng, 鞠了一个躬, **bowed one body**

lǐguo fà, 理过发, **manages sent**

lǐguo sān cì fà, 理过三次发, **manages three times has sent**

Verb Compliment Compounds

If one verb and it's complement verb are both monosyllabic and form a compound, they are written as one Hanyu Pinyin

Examples:

gǎohuài, 搞坏, **causes to break down**

jiànchéng, 建成, **completes (such as a project)**

shútòu, 熟透, **thoroughly ripe**

huàwéi, 化为, **changes into**

dǎsǐ, 打死, **beat kill**

If the verb or the compliment are polysyllabic they are written separately and two or more distinct Hanyu Pinyin are formed.

Examples:

zǒu jìnlái, 走进来, **go forth enter come / go forth into**

zhěnglǐ hǎo, 整理好, **reorganizes well**

jiànshè chéng, 建设成, **construction becoming, constructs, builds**

gǎixiě wéi, 改写为, **rewrite for**

[Type text]

Adjectives
Xíngróngcí
形容词

A one syllable adjective and its duplication are written as one and the complement is added to it to form one continuous Hanyu Pinyin.

Example:

mēngmēnglìang, 蒙蒙亮, **cover cover light, dim, dawn**

lìangtāngtāng, 亮堂堂, **shining bright**

Complement of Size or Degree Adjectives

Complements of size or degree are written separated from the word they qualify. They are written after the involved verb. Duplication acts to increase the quality of the duplicated adjective. Duplicates are written continuously.

Example:

Yīdiǎndiǎnr, 一点点儿, is less than **yīdiǎnr**, 一点儿.

Examples:

xiē 些, **few, some**

yīxiē, 一些, **a few**

diǎnr, 点儿, **little**

yīdiǎnr, 一点儿, **a little**

yīdiǎndiǎnr, 一点点儿, **a little**

dà xiē, 大些, **big some,**

dà yīxiē, 大一些, **big a little**

kuài yīdiǎnr, 快一点儿, **fast a little**

kuài diǎnr, 快点儿, **fast a little**

Pronouns
Dàicí
代词

Personal Pronouns

(们, **men**, **plural suffix for pronouns and human nouns**), the plural suffix is compounded with the root noun or pronoun to form a compound Hanyu Pinyin word written continuously.

Examples:

wǒmen, 我们, **we / us**

tāmen, 他们, **they**

nǐmen, 你们, **you (plural)**

zánmen, 咱们, **we / us**

háizimen, 孩子们, **children**

lǎoshīmen, 老师们, **teachers**

nánshìmen, 男士们, **gentlemen**

nǔshìmen, 女士们, **ladies**

Demonstrative Pronouns
指示代词
Zhǐshì Dàicí

Demonstrative pronouns acting as definite articles are written separately from the target subject or object of a sentence. The grammatical affixes 些, 里, 儿, 边, and 个 are added continuously with the demonstrative pronouns.

zhè / zhèi, 这, this

zhèxiē, 这些, these

zhèr, 这儿, here

nà / nèi, 那, that

nàxiē, 那些, those

nàli, 那里, there

gāi, 该, this

zhèli, 这里, here

zhèbian, 这边, this side / here

zhège / zheige, 这个, this one

nèige, 那个, that one / that piece

nàr, 那儿, there

běn, 本市, this

Examples:

zhè rén, 这人, this person

zhèxiē rén, 这些人, these person

dào zhèr lái, 到这儿来, to here come

dào nàr qù, 到那儿去, to there go

tā yào nàge, 他要那个, he want that one

wǒ yào zhège, 我要这个, I want this one

běn bùmén, 本部门, this department

nà cì huìyì, 那次会议, that conference

gāi kān, 该刊, this publication

gāi gōngsī, 该公司, this company

nàxiē cì huìyì, 那些次会议, those conference

[Type text]

Quantitative Adjectives

Modifers of nouns that add a quantitative adjectival quality are written separate from the target noun. As these can modify countable nouns, the Countable Noun Indicator is also written separately.

gè, 各, **each**

měi, 每, **each**

mǒu, 某, **some, a certain**

Examples:

gè gè, 各个, **each**

gè guó, 各国, **each country**

měi nián, 每年, **every year**

mǒu rén, 某人, **somebody**

měi cì, 每次, **each time**

gè rén, 各人, **each person**

gè xuékē, 各学科, **various disciplines**

[Type text]

Numbers

For numbers between eleven and one hundred, write them continuously.

Examples:

shíyī, 十一, **eleven**   **sānshísān**, 三十三, **thirty three**

shíwǔ, 十五, **fifteen**   **jiǔshíjiǔ**, 九十九, **ninety nine**

For one hundred, one thousand, ten thousand, and one hundred million, the number in the first position is continuous with the larger number.

Examples:

jiǔbǎi, 九百, **900**

sānqiān, 三千, **3000**

liùwàn, 六万, **60,000**

sìyì, 四亿, **400,000,000**

Ordinal numbers are separated with a hyphen.

Examples:

dì-yī, 第一, **first**

dì-èrshíbā, 第二十八, **28th**

dì-shísān, 第十三, **13th**

dì-sānbǎi wǔshíliù, 第三百五十六, **356th**

Number, Countable Noun Indicator and Target Noun

Countable Nouns (**CN**) are preceded by a Quantitative Adjective (**QA**) and a Countable Noun Indicator (**CDI**). **CNI's** are variably called measure words or classifiers. The **QA**, **CNI** and **CN** are all separated. The **QA** can be an absolute number such as (两, **liǎng**, **two**) or can be a relative numeric indicator such as (多, **duō**, **many**), (几, **jǐ**, **several**) and (些, **xiē**, **a few**).

Examples:

liǎng gè rén, 两个人, **two people**

liǎng jiān bàn wūzi, 两间半屋子, **two-and-a-half rooms**

yī dà wǎn fàn, 一大碗饭, **a large bowl food**

wǔshísān réncì, 五十三人次, **53 people**

yībǎi duō gè, 一百多个, **100 more, more than one hundred, 100 plus**

jǐ jiā rén, 几家人, **several family members**

shí lái wàn rén, 十来万人, **ten come ten thousand people**

jǐ tiān gōngfu, 几天工夫, **several day of free time**

jǐshí, 几十, **several dozen**

shíjǐ gè rén, 十几个人, **several people**

jǐshí gēn gāngguǎn, 几十根钢管, **several dozens steel pipes**

Adverbs
副词
Fùcí

Adverbs are written separately from other words.

Examples:

hěn hǎo, 很好, **very good** **fēicháng kuài**, 非常快, **very quick**

bù lái, 不来, **not come** **dōu lái**, 都来, **always comes**

zuì dà, 最大, **most big** **gèng měi**, 更美, **more beautiful**

Prepositions
介词
Jiècí

Prepositions are written separately.

Examples:

zài qiánmiàn, 在前面, **at frontside**

wèi rénmín fúwù, 为人民服务, **for people serves**

shēng yú 1940 nián, 生于1940年, **born in 1940 year**

xiàng dōngbiān qù, 向东边去, **toward eastside go**

cóng zuótiān qǐ, 从昨天起, **from yesterday**

guānyú zhègè wèntí, 于这个问题, **about this question**

Conjunctions
连词
Liáncí

Conjunctions are always written separately.

Examples:

gōngrén hé nóngmín, 工人和农民, **worker and farmer**

guāngróng ér jiānjù, 光荣而艰巨, **honorable and arduous**

bùdàn kuài érqiě hǎo, 不但快而且好, **not only quick moreover good**

Nǐ lái háishi bù lái, 你来还是不来, **you come or not come**

[Type text]

Structural Auxiliaries
结构助词
Jiégōu Zhùcí

的, de, possessive, modifying, or descriptive particle, of

地, de, subordinate particle adverbial, -ly

得, dé, adverbial particle

之, zhī, literary equivalent of 的 as a subordinate particle

Examples:

dàdì de nǚ' ér, 大地的女儿, earth daughter

zhè shì wǒ de shū, 这是我的书, this is my book

wǒmen guòzhe xìngfú de shēnghuó, 我们过着幸福的生活, we happy life

mài qīngcài luóbo de, 卖青菜萝卜的, sells green vegetables radish

tā mànman de zǒu, 他慢慢地走, he walk slowly

tǎnbái de gàosù nǐ ba, 坦白地告诉你吧, tells you honestly

dǎsǎo de gānjìng, 打扫得干净, cleans cleanly

hóng de hěn, 红得很, red very

xiě de bù hǎo, 写得不好, writes not good

lěng de fādǒu, 冷得发抖, is cold trembles

shàonián zhī jiā, 少年之家, children's club

zuì fādá de guójiā zhī yī, 最发达的国家之一, one of most developed national

[Type text]

Modal Particles
语气助词
Yǔqì Zhùcí

Particles indicating moods are written separately.

Examples:

Nǐ zhīdào ma?, 你知道吗, **You know?**

Zěnme hái bù lái a?, 怎么还不来啊, **How yet not come?**

Kuài qù ba!, 快去吧!, **Quick go!**

Tā shì bù huì lái de. 他是不会来的, **He is not able to come.**

Interjectives
叹词
Tàncí

Examples:

A! Zhēn měi!, 啊!真美, **Ah!, Really beautiful!**

Nnng, nǐ shuō shénme?, 嗯,你说什么, **You say what?**

Hmmph!, zǒuzhe qiáo ba!, 哼走着瞧吧, **Humph!, wait and see!**

[Type text]

Onomatopoeia
拟声词
Nǐshēngcí

pā!, 啪, **pa!**

jīji-zhāzhā, 叽叽喳喳, **chirp chirp**

huá huá, 哗哗, **whish whish**

hōnglōng yī shēng, 轰隆一声, **bang!**, **One time**

Dà gōngjī wō-wō-tí., 大公鸡喔喔啼, **Big cockerel wo-wo cries.**

Dū, qìdí xiǎng le. 嘟,汽笛响了, "*du*", **the steam whistle made a sound.**

Idioms
成语
Chéngyǔ

Four word idioms are divided into two double syllables interpersed with a hyphen.

céngchū-bùqióng, 层出不穷, **emerges one after another incessantly**

àizēng-fēnmíng, 爱憎分明, **is clear about what to love and what to hate**

yángyáng-dàguān, 洋洋大观, **spectacular**

guāngmíng-lěiluò, 光明磊落, **frank**

fēngpíng-làngjìng, 风平浪静, **uneventful**

píngfēn-qiūsè, 平分秋色, **shares half and half**

diānsān-dǎosì, 颠三倒四, **disorderly**

[Type text]

There are four word idioms which are written continuously.

bùyìlèhū, 不亦乐乎, **delight**

àimònéngzhù, 爱莫能助, **wants to help but not be able**

húlihútu, 糊里糊涂, **bewildered**

diàoerlángdāng, 吊儿郎当, **careless**

zǒngéryánzhī, 总而言之, **in brief**

yīyīdàishuǐ, 一衣带水, **close**

hēibuliūqiū, 黑不溜秋, **swarthy**

Capital Letters
大写
Dàxiě

The first word in sentences and poetry each begin with a capital letter. Proper Nouns each begin with a capital letter.

Examples:

Běijīng, 北京, **Beijing**

Chángchéng, 长城, **Great Wall (long wall)**

Qīngmíng, 清明, **Pure Brightness (a city)**

For a Proper Noun which is composed of several words, each words first letter has a capital letter.

[Type text]

Examples:

Guójì Shūdiàn, 国际书店, **International Bookstore**

Guāngmíng Rìbào, 光明日报, **Guangming Daily**

Hépíng Bīnguǎn, 和平宾馆, **Peaceful Guesthouse**

When a Proper Noun forms a word with a Common Noun the word is written continuously. The Proper Noun is capitalized and the common noun is not.

Examples:

Zhōngguórén, 中国人, **Chinese person**

Míngshǐ, 明史, **Ming Dynasty history (Ming Dynasty is** 明朝, **Míng cháo)**

Guǎngdōnghuà, 广东话, **Cantonese (the spoken language of Guangdong province)**

There are some words that through common use have changed into common nouns. The first letter is therefore a small letter.

Examples:

guǎnggān, 广柑, **sweet orange**

zhōngshānfú, 中山服, **Chinese tunic**

chuānxiōng, 川芎, **rhizome of Ligusticum wallichii**

zàngqīngguǒ, 藏青果, **terminalia**

Dividing and Hyphenating Words

Dividing and hyphenating words to carry on to the next sentence must be done at the completion of a syllable. A hyphen is used between the two syllables.

Example:
(光明, **guāngmíng**, **bright**, **promising**)

Guāngmíng is split between the syllables forming the compound word, **guāng-míng**. The format **gu-āngmíng** cannot be used.

Tone Marker Placement

1. First, look for an *a* or an *e*. If either vowel appears, it takes the tone mark. There are no possible Pinyin syllables that contain both an *a* and an *e*.
2. If there is no *a* or *e*, look for an *ou*. If *ou* appears, then the *o* takes the tone mark.
3. If none of the above cases hold, then the last vowel in the syllable takes the tone mark.

The reasoning behind these rules is in the case of diphthongs and triphthongs, *i*, *u*, and *ü* are considered medial glides rather than part of the syllable nucleus in Chinese phonology. The rules ensure that the tone mark always appears on the nucleus of a syllable.

Another way to find the vowel for a tone mark is to apply the tone mark in the following order: *a*, *e*, *o*, *i*, *u*, except for *iu*, in which case *u* takes the tone mark.

The Character Ü

An umlaut is placed over the letter *u* when it occurs after the initials *l* and *n*. This is necessary in order to distinguish the front high rounded vowel in *lü* from the back high rounded vowel in *lu*. Tonal markers are added on top of the umlaut, as in *lǖ*.

However, the *ü* is *not* used in other contexts where it represents a front high rounded vowel, namely after the letters *j*, *q*, *x* and *y*. Genuine ambiguities only happen with *nu / nü* and *lu / lü*, which are then distinguished by an umlaut diacritic.

Chinese Learning Websites

Cautionary Statement, Internet Rules

1) That which is on the internet today may not be there tomorrow.

2) The internet is the final resting ground for opinion, errors and misdirection.

3) Wikipedia is particularly unreliable as any enthusiast can edit it.

4) Self declared experts with grammar and spell check can seem very authoritative.

5) Some sites offering audio clips of Pinyin phonemes are particularly unreliable and entertaining.

6) University sites seem more reliable but less visually interesting.

7) It is far easier to find fee sites than free sites.

8) Much of what you need is there for free if you can find it but it is scattered across many sites.

9) Most sites you sign up for do not offer a simple cancellation, they will keep auto debiting your credit card.

10) The web site with pictures of me in a brothel with three girls in Chengdu was an interview I was doing.

[Type text]

How to Find the Ultimate Tools

There are many poor quality books, tapes, CD's, DVD's and flashcards on the market, many that I have bought. Learn from my mistakes. Some rules.

1) If it can fit in your pocket it is not good because the font is too small to read.

2) If it does not have English, Pinyin and Characters it is relatively useless.

3) If it gets too creative with translations it will impede your understanding of grammar.

4) If it is made of that super thin onion skin paper it makes excellent toilet paper. Which, when you go to China, you will always find a shortage of.

5) If you buy a character book and it does not have the characters for rice, eat, train and middle, the writer has never been to China and the book may be useless.

6) Nobody has cassette tape players anymore, why buy cassettes?

7) Big multi-coloured boxes can have surprisingly little in them. Open and inspect.

8) Eight CD sets often have enough information to be all fit onto one CD, with lots of room left over.

9) Do not assume that a position at a university or a Ph.D. makes the book better. The worst grammar books I have are written by grammar professors. Even my Chinese friends do not understand some of the grammar constructions.

10) Books written by Cantonese Chinese may have slightly different sentence constructions.

11) Introductory character writing or grammar books with sentences with more than five words or characters are too advanced for a beginner.

My Personal Favorite Web Sites

www.SpeakandWriteChinese.com

This is my website. It is in the building phase. I am going to try and gradually introduce everything that you will need. I am working on building a database that anyone can add to to add words, sentences and phrases. Ultimately I will write a program to write English, Hanzi and Pinyin at the same time. It will also have a review for books, CDs, DVDs, websites and other learning resources. You will be able to order any of my books, flash cards and CD's from this site. First I have to learn to use a computer.

www.mandarintools.com

This is hands down the best web site for character information in a dictionary format and it is free. Everything you need is there, dictionary, conversion utilities, the CEDICT database. There is even some useful grammar and sentence structure. The interface is a little awkward and unrevealing. If you delve into it and open everything it is a treasure of information and programs. They accept contributions. You can download their great stand alone program **DimSum** for free. You can also download the CEDICT database.

www.zhongwen.com

This is a great website for researching the Radicals and etymology of characters. The interface is easy to use. It also links to the Ocrat database, sometimes. The interface makes it easy to navigate quickly. The site is a no charge site. I feel that this

[Type text]

is the best site for research and it shows the learner a fascinating look at how characters within a group evolved.

http://lost-theory.org/ocrat

This site has an easy to use interface and provides animated stroke order access. This side has common family names, P.R.C. provinces and other difficult to find but interesting characters. This site is a no charge site. Personally, I do not feel a great need to watch the stroke order of every character. I feel it is better to learn the rules of stroke order.

www.sexybeijing.tv

This website details the adventures of Su Fei, a hot Jewish girl from California who goes around creating adventure in Beijing. She takes her name from a brand name product line of women's sanitary pads. She is so funny and it is a great place to learn conversational Mandarin. Her videos are easiest to access at www.sexybeijing.tv. These videos give you a nice exposure to the real life for citizens of a big Chinese city.

www.chinesesavvy.com

This site has a nice profile of everything you need to learn to function in China. It is expensive and in some of the paid features the native Beijingers talk so fast it is hardly an introduction to spoken Mandarin. There is little English translation of these conversations.They have a great forum for discussing any issues in China. However, the moderator edits out any issues that are controversial in China.

[Type text]

www.chineselearner.com

This is a great website and is rapidly getting bigger and better. It is being updated often so sometimes is does not fire up immediately. The moderators are friendly and they respond to e-mails quickly. Most of what they offer is currently free. Oddly there are lessons offered in the Hanyu Pinyin section that are not translated from Hanzi.

http://www.csulb.edu/~txie/Pinyin/Pinyin.htm

This is a great website that has all you need to get your computer to type Pinyin and convert to Hanzi; in fact, it is more useful than the Microsoft embedded utility. If you have a bootleg Windows and cannot access Microsoft free downloads, this is the solution. I carry it on my USB wherever I go.

http://www.globechinese.com/

Chinese Character Bible or Hanzi Explorer 9.2 is an animated character writing program with pronunciation. It is a free shareware download. It has a colourful interface and is easy to use. Oddly, it does not show Pinyin when it demonstrates a character. So you are left to try and figure out the Pinyin or plug it into another program.

http://babelfish.yahoo.com/

This is a translator program that can interconvert Hanzi and English. Like all such programs the Hanzi to English and English to Hanzi is somewhat speculative.

[Type text]

http://xenomachina.com/toys/Pinyin2hanzi.html

This site has a program that takes Pinyin and converts it to Hanzi to give you choices of characters.

http://technology.chtsai.org/

This is a great website for statistics of word frequency and links to useful word lists. There is also a hard to find list of Chinese names. These lists can save you hundreds of hours if you are writing a book. This is a must have site for the committed learner.

http://www.Pinyin.info/

This website is full of useful tools for manipulating Pinyin. It has all the official rules of Pinyin along with conversion tools, spell checker and how to set up your computer for Chinese usage. There is also a comparison of the different Romanisation systems, which is very comprehensive

http://www.uni.edu/becker/chinese2.html

This website offers links to multitudes of other Chinese learning websites. The interface is easy and very colourful.

http://www.rci.rutgers.edu/~rsimmon/chingram/

This site has a good section on Mandarin Grammar but it lacks explanation. It appears to be a slide presentation that served as highlights to the speaker. It does cover all the relevant areas of Mandarin Chinese grammar.

[Type text]

http://www.askbenny.cn

Benny, the world's most famous Chinese teacher, is a great site that introduces very useful sentence constructions and vocabulary. He is very personable and has more energy than is possible. This site is free!!!!, but please donate. I would rank this site number one in ease of access, utility and fun for a speaking tool.

http://www.chinese-tools.com/

This website has a good dictionary and a translator that converts characters to Hanyu Pinyin with tone markers. There is also a idiom dictionary with 30,000 idioms.

http://chinesepod.com/

This website is a audio video site based on progressive learning of Standard Mandarin. There are various levels of membership and the price is very reasonable at the beginner level. The higher priced long winded explanations are too complex for learners. Some of the speakers speak far too fast to make it a learning experience. However, the transcripts in English and Hanyu Pinyin available with the sound files are excellent. The moderator **Ken** gives some very incorrect grammatical translations. These can be a huge barrier to learning Mandarin Grammar as he mixes up both word order and word usage.

[Type text]

Using a Computer in China

Using a computer in China at an internet café is full of risk. First, they are common sites for thieves and I have had young boys crawl on their hands and knees and try and unplug my USB, take by backpack, wallet, passport etc. Often the computers are set up with keystroke copy programs and will copy your credit card, bank account and e-mail passwords. I have had bank accounts emptied twice and charge cards emptied twice.

If you bring your own computer it is a target for thieves and you cannot fall asleep on a bus or train without risk. To safely prepare a computer for use is no short or simple task. I always carry a USB with **CCleaner** on it from www.ccleaner.com, a free registry cleaner. I clean the registry both before and after I use the computer.

I also carry the free download **Counter Spy** from www.sunbelt-software.com and I run the program to find viruses and spyware. Chinese computers can be very slow and it can take from 20 minutes to 2 hours to make a computer safe. Many Chinese chat programs open the IP address and will take whatever information you have to steal. **QQ** is the most popular chat program in China. Chinese people do not realize that the purpose of the program is to take your information for marketing purposes and sell it to advertisers. The chat utility is a cover. So I remove it.

Programs such as **Windows Password Reset** will allow you to bypass security functions and remove malicious programs. I always remove **QQ** and the entire **Tencent** family of programs. I install my registry cleaner and spyware program and sometimes take out dozens of Trojans and viruses. I have found that most computers in China are not secured and they have no administrator passwords anyhow.

It is very important to have **Skype** on your USB, a headset and a **Skype** account. Calling out of China can be a real challenge in remote areas. **www.Skype.com**

[Type text]

How to Spend Your Money Wisely

If you have money to spend I would highly recommend;

1) My books, CD's and website. www.SpeakandWriteChinese.com

2) Beginner's Chinese by Yong Ho. 1977   ISBN 0-7818-0566-X

    There are multitudes of introductory books on the market but this book has more useful methods to learn in this book of 174 pages than a huge pile of other books I have. I carried this book in China for a long time.

3) Chinese Grammar by Claudia Ross. 2004   ISBN 0-07-137764-6

    I have all the classic grammar texts, Chao, Li, etc. but this book has all the relevant grammar in it. If you master this book you do not need any other grammar to speak Mandarin. The book is structured in a very practical way.

4) Wenlin DVD available at www.languageworld.com

    Of the multitude of Chinese learning DVD's I have, this replaces them all. You can learn everything here in an easy interface, stroke order, Radicals, Words versus characters. You can search specific Radicals within characters and words. For the beginner or researcher this is the best bang for the buck. Rather than randomly buy 10 different tools, buy this one.

5) e-Stroke available at www.eon.com

    This program allows you to cut, paste, and drop a character into their tool and it gives you an animated stroke order, Pinyin and definition. It is indispensible for identifying obscure characters.

[Type text]

Cut these out or photocopy them and put your phone number in the columns and get these babies plastered all over China Town or the Faculty of Computer Science at your local university.

我 教 你 英 文 你 教 我 汉 語

Wǒ jiāo Nǐ Yīngwén, Nǐ jiāo Wǒ Hànyǔ.
I teach you English, You teach me Han language.

我 教 你 英 文 你 教 我 汉 語

Wǒ jiāo Nǐ Yīngwén, Nǐ jiāo Wǒ Hànyǔ.
I teach you English, You teach me Han language.

[Type text]

Notes:

Notes:

Notes:

Notes:

Notes:

Notes:

Notes: